Encyclopedia of MATLAB: Science and Engineering

Volume I

Encyclopedia of MATLAB: Science and Engineering

Volume I

Edited by **Louis Young**

New Jersey

Published by Clanrye International,
55 Van Reypen Street,
Jersey City, NJ 07306, USA
www.clanryeinternational.com

Encyclopedia of MATLAB: Science and Engineering
Volume I
Edited by Louis Young

International Standard Book Number: 978-1-63240-189-2 (Hardback)

Printed in the United States of America.

Contents

Preface

In my initial years as a student, I used to run to the library at every possible instance to grab a book and learn something new. Books were my primary source of knowledge and I would not have come such a long way without all that I learnt from them. Thus, when I was approached to edit this book; I became understandably nostalgic. It was an absolute honor to be considered worthy of guiding the current generation as well as those to come. I put all my knowledge and hard work into making this book most beneficial for its readers.

This book analyzes applications of MATLAB in roughly every division of science. This book covers applications based on the engineering of MATLAB as a tool for computing. The book has several chapters dealing with numerous professional fields and can be utilized by experts for their researches.

I wish to thank my publisher for supporting me at every step. I would also like to thank all the authors who have contributed their researches in this book. I hope this book will be a valuable contribution to the progress of the field.

Editor

MATLAB Applications in Engineering

Simulation of Power Converters Using Matlab-Simulink

Christophe Batard, Frédéric Poitiers, Christophe Millet and Nicolas Ginot

Additional information is available at the end of the chapter

1. Introduction

A static converter is an electrical circuit which can control the transfer of energy between a generator and a receiver. The efficiency of a converter should be excellent. The components constituting a converter are:

-   Capacitors, inductors and transformers with minimum losses,
-   Power semiconductors operating as switches.

The design of power converter consumes time with a significant cost. Performance is generally determined after testing converters at nominal operating points. Thus, simulation can substantially reduce development cost.

The development of specific software dedicated to simulation of power electronic systems (PSIM, SABER, PSCAD, "SimPowerSystems" toolbox of Simulink…) allows simulating fast and accurately the converter behavior. Unfortunately, the designers of converters don't always have such available software. In many cases, they have to simulate power electronics devices for occasional need. So they don't want to buy the SimPowerSystems toolbox in addition to Matlab and Simulink. The purpose of this chapter is to present the ability to simulate power converters using only Simulink. Simulink is a graphical extension to MATLAB for representing mathematical functions and systems in the form of block diagram, and simulate the operation of these systems.

Traditionally two approaches are used to simulate power electronic systems:

-   The first, so called fixed topology, where semiconductors are impedances with low or high values based on their on-state or off-state. Equations system does not depend on the state of the semiconductor. Despite its simplicity, this approach raises problems of compromise between accuracy of the results and stability of numerical integration methods.

- The second, so called variable topology, assimilates the switches to open-circuits or short-circuits. The system equations then depend on the state of the semiconductor. There are no accuracy problems but writing the equations of different configurations can be laborious as well as obtain switching conditions of the semiconductor.

In this chapter, we propose a method for simulating static converters with Simulink based on the variable topology approach where switching conditions of semiconductor are realized by switching functions.

2. Linear load modeling in Simulink

This paragraph deals with the modelling of linear elements commonly encountered in the electrical energy conversion. Elementary linear dipoles are described by a system of linear differential equations. There are several different ways to describe linear differential equations. The state-space representation (SSR) is the most easy to use with Matlab. The SSR is given by equations (1) and (2).

$$\dot{X} = A\,X + B\,U \tag{1}$$

$$Y = C\,X \tag{2}$$

where X is an n by 1 vector representing the state (commonly current through an inductance or voltage across the capacitance), U is a scalar representing the input (voltage or current), and Y is a scalar representing the output. The matrices A (n by n), B (n by 1), and C (1 by n) determine the relationships between the state and input and output variables.

The commonly elementary dipoles encountered in power electronics are:

- RL series dipole
- RLC series dipole
- RC parallel dipole
- L in series with RC parallel dipole

2.1. RL series dipole

The variation of the current through the dipole is governed by equation (3).

$$v(t) = R\,i(t) + L\,di/dt \;\Rightarrow\; i(t) = \frac{1}{L}\int \big(v(t) - R\,i(t)\big)\,dt \tag{3}$$

The RL series dipole is modelled by the scheme illustrated in figure 1.

2.2. RLC series dipole

The variation of the current through the dipole is governed by equation (4) and the variation of the voltage across the capacity is governed by equation (5).

$$v(t) = R\,i(t) + v_C(t) + L\,di/dt \quad \Rightarrow \quad i(t) = \frac{1}{L}\int\big(v(t) - Ri(t) - v_C(t)\big)\,dt \qquad (4)$$

$$i(t) = C\,dv_C/dt \quad \Rightarrow \quad v_C(t) = \frac{1}{C}\int i\,dt \qquad (5)$$

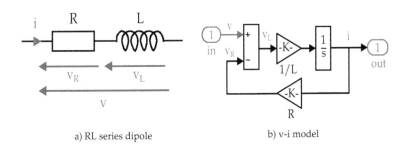

a) RL series dipole

b) v-i model

Figure 1. Model of a RL series dipole

The RLC series dipole is modelled by the scheme illustrated in figure 2.

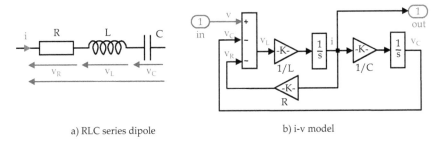

a) RLC series dipole

b) i-v model

Figure 2. Model of a RLC series dipole

2.3. RC parallel dipole

The variation of the voltage across the dipole is governed by equation (6).

$$i(t) = C\,dv/dt + v(t)/R \quad \Rightarrow \quad v(t) = \frac{1}{C}\int\big(i(t) - v(t)/R\big)\,dt \qquad (6)$$

The RC parallel dipole is modelled by the scheme illustrated in figure 3.

2.4. L in series with RC parallel dipole

In a L in series with RC parallel dipole, the variation of the current through the inductance is governed by equation (7) and the variation of the voltage across the capacity is governed by equation (8).

$$v_i(t) = v_o(t) + L\frac{di_L}{dt} \Rightarrow i_L(t) = \frac{1}{L}\int\left(v_i(t) - v_o(t)\right)dt \qquad (7)$$

$$i_L(t) = i_R(t) + C\frac{dv_o}{dt} \Rightarrow v_o(t) = \frac{1}{C}\int\left(i_L(t) - i_R(t)\right)dt \qquad (8)$$

$$i_R(t) = v_o(t)/R \qquad (9)$$

The L in series with RC parallel dipole is modelled by the scheme illustrated in figure 4.

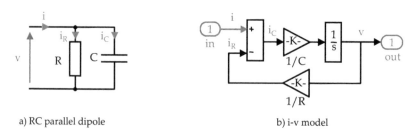

a) RC parallel dipole   b) i-v model

Figure 3. Model of a RC parallel dipole

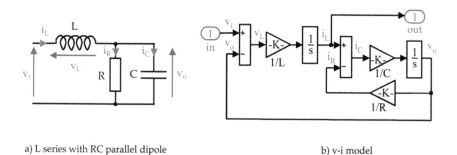

a) L series with RC parallel dipole   b) v-i model

Figure 4. Model of a L in series with RC parallel dipole

3. DC-DC converter model in Simulink

This part will be dedicated to the DC-DC converter modelling with Simulink. The input generator is a DC voltage source and the output generator is also a DC voltage source. The output voltage is always smoothed by a capacitor. Only the non-isolated DC-DC converters are studied in this paragraph. The switches are assumed ideal, as well as passive elements (L, C)

3.1. Buck converter

3.1.1. Operating phases

The buck converter circuit is illustrated in figure 5a. The most common strategy for controlling the power transmitted to the load is the intersective Pulse Width Modulation (PWM). A control voltage v_m is compared to a triangular voltage v_t. The triangular voltage v_t determines the switching frequency f_t. The switch T is controlled according to the difference $v_m - v_t$ (figure 5b). Three operating phases are counted (figure 5c):

- T state-on and D state-off
- T state-off and D state-on
- T and D state-off

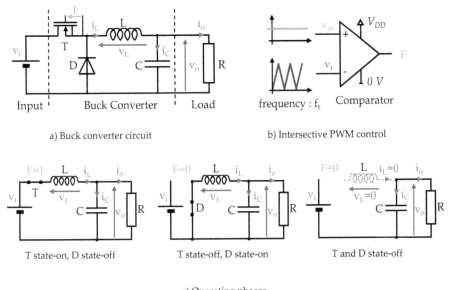

a) Buck converter circuit   b) Intersective PWM control

T state-on, D state-off   T state-off, D state-on   T and D state-off

c) Operating phases

Figure 5. Buck converter

The variation of the current through the capacitor C is governed by equation (10). The variation of the voltage across the capacity is governed by equation (11). Equation (12) describes the variation of the voltage across the inductance which depends on the operating phase. F is a logical variable equal to one if v_m is greater than or equal to v_t, F equal to zero if v_m is less than v_t. Sign(i_L) is also a logical variable which is equal to one if i_L is positive, sign (i_L) equal to zero if i_L is zero.

$$i_C(t) = i_L(t) - i_o(t) = C \frac{dv_o}{dt} \tag{10}$$

$$v_o(t) = \frac{1}{C} \int i_C(t) \, dt = \frac{1}{C} \int \left(i_L(t) - i_o(t) \right) dt \tag{11}$$

$$v_L(t) = \left(v_i(t) - v_o(t) \right) * F - v_o(t) * \overline{F} * sign(i_L) \tag{12}$$

3.1.2. Open-loop buck converter

Simulink model of the open-loop buck converter is shown in figure 6a. The Buck block is illustrated in figure 6c. Equation (12) is modelled by blocks addition, multiplication and logic. The structure of the converter requires a current iʟ necessarily positive or zero. Also, the inductance current is modelled by an integrator block that limits the minimum value of iʟ to zero.

The PWM control block is illustrated in figure 6b.

In the case of a resistive load, the load block is constituted by a gain block (value 1/R).

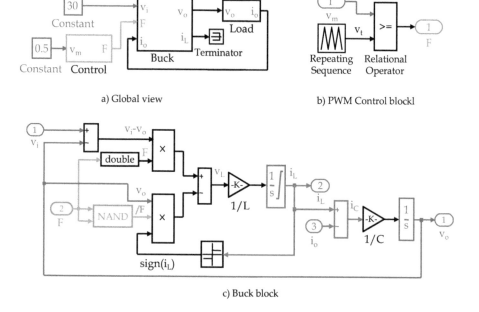

a) Global view

b) PWM Control blockl

c) Buck block

Figure 6. Buck converter described in Simulink

3.1.3. Closed-loop buck converter

A closed-loop buck converter circuit is illustrated in figure 7a. The measurement of the output voltage is realized by 2 resistances R_1 and R_2. The regulation is achieved by a PID controller. Simulink model of the closed loop converter is shown in figure 7b. Simulink PID control block is illustrated in figure 7c.

The parameters used for the closed-loop simulation are :

$V_i = 12$ V	$L = 300$ μH	$C = 5$ μF	$R = 3$ Ω	$f_t = 50$ kHz
Output voltage measurement:		$R_1 = 10$ kΩ	$R_2 = 10$ kΩ	
PID block :		$K_p = 10$	$T_i = 0.2$ ms	

The voltage reference was fixed to 2.5 V. The simulation of the closed-loop buck converter is illustrated in figure 7d. The list of configuration parameters used for is:

Start time : 0	Stop time : 0.5 e-3
Type : Variable-step	Solver : ode15s (stiff/NDF)
Max step size : 1e-6	Relative tolerance : 1e-3
Min step size : auto	absolute tolerance : auto

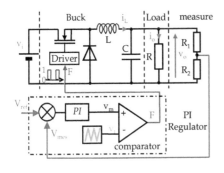

a) Closed-loop buck converter circuit

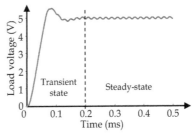

b) Buck Simulink diagram

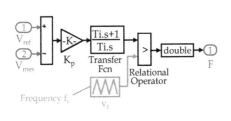

c) Simulink PI regulator

d) Output voltage of the buck converter

Figure 7. Modeling a closed loop DC / DC converter

In steady-state, $V_{ref} = V_{mes} = 2.5$ V. From figure 7a, we deduce the theoretical value of V_o:

$$V_o\big|_{steady-state} = \frac{R_1 + R_2}{R_2} V_{ref} = 5\,V \tag{13}$$

Simulation is in good agreement with theoretical value. From figure 7d, we deduce that the transient state last roughly 0.2 ms.

3.2. Boost converter

3.2.1. Operating phases

The boost converter circuit is illustrated in figure 8a. The principle of the switch control is described in figure 5b Three operating phases are counted (figure 8c) :

-   T state-on and D state-off
-   T state-off and D state-on
-   T and D state-off

The variation of the voltage across the inductance L (equation 14) and the current through the capacity (equation 15) depend on the operating phase.

$$v_L(t) = v_i(t) * F + \left(v_i(t) - v_o(t)\right) * \overline{F} * sign(i_L) \tag{14}$$

$$i_C(t) = -i_o(t) * F + i_L(t) * \overline{F} * sign(i_L) = C\frac{dv_o}{dt} \tag{15}$$

$$v_o = \frac{1}{C}\int i_C(t)\,dt = \frac{1}{C}\int\left(-i_o(t).F + i_L.\overline{F}.sign(i_L)\right)dt \tag{16}$$

3.2.2. Open-loop operation

Simulink model of a open-loop boost converter is shown in figure 9a. The Boost block is illustrated in figure 9b. Equation (14), (15) and (16) are modeled by addition blocks, multiplication blocks and logic blocks. The structure of the converter requires a current i_L necessarily positive or zero. Also, the inductance current is modeled by an integrator block that limits the minimum value of i_L to zero.

The PWM control block is illustrated in figure 6b.

In the case of a resistive load, the load block is constituted by a gain block (value 1/R).

Simulation example:

The parameters used for of an open-loop simulation are :

$V_i = 12$ V	$L = 200$ µH	$C = 50$ µF	$R = 5\,\Omega$	$f_t = 50$ kHz
Control blok:	$V_{t\,max} = 1$ V	$V_{t\,min} = -1$ V	$V_m = 0$	

The simulation of the open-loop boost converter is illustrated in figure 9c. The list of configuration parameters used is:

Start time : 0   Stop time : 7 e-3
Type : Variable-step   Solver : ode15s (stiff/NDF)
Max step size : 1e-6   Relative tolerance : 1e-3
Min step size : auto   absolute tolerance : auto

Knowing that v_t varies from -1 V to $+1$ V and $v_m = 0$, we deduce that the duty cycle α is equal to 0.5. In steady-state, we deduce theoretical value of V_o :

$$V_o\big|_{steady-state} = \frac{V_i}{\alpha} = 24\ V \tag{17}$$

Simulation is in good agreement with theoretical value. From figure 9c, we deduce that the transient state last roughly 2.5 ms.

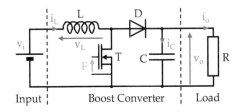

a) Boost converter circuit

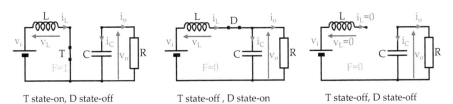

T state-on, D state-off   T state-off , D state-on   T state-off, D state-off

b) Operating phases

Figure 8. Boost converter

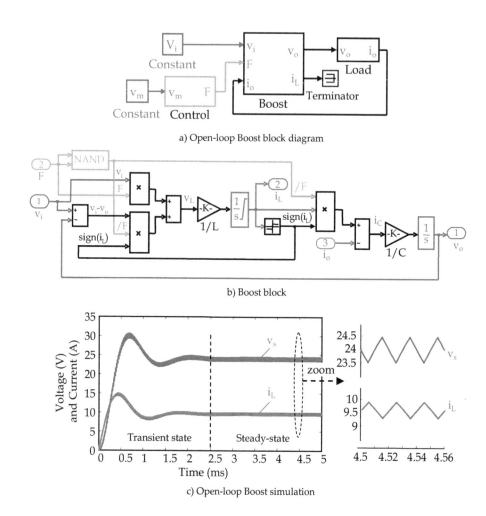

a) Open-loop Boost block diagram

b) Boost block

c) Open-loop Boost simulation

Figure 9. Boost converter described in Simulink

4. DC-AC converter model in Simulink

An inverter is a DC – AC power converter. This converter obtains AC voltage from DC voltage. The applications are numerous: power backup for the computer systems, variable speed drive motor, induction heating... In most cases, the dead times introduced into the control of the switches do not change the waveform of the inverter.

This paragraph is dedicated to the simulation of a three-phase inverter without taking into account the dead times introduced into the control of the switches.

4.1. Electrical circuit

A variable speed drive for AC motor is shown in figure 10. It consists on a continuous voltage source and a three-phase inverter feeding an AC motor.

In order to simplify the modelling, the electrical equivalent circuit of the AC motor is described by an inductance L_M in series with a resistance R_M. The motor runs with delta connection of the stator.

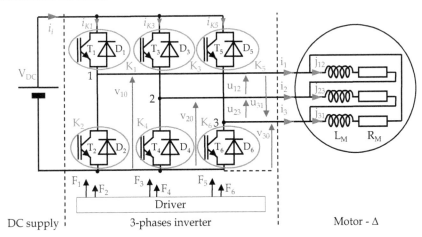

Figure 10. Electrical circuit

There are many strategies for controlling the switches. The most common control strategy is the intersective PWM. Its principle is reminded in figure 11. The switch control signals are generated by comparing three sinusoidal voltages (modulating) which are phase-shifted through $2\pi/3$ [rad] with a same triangular voltage waveform (carrier).

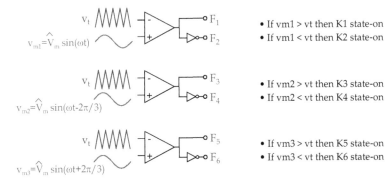

Figure 11. Three phase PWM control

Knowing the conduction intervals of the switches, it is then possible to determine the waveform of different voltages and currents.

The line to neutral voltage v_{10}, v_{20} et v_{30} are dependent on the state of the switches. Examples:

K_1 state-on and K_2 state-off: $v_{10} = + V_{DC}$ K_1 state-off and K_2 state-on: $v_{10} = 0$

K_3 state-on and K_4 state-off: $v_{20} = + V_{DC}$ K_3 state-off and K_4 state-on: $v_{20} = 0$

K_5 state-on and K_6 state-off: $v_{30} = + V_{DC}$ K_5 state-off and K_6 state-on: $v_{30} = 0$

The phase-phase voltage can be deduce from the line to neutral voltage:

$$u_{12} = v_{10} - v_{20} \tag{18}$$

$$u_{23} = v_{20} - v_{30} \tag{19}$$

$$u_{31} = v_{30} - v_{10} \tag{20}$$

The input current i_i is deduced from the current of switches K_1, K_3 and K_5:

$$i_i = i_{K1} + i_{K3} + i_{K5} = F_1 \cdot i_1 + F_3 \cdot i_2 + F_5 \cdot i_3 \tag{21}$$

4.2. Simulink model

Simulink model of the three-phase inverter is shown in figure 12a. The control block is illustrated in figure 12b. It models a three phases PWM control. The inverter block is illustrated in figure 12c.

In the case of a resistive load, the load block is constituted by a gain block (value 1/R).

4.3. Simulation example

The parameters used for of an open-loop simulation are :

Power Circuit :	$V_{DC} = 400$ V	$L_M = 10$ mH	$R_M = 5\ \Omega$
Control blok:	$f_t = 20$ kHz	$V_{t\,max} = 1$ V	$V_{t\,min} = -1$ V
	$f_m = 50$ Hz	$V_{m\,max} = 0.5$	

The simulation of the open-loop three-phase inverter is illustrated in figure 13. The list of configuration parameters used is:

Start time: 0	Stop time: 1.5
Type: Variable-step	Solver: ode15s (stiff/NDF)
Max step size: 1e-5	Relative tolerance: 1e-3
Min step size: auto	absolute tolerance: auto

The relation between the amplitude of the sinusoidal voltage and the triangular voltage determines the maximum value of the fundamental line-line voltage of the inverter:

$$U_{max} = \frac{\sqrt{3}}{2} \frac{V_{m\,max}}{V_{t\,max}} V_{DC} = \frac{\sqrt{3}}{2} \frac{0.5}{1} 400 = 173\ V \tag{22}$$

Neglecting the current harmonics, the maximum value of the line current is deduced from equation (22) :

$$I_{1\,max} = \sqrt{3}\, J_{12\,max} = \frac{\sqrt{3}\, . U_{max}}{\sqrt{R_M{}^2 + (L_M\, 2\,\pi\, f_m)^2}} = \frac{\sqrt{3}\, . 173}{\sqrt{4^2 + (10^{-2}\, 2\,\pi\, 50)^2}} = 59\ A \tag{23}$$

Simulations are in good agreement with theoretical values.

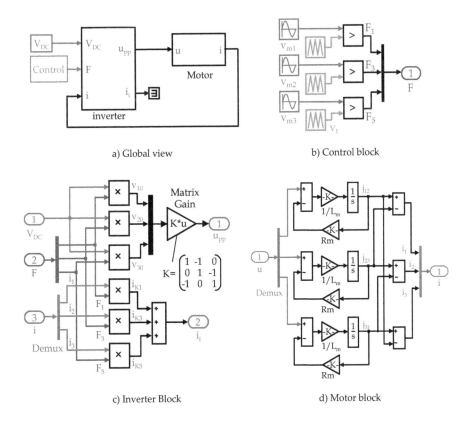

a) Global view

b) Control block

c) Inverter Block

d) Motor block

Figure 12. Three phase inverter

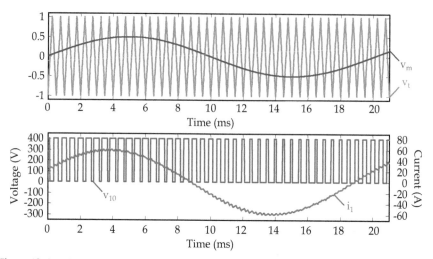

Figure 13. Simulation example of a three-phase inverter with PWM control

5. Modeling and simulation of diode rectifiers

Three-phase AC to DC converters are widely used in many industrial power converters in order to obtain continuous voltage using a classical three-phase AC-line. These converters, when they are used alone or associated for specific applications, can present problems due to their non-linear behaviour. It is then important to be able to model accurately the behaviour of these converters in order to study their influence on the input currents waveforms and their interactions with the loads (classically inverters and AC-motors).

Several studies have shown the importance to have tools to simulate the behaviour of complex power electronics systems (Ladoux et al., 2005), (Qijun et al. 2007), (Zuniga-Haro & Ramirez, 2009) and several methods have been also presented in order to reduce the simulation time or to improve the precision. Although constant topology methods have been developed (Araujo et al., 2002), variable topology methods seem to be very suitable for simulation of power-electronics converters (Terrien et al., 1999).

In this chapter, an original and simple method is developed to model and simulate AC-DC converters taking into account overlap phenomenon with continuous and discontinuous conduction modes using Matlab-Simulink. The diodes are assumed ideal ($v_d = 0$ when the diode is state-on, $i_d = 0$ when the diode is state-off)

If the electrical network is considered as ideal (no line inductance) and the conduction is maintained continuous, ($i_d>0$), the modelling of the converters can be realised very simply by a functional approach (commutation functions) where the switches are opened or closed. An example is presented in figure 14.

$v_O = F_1 \cdot v_i - F_2 \cdot v_i$ With : $F_1 = 1$ if $v_i > 0$ and $F_1 = 0$ if $v_i < 0$

$F_2 = 0$ if $v_i > 0$ and $F_2 = 1$ if $v_i < 0$

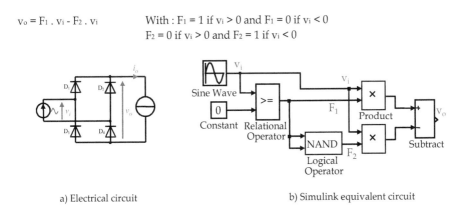

a) Electrical circuit   b) Simulink equivalent circuit

Figure 14. Basic model of a single-phase rectifier.

In this chapter, the proposed approach is completely different from the approach based on commutation functions. It permits to simulate accurately the commutation in the six-pulse AC-DC converter, even under unbalanced supply voltages (the influence of voltages unbalances on AC harmonic magnitudes currents has been demonstrated (de Oliveira & Guimaraes, 2007) or line impedances conditions.

The overlap phenomenon and the unbalance of line impedances can be taken into account by modifying the commutation functions to correspond to the real behaviour of the rectifiers in these conditions. Indeed, the commutations are not instantaneous. Several contributions have already been proposed in scientific literature to refine the modelling of rectifiers. Most of these contributions show good simulation results but the analytical models used are complex and not reflecting precisely the real behaviour of the converter (Hu & Morrison, 1997), (Arrillaga et al., 1997). Some methods have been developed in order to model and simulate power factor corrected single-phase AC-DC converters (Pandey et al., 2004).

5.1. Electrical model

The six-pulse AC-DC converter is illustrated in figure 15a. Inductances L_i characterize the line inductances and L_o characterizes the output inductance. The AC-DC converter modelling is based on the variable topology approach. The diodes are modelled by an ideal model which traduces the state of the switch:

-   $v_D = 0$ when the diode is state-on;
-   $i_D = 0$ when the diode is state-off.

There are 13 operating phases:

-   1 phase of discontinuous conduction mode (P_0)

All the diodes are state-off (figure 15b)

- 6 phases of classical conduction P_1 to P_6 (figure 15c)

$P_1 : D_1$ and D_5 state-on $P_2 : D_1$ and D_6 state-on $P_3 : D_2$ and D_6 state-on

$P_4 : D_2$ and D_4 state-on $P_5 : D_3$ and D_4 state-on $P_6 : D_3$ and D_5 state-on

- 6 phases of overlap O_1 to O_6 (figure 15d)

$O_1 : D_1, D_5$ and D_6 state-on $O_2 : D_1, D_2$ and D_6 state-on $O_3 : D_2, D_4$ and D_6 state-on

$O_4 : D_2, D_3$ and D_4 state-on $O_5 : D_3, D_4$ and D_5 state-on $O_6 : D_1, D_3$ and D_5 state-on

For an operating phase, we determinate the di/dt through each inductance (L_i and L_o) and the voltage across each diode. In order to simplify results presentation, we consider that the line is balanced (same RMS voltages and line inductances L_i) and have no resistive part.

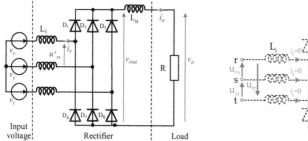

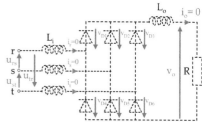

a) Six-pulse AC-DC converter   b) Discontinuous conduction phase

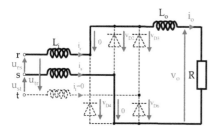

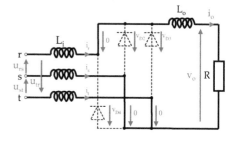

c) Conduction phase P1 : D1 et D5 state-on   d) Overlap phase O1 : D1 D5 et D6 state-on

Figure 15. Six-pulse diode rectifier.

Naturally, the method is equivalent under unbalanced conditions but the mathematical expressions of the different variables are more complex.

As an example, we will consider the following succession of phases: $P_0, P_1, O_1, P_2, O_2, P_3...$:

To shift from phase P_0 (diodes state-off) to phase P_1 ($D_1 D_5$ state-on), the voltage across diodes D_1 and D_5 have to be equal to zero.

To shift from phase P_1 (D_1 D_5 state-on) to overlap phase O_1 (D_1 D_5 D_6 state-on), the voltage across the diode D_6 has to be equal to zero.

To shift from overlap phase O_1 (D_1 D_5 D_6 state-on) to phase P_2 (D_1 D_6 state-on), the current through the diode D_5 has to be equal to zero.

And so forth ...

5.1.1. Discontinuous conduction mode

This mode corresponds to the case where $i_o = 0$ (figure 15b). In this case, all diodes are opened. Equation (24) describes this mode.

$$\frac{di_r}{dt} = \frac{di_s}{dt} = \frac{di_t}{dt} = 0 \tag{24}$$

5.1.2. Continuous conduction mode

Let's take example of the continuous conduction mode P_1. From the figure 15c, we can write equations (25), (26) and (27) :

$$\frac{di_r}{dt} = -\frac{di_s}{dt} = \frac{di_o}{dt} = \frac{u_{rs} - v_o}{2L_i + L_o} \tag{25}$$

$$\frac{di_t}{dt} = 0 \tag{26}$$

$$v_{D6} = u_{st} \frac{L_i}{2L_i + L_o}\left(u_{rs} - v_o\right) \tag{27}$$

We obtain the di/dt corresponding to the other continuous conduction modes by making circular permutations of indexes. For example, for conduction mode P_2: D_1 and D_6 are state-on. The indexes s and t are permuted as presented below:

$$\frac{di_r}{dt} = -\frac{di_t}{dt} = \frac{di_o}{dt} = \frac{u_{rt} - v_o}{2L_i + L_o} \tag{28}$$

$$\frac{di_s}{dt} = 0 \tag{29}$$

5.1.3. Overlap phases

Let's take example of the overlap phase O_1. From the figure 15c, we can write equations (30) and (31) :

$$\frac{di_r}{dt} = \frac{di_o}{dt} \tag{30}$$

$$i_s + i_t = -i_0 \iff -\frac{di_s}{dt} - \frac{di_t}{dt} = \frac{di_0}{dt} \tag{31}$$

The expression of the di/dt as a function of the device parameters is more complicated to obtain here than in the case of a classical operating phase. Equations have been detailed in (Batard et al., 2007) and the final result is recalled below:

$$\frac{di_r}{dt} = \frac{di_0}{dt} = \frac{1}{3 L_i + 2 L_0} \left[u_{rs} + u_{rt} - 2 v_0 \right] \tag{32}$$

$$\frac{di_s}{dt} = \frac{1}{3 L_i + 2 L_0} \left(-\frac{2 L_i + L_0}{L_i} u_{rs} + \frac{L_i + L_0}{L_i} u_{rt} + v_0 \right) \tag{33}$$

$$\frac{di_t}{dt} = \frac{1}{3 L_i + 2 L_0} \left(\frac{L_i + L_0}{L_i} u_{rs} - \frac{2 L_i + L_0}{L_i} u_{rt} + v_0 \right) \tag{34}$$

We obtain the di/dt corresponding to the other overlap modes by making circular permutations of indexes. For example, for overlap mode O_2: D_1, D_2 and D_6 are state-on. The indexes r and t are permuted and the sign of v_s and di_0/dt are changed:

$$\frac{di_r}{dt} = \frac{1}{3 L_i + 2 L_0} \left(\frac{L_i + L_0}{L_i} u_{ts} - \frac{2 L_i + L_0}{L_i} u_{tr} - v_0 \right) \tag{35}$$

$$\frac{di_s}{dt} = \frac{1}{3 L_i + 2 L_0} \left(-\frac{2 L_i + L_0}{L_i} u_{ts} + \frac{L_i + L_0}{L_i} u_{tr} - v_0 \right) \tag{36}$$

$$\frac{di_t}{dt} = -\frac{di_0}{dt} = \frac{1}{3 L_i + 2 L_0} \left[u_{ts} + u_{tr} + 2 v_0 \right] \tag{37}$$

5.2. Simulink model

The simulink model of the six-pulse diode rectifier is illustrated in figure 16a. The resistive load is modelled as a gain. The internal structure of the diodes rectifier block is presented in figure 16b. Four different blocks can be seen on this scheme.

The first one called MF1 is a Matlab function which computes each diode voltage. The inputs of this block are the initial phase and the three-phase network voltages.

The second one called MF2 is also a Matlab function which computes the new operating phase and each inductance di/dt. Its computing algorithm is shown in figure 16d. The new operating phase depends on the initial phase, the diode voltages and currents.

The third, called "Initial Phase" extract the operating phase of the MF2 block, this operating phase becomes the initial phase of the next calculation step (the Simulink block "memory" is used).

The Current block computes each diode current which permits to obtain the DC current and the line currents.

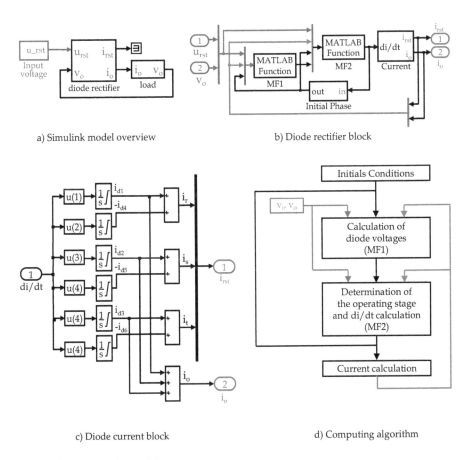

a) Simulink model overview   b) Diode rectifier block

c) Diode current block   d) Computing algorithm

Figure 16. Diode rectifier model

The internal structure of the Current block is shown in figure 16c. The originality of our approach is the calculation of the values of each diode current with the values of di/dt of inductances L_i and L_o. We use then six integrator blocks (one for each diode). The integrator blocks are set to limit their minimal output value to zero (lower saturation limit), this feature permits to avoid the problem of accurate determination of the instant when diodes currents reach to zero.

It is then possible to determinate the output current of the rectifier ($i_o = i_{D1} + i_{D2} + i_{D3}$) and the input line currents ($i_r = i_{D1} - i_{D4}$, $i_s = i_{D2} - i_{D5}$, $i_t = i_{D3} - i_{D6}$).

5.3. Experimental validation

Simulations and experimental waveforms related to figure 15 are shown in figure 17. The simulation parameters are adjusted as follows:

$$U_{RMS} = 230 \text{ V} ; R = 58 \text{ } \Omega ; L_i = 800 \text{ } \mu H ; L_o = 800 \text{ mH}$$

It can be seen that the simulated waveforms are very close to the experimental ones. The overlap interval υ_1 is equivalent for simulation and experimental results ($\upsilon_1 \cong 0.7$ ms).

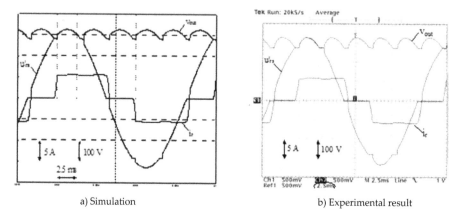

a) Simulation   b) Experimental result

Figure 17. Comparison of Simulation and Experimental Waveforms in a six-pulse diode rectifier

The list of configuration parameters used for Matlab simulation is:

Start time : 0   Stop time : 0.2s
Type : Variable-step   Solver : ode15s (stiff/NDF)
Max step size : 1e-4   Relative tolerance : 1e-5
Min step size : auto   absolute tolerance : auto

Using a PC with an Intel core 2 duo CPU running at 2.19 GHz with 1 Go de RAM, the simulation time was 4 s.

This model has also been tested with a load constituted of an inverter and an induction machine. The results of this test have validated operations for discontinuous conduction mode. For the same configuration parameters, the simulation time was 5 s.

6. Modeling and simulation of thyristor rectifiers

The Simulink model of the controlled rectifier is very close to the Simulink model of the diode rectifier. Only the condition to turn the thyristor on is different to the condition to turn the diode on. For an ideal thyristor, it is recalled that the thyristor turn-on if its voltage is positive and if a current pulse is sent to the gate.

To illustrate the modelling of controlled rectifier with Simulink, let's look at one of the principles of speed control of DC machines.

6.1. Electrical model

Let us consider the electrical scheme presented on figure 18a. It represents a DC motor fed by a six-pulse rectifier. The electrical equivalent circuit of the DC motor is described by an inductance L_a in series with a resistance R_a in series with an induced voltage V_a which characterizes the electromotive force, as illustrated in figure 18b.

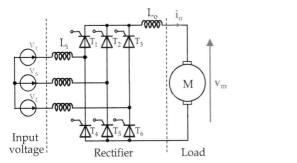
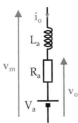

a) Electrical circuit   b) Simplified electrical circuit of a DC motor

Figure 18. Controlled rectifier with inductive load

The thyristor are modelled by an ideal model which traduces the state of the switch:

- $V_T = 0$ when the thyristor is state-on
- $I_T = 0$ when the thyristor is state-off

Similar to the diode rectifier, there are 13 operating phases to describe:

- 1 phase of discontinuous conduction mode (P_0)

All the thyristor are state-off

- 6 phases of classical conduction P_1 to P_6 (figure 15c)

P_1 : T_1 and T_5 state-on P_2 : T_1 and T_6 state-on P_3 : T_2 and T_6 state-on

P_4 : T_2 and T_4 state-on P_5 : T_3 and T_4 state-on P_6 : T_3 and T_5 state-on

- 6 phases of overlap O_1 to O_6 (figure 15d)

O_1 : T_1, T_5 and T_6 state-on O_2 : T_1, T_2 and T_6 state-on O_3 : T_2, T_4 and T_6 state-on

O_4 : T_2, T_3 and T_4 state-on O_5 : T_3, T_4 and T_5 state-on O_6 : T_1, T_3 and T_5 state-on

The different operating phases are illustrated in figure 15. The equations that governs an operating phase are the same whatever we work on a diode rectifier or a controlled rectifier.

6.2. Simulink model

The simulink model of the controlled rectifier with inductive load is presented in figure 19. It consists of four blocks:

- Input Voltage block characterizes the mains supply,
- teta_r block models the thyristor control,
- Controlled rectifier block computes the different operating phases.
- The load block represents the motor resistance R_a and the induced voltage V_a.

The motor inductance L_a is regrouped with the output line inductance L_o to have a single output inductor L_{oeq}.

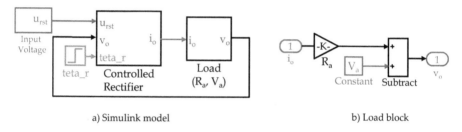

a) Simulink model   b) Load block

Figure 19. Simulink model of the controlled rectifier with inductive load

6.2.1. Internal structure of the rectifier block

The structure of the rectifier block is presented on figure 20a. Four different blocks can be seen on this scheme: the first one called "Control T" is used for the control of the thyristor gate. The second one called MF1 is used to compute the inductances state and voltage. The third called Current computes inductances currents. Then, the Initial Phase block computes the initial state for next computing phase.

The computing algorithm has been created in accordance with figure 20b. For each computing step, the new operating phase is calculated. This phase is a function of the initial phase, the sign of the inductance currents and the diode voltages. For each operating phase, the value of each inductance di/dt is calculated and permits to know the diodes currents with the integrator function.

The current block is strictly identical to the current block shown in figure 16.

6.2.2. Thyristor control

The control device for thyristor T_1 is presented in figure 21. The switch-on of T_1 is delayed of θ_r after u_{rt} has reached to zero (block "Delay 1"). The control thus carried out is a pulse train (the width of a pulse is computed by block "Delay 2").

The same principle is applied to the other thyristor.

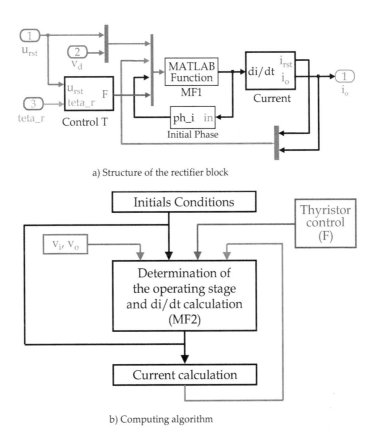

a) Structure of the rectifier block

b) Computing algorithm

Figure 20. Structure of the rectifier block

6.3. Experimental validation in continuous conduction mode

Simulations and experimental waveforms related to the electrical circuit presented in figure 18 are shown in figure 22. The simulation parameters are adjusted as follows:

$$U_{RMS} = 230 \text{ V}; R_a = 4 \ \Omega; V_a = 145 \text{ V}; L_i = 800 \ \mu\text{H}; L_{oeq} = 800 \text{ mH}$$

The list of configuration parameters used for Matlab simulation is:

Start time : 0   Stop time : 0.2s

Type : Variable-step   Solver : ode15s (stiff/NDF)

Max step size : 1e-4   Relative tolerance : 1e-5

Min step size : auto   absolute tolerance : auto

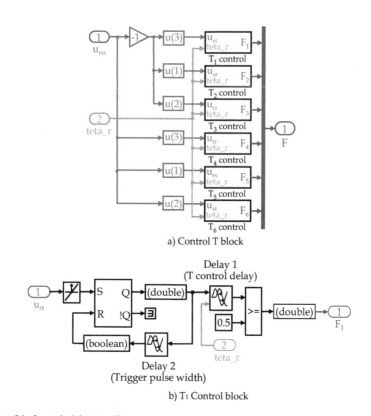

a) Control T block

b) T₁ Control block

Figure 21. Control of thyristor T₁

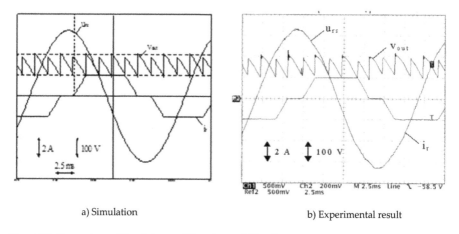

a) Simulation   b) Experimental result

Figure 22. Comparison of Simulation and Experimental Waveforms

We can see that simulation results are in good agreement with experimental waveforms. The overlap delays are equivalent for simulation and experimental results.

7. Conclusion

This chapter has shown that it is possible to simulate many electrical power converters only using Simulink toolbox of Matlab, thus avoiding the purchase of expensive and complex dedicated software. The simulation method is based on the variable topology approach where switching conditions of semiconductor are realized by switching functions.

The first part of this chapter is dedicated to the modelling of linear loads: RL series, RLC series and L in series with RC parallel dipoles are considered. The second part deals with the simulation of DC-DC converters. The buck converter is first studied: after describing the operating phases, open-loop and closed-loop models are presented. A simulation is realised for closed-loop model showing good agreement with theoretical values. The third part shows how to model three-phases DC-AC converters. The electrical circuit and his complete Simulink model are presented and simulation results on RL series load with PWM control are shown. The fourth part presents the modelling of a six-pulse AC-DC converter which is frequently used in industrial applications. The complete model of this converter and his Simulink equivalent circuit are accurately described taking into account overlap phenomenon. A simulation result on RL series load is presented and compared to experimental result. The similarity of the two results shows the validity of the proposed model. The fifth part extends the method to controlled rectifier. The structure studied here is a six-pulse thyristor rectifier feeding a DC motor. The difference with the diode rectifier is presented with the introduction of a thyristor control block in the simulation. Simulations results are showed in continuous condition mode and are in good agreement with experimental results.

Many of the results presented in this chapter are computed with short simulation times (few seconds). This can be achieved thanks to the simplicity of the proposed method. The power electronics converters presented are used alone but the method can be easily extended to cascaded devices allowing the simulation of complex power electronic structures such as, for example, active filters with non-linear loads.

Author details

Christophe Batard, Frédéric Poitiers, Christophe Millet and Nicolas Ginot
Lunam University - University of Nantes, UMR CNRS 6164 ,
Institut d'Electronique et de Télécommunications de Rennes (IETR), France

8. References

Ladoux, P.; Postiglione, G.; Foch, H.; & Nuns, J.; "A Comparative Study of AC/DC Converters for High-Power DC Arc Furnace," *IEEE Trans. Indus. Electron.*, vol. 52, no. 3, pp. 747-757, June 2005.

Qijun, P.; Weiming, M.; Dezhi, L.; Zhihua, Z. & Jin, M.; "A New Critical Formula and Mathematical Model of Double-Tap Interphase Reactor in a Six-Phase Tap-Changer Diode Rectifier," *IEEE Trans. Indus. Electron.*, vol. 52, no. 1, pp 479-485, Feb. 2007.

P. Zuniga-Haro, J. M. Ramirez, "Multi-pulse Switching Functions Modeling of Flexible AC Transmission Systems Devices", Electric Power Components and Systems, Volume 37, Issue 1 January 2009 , pages 20 – 42.

R. E. Araujo, A. V. Leite and D. S. Freitas, "Modelling and simulation of power electronic systems using a bond graph formalism," *Proceedings of the 10th Mediterranean Conference on Control and Automation* - MED2002 Lisbon, Portugal, July 9-12, 2002.

F. Terrien, M. F. Benkhoris and R. Le Doeuff, "An Approach for Simulation of Power Electronic Systems," *Electrimacs' 99*, Saint Nazaire, France, vol. 2, pp 201-206.

S. E. M. de Oliveira and J. O. R. P. Guimaraes, "Effects of Voltage Supply Unbalance on AC Harmonic Current Components Produced by AC/DC Converters", *IEEE Trans. on Power Delivery*, vol. 22, no. 4, pp. 2498-2507, Oct. 2007.

L. Hu and R. E. Morrison "The use of modulation theory to calculate the harmonic distorsion in HVDC systems operating on an unbalanced supply," *IEEE Trans. on Power Delivery.*, vol. 12, no. 2, pp. 973-980, May 1997, Letters to editor.

J. Arrillaga, B. C. Smith, N. R. Watson and A. R. Wood, "Power system harmonic analysis," ed *John Wiley & Sons, 1997*.

A. Pandey, D. P. Kothari, A. K. Mukerjee, B. Singh, "Modelling and simulation of power factor corrected AC-DC converters", International Journal of Electrical Engineering Education, Volume 41, Issue 3, July 2004, pp 244-264.

C. Batard, F. Poitiers and M. Machmoum, "An Original Method to Simulate Diodes Rectifiers Behaviour with Matlab-Simulink Taking into Account Overlap Phenomenon," *IEEE International Symposium on Industrial Electronics 2007, ISIE 2007*, pp 971-976, Vigo, Spain, 4-7 June 2007

Chapter 2

PID Control Design

A.B. Campo

Additional information is available at the end of the chapter

1. Introduction

Many industrial applications have digital closed loop control systems and the main algorithm used at these applications is the Proportional Integral Derivative structure (PID). This chapter presents some useful MATLAB commands that might be used as an instrument to analyze the closed loop and also to help the control system design. The first part presents the general standard structure of this controller, whereas MATLAB/SIMULINK programs are used to illustrate some design aspects. Script codes are used to describe the dynamic systems through the Laplace Transform and time response analysis of the system with time delays. Block diagram descriptions employed to represent the distillation process are used to analyses the Proportional Integral controller (PI) applied to the system. Performance analysis is conducted to implement an exhaustive searching algorithm applied in tuning PI parameters. At the second part a Smith Predictor structure is designed and presented to enhance the system performance. Some common feedback structures are presented and the classical literature will be referenced to present the main topics.

Along the chapter the tuning algorithms and the system analyses tools are presented through a specific application. This example is related to the tuning of PI control system applied to the temperature and pressure control in a distillation process designed to obtain the anhydrous ethanol and the hydrated ethanol from the sugarcane fermentation and distillation.

2. PID structures

In the literature, several works has describing the PID structure (Åström & Hägglund, 1995), (Ang, 2008), (Mansour, 2011) and (Alfaro, 2005). According to the authors the three term form is the standard PID structure of this controller. The structure is also known as parallel form and is represented by:

$$G(s) = K_p + K_I \frac{1}{s} + K_D s = K_p \left(1 + \frac{1}{T_I s} + T_D s \right) \tag{1}$$

Where:

K_P: proportional gain;
K_I : integral gain;
K_D: derivative gain;
T_I : integral time constant and
T_D: derivative time constant.

In MATLAB, the script code of parallel form may be represented by:

```
s = tf('s');
% PID Parallel form
Kp=10;
Td=0.1;
Ti=0.1;
G=Kp*(1+(1/(Ti*s))+Td*s);
```

The control parameters are:

-   The proportional term: providing an overall control action proportional to the error signal through the constant gain factor.
-   The integral term: the action is to reduce steady-state errors through low-frequency compensation by an integrator.
-   The derivative term: improves transient response through high-frequency compensation by a differentiator.

The very same system may be designed at SIMULINK Toolbox, represented in figure 1.

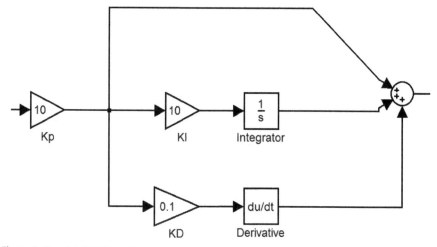

Figure 1. Simulink PID Control

To minimize the gain at high frequencies, the derivative term is usually modified to:

$$G(s) = K_p \left(1 + \frac{1}{T_I s} + \frac{T_D s}{1 + \alpha T_D s} \right) \tag{2}$$

Where α is a positive parameter adjusted between 0.01 and 1. This formulation is also used to obtain a causal relationship between the input and the output of the controller. Another usual structure employed at the PID controller is presented in figure 2.

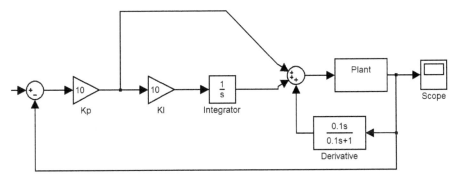

Figure 2. PID Controller with derivative term at the feedback branch.

According to this configuration, the derivative term is inserted out of the direct branch. The structure is carried to minimize the effect of set-point changes at the output of the control algorithm. By using this configuration only variations at the output signal of the plant will be added with the integral and proportional actions.

2.1. Tuning methods

Several tuning methods are described in (Åström & Hägglund, 1995) and in (Ang, 2007). The tuning methods are employed to obtain the stability of the closed-loop system and to meet given objectives associated with the following characteristics:

- stability robustness;
- set-point following and tracking performance at transient response, including rise-time, overshoot, and settling time;
- regulation performance at steady-state, including load disturbance rejection;
- robustness against plant modelling uncertainty;
- noise attenuation and robustness against environmental uncertainty.

In (Ang, 2007), the PID controllers tuning methods are classified and grouped according to their nature and usage. The groups that describe each tuning method are:

- Analytical methods—at these methods the PID parameters are calculated through the use of analytical or algebraic relations based in a plant model representation and in some design specification.

- Heuristic methods—These methods are evolved from practical experience in manual tuning and are coded trough the use of artificial intelligence techniques, like expert systems, fuzzy logic and neural networks.
- Frequency response methods—the frequency response characteristics of the controlled process is used to tune the PID controller. Frequently these are offline and academic methods, where the main concern of design is stability robustness since plant transfer function have unstructured uncertainty.
- Optimization methods—these methods utilize an offline numerical optimization method for a single composite objective or use computerised heuristics or, yet, an evolutionary algorithm for multiple design objectives. According to the characteristics of the problem, an exhaustive search for the best solution may be applied. Some kind of enhanced searching method may be used also. These are often time-domain methods and mostly applied offline. This is the tuning method used at the development of this work.
- Adaptive tuning methods—these methods are based in automated online tuning, where the parameters are adjusted in real-time through one or a combination of the previous methods. System identification may be used to obtain the process dynamics over the use of the input-output data analysis and real time modelling.

2.2. Measures of controlled system performance

A set of performance indicators may be used as a design tool aimed to evaluate tuning methods results. These performance indicators are listed from (3) to (6) equations.

Integral Squared Error (ISE)

$$J_{ISE} = \int_0^T \left(e(t)\right)^2 dt \tag{3}$$

Integral Absolute Error (IAE)

$$J_{IAE} = \int_0^T \left|e(t)\right| dt \tag{4}$$

Integral Time-weighted Absolute Error (ITAE)

$$J_{ITAE} = \int_0^T t\left|e(t)\right| dt \tag{5}$$

Integral Time-weighted Squared Error (ITSE)

$$J_{ITSE} = \int_0^T t\left(e(t)\right)^2 dt \tag{6}$$

These indicators can help the design engineer to decide about the best adjustment for the PID control parameters. In (Cao, 2008) it is presented some MATLAB codes to obtain these indicators.

3. Distillation column dynamics

In Brazil approximately 50% of vehicle fleet is composed of flex vehicles, resulting in 30 million of vehicles. This kind of vehicle uses fossil fuel and/or ethanol. The ignition system is adjusted automatically depending of the proportion of each fuel kind. To attend the national ethanol demand there are several ethanol distillation facilities across the country. In each of these facilities the fermented sugarcane is distilled, obtaining two products: the anhydrous ethanol and the hydrated ethanol.

The hydrated ethanol is obtained from link between the second and the third column. The anhydrous ethanol is obtained at the base of the third column, see Figure 3. The production process is composed of a series of columns where two variables are controlled to generate the hydrated ethanol and the anhydrous ethanol at the standardized specification: the pressure at the column A and the temperature at the distillation tray A20 (Santos et al., 2010). The hydrated ethanol has to have a concentration of 92,6 °INPM (°INPM is a measurement of the weight of pure ethanol fuel in 100g of ethanol fuel – water mixture). So as near the concentration is about this value, the best will be the quality of the hydrated ethanol and the anhydrous ethanol.

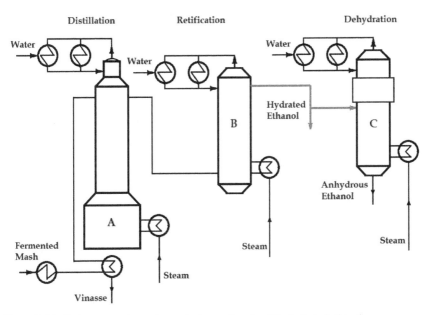

Figure 3. Distillation process to produce anhydrous ethanol and the hydrated ethanol.

These variables depend respectively on the steam flow at the basis of the column A and on the flow of fermented mash applied at the column A. The minimization of the variability of the alcoholic content according the brazilian standard NBR 5992-80 is the main design objective of the control system.

The distillation process is characterized by a high coupling through the system variables and by a non-linear relationship between them. According (Santos, 2010) the models that represent the relationship between the main process variables is FOTD (First Order with Time Delay).

$$G(s) = \frac{Ke^{-\theta s}}{\tau s + 1} \tag{7}$$

In this work the modeling procedure was developed and the following equation was obtained from the relationship of the pressure variation at the A column and the steam flow valve actuation:

$$K = \frac{\Delta PV}{\Delta MV} = \frac{(0,36 - 0,44).110\%}{55 - 85,91}$$
$$K = 0,26\% bar \ / \ \% opennig \tag{8}$$
$$\theta = t_1 - t_0 = 3s$$
$$\tau = t_2 - t_1 = 23s$$

Where MP is the Manipulated Variable e PV is the Process Variable.

So, the FODT representation is:

$$G(s) = \frac{0,26e^{-3s}}{23s + 1} \tag{9}$$

The same modeling procedure was developed to obtain the relationship among the variation of the temperature at the distillation tray A20 and the variation of the flow of fermented mash applied at the column A:

$$K' = \frac{\Delta PV}{\Delta MV} = \frac{\dfrac{(97,8 - 95,8)}{150}.110\%}{23\% - 33\%}$$
$$K' = -0,133\%^{\circ}C \ / \ \%_{opennig} \tag{10}$$
$$\theta' = t_1 - t_0 = 85s$$
$$\tau' = t_2 - t_1 = 174s$$

So, the FODT representation is:

$$G(s) = \frac{-0,133e^{-85s}}{174s + 1} \tag{11}$$

3.1. Tuning methods

The above systems were described in (Santos, 2010) and at that work there also were described and applied four tuning methods of the PI control: Ziegler-Nichols (First Method), CHR, Cohen-Coon and IMC (Internal Model Control).

Each method was analyzed through the use of Integral Absolute Error (IAE) and the best results are described at Table 1.

	Method	Kp	TI	IAE	Overshoot (%)
Pressure Control Loop	IMC	13	24	7,5	0%
Temperature Control Loop	Ziegler-Nichols	13.8	283	190	18%

Table 1. PI Tuning parameters

The simulation results presented (Santos, 2010) were used at the real process and another manual calibration was made. The new tuning parameters are presented at Table 2.

	Kp	T_I
Pressure Control Loop	13	2
Temperature Control Loop	12	30

Table 2. Manual PI Tuning parameters adjusted at the process.

The process where the temperature and pressure loops were modelled is described at figure 4 (Santos, 2010).

3.2. Exhaustive search solution

Both transfer functions represent a First Order plus Dead Time (FODT). So, for both systems it was applied the same procedure to tune the PI parameters. A Pade approximation is applied to generate a polynomial approximation to the delay time and a MATLAB program was designed to search the PI parameters.

The delay time of the system may be represented as a polynomial ratio according the Pade approximation. MATLAB has a specific function to generate this ratio, given the time delay and the order of the desired polynom. This function is:

$$[num,den] = pade(T,N)$$

Using this function and the transfer function of the pressure variation at the A column and the steam flow valve actuation, it was built an exhaustive searching algorithm to obtain the minimum Integral Absolute Error (IAE) using a Proportional Integral (PI) control system. At the next program it may be seen that the Pade approximation was built with two second order polynomial ratio.

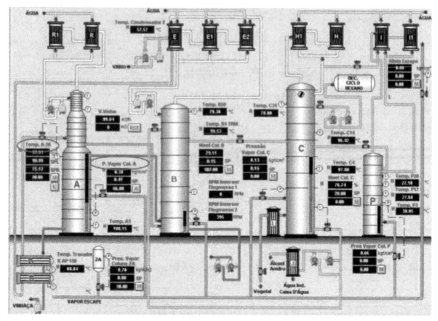

Figure 4. Piping and instrumentation diagram.

At the end of the execution, the minimum K_P obtained was equal to 17.3 and the minimum T_i was 23, and IAE equal 6.35. This is a better result than that presented at (Santos, 2010).

MATLAB program uses a Transfer Function representation for the Dead Time and for the plant. Both are associated in series through a specific MATLAB function and a unitary feedback loop is calculated to analyses the system response to several pairs of K_P and T_i values.

```
clc
close all
s = tf('s')
t=0:0.1:1000; tam=length(t);
T = 3;
% Plant - Transfer Function
plant = (0.26*((1-(T/2)*s+((T*s)^2)/12)/(1+(T/2)*s+((T*s)^2)/12)))/(23*s+1)
Kc = 12.00:0.01:18.00;
Ti = 22.00:0.01:25.00;
tamKp = length(Kp);
tamTi = length(Ti);
count = 1;
for i = 1:tamKc,
        for j = 1:tamTi,
```

```
                        PI = Kp(i)*(1+1/(Ti(j)*s));
                        H=series(PI,plant);
                        L=feedback(H,1);
                         [output, t] = step(L,t);
                        MP = Calcul_MP(output);
                        IAE = IAE_U_Step(output,0.1);
                        result(count,1) = Kp(i);
                        result(count,2) = Ti(j);
                        result(count,3) = MP;
                        result(count,4) = IAE;
                        count = count+1;
        end
        count
end
% Search for minimum Kc and minimum Ti
tam = length(result)
minimumIAE = 1000
for i=1:tam(1),
        if  minimumIAE > result(i,4)
                minimumIAE = result(i,4);
                minimumKp = result(i,1);
                minimumTi = result(i,2);
        end
end
minimumIAE
minimumKp
minimumTi
```

At the program listed above, two other functions were developed: *Calcul_Mp* and *IAE_U_Step*.

These functions are listed below:

```
function [MP] = CalculMP(output)
        tam = length(output);
        MP = (max(output)-output(tam))/output(tam)*100;
end
```

At the function CalculMP the output length is obtained to take the last value of the output variable to the step response. It is used to calculate the overshoot of the system.

At the next function the Integral Absolute Error (IAE) is numerically obtained using the output generated at the main mathscript code.

```
function [IAE_Value] = IAE_U_Step(output,int_T)
        Tam = length(output);
        IAE_Value = 0;
```

```
for i=1:Tam,
    if output(i) < 1
        IAE_Value = IAE_Value + (1-output(i))*int_T;
    else
        IAE_Value = IAE_Value + (1-output(i))*(-1)*int_T ;
    end
end
end
```

The closed loop system model with a PI control was built at SIMULINK as represented at figure 5.

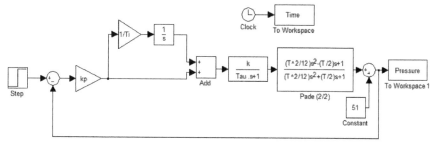

Figure 5. Closed loop Pressure Control with Pade approximation.

Applying a step function from 51 bar to 85 bar at the input of the system presented at figure 5, the output is presented at figure 6 for the tuning parameters obtained at the exhaustive search algorithm.

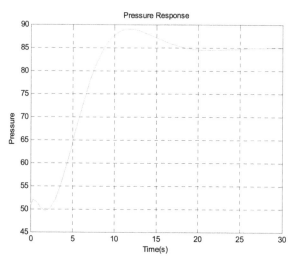

Figure 6. Step response of the closed loop pressure control system.

The step response presented at Figure 6 represents a fast response with low overshoot than that presented at (Santos, 2010). It is possible to verify the delay time at the output signal.

The same procedure was used to design the control algorithm to the temperature loop and best results were obtained when compared with those presented at (Santos, 2010). In both closed loops the exhaustive search for the best response was executed near the initial solution obtained through the experimental tuning procedure.

4. Smith Predictor design

A design tool very useful to control engineers when it is necessary to design a control system with delay at time response is the Smith Predictor (Ogata, 2009). At the distillation plant both SISO systems are represented by transfer functions with time delays. At this item it is done some considerations about the use of this technique to generate better results for the time response of the system. The control structure of the Smith Predictor is presented at figure 7.

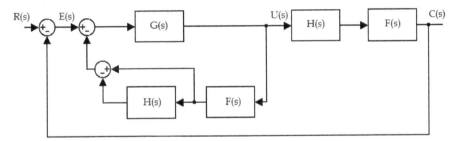

Figure 7. Smith Predictor Structure.

In the system presented at figure 7, H(s) represents the pure delay time and F(s) represents the plant transfer function without delay. Analysing as separated parts, it is proposed a controller with input E(s) and output U(s) that has the delay time transfer function H(s) and F(s) modelled in its structure. It is possible to analyse the system proposed and verify that its transfer function C(s)/R(s) is equal to the transfer function of the system presented at figure 8.

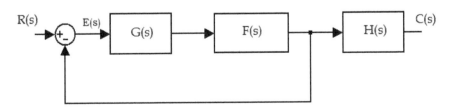

Figure 8. Equivalent system.

At figure 8 it is possible to verify that G(s) may be designed considering the transfer function F(s) without the time-delay. The transfer function of the complete system has the design specification plus the dead time present at the original plant.

4.1. MATLAB code implementing Smith Predictor

To analyse the system performance with a Smith Predictor structure it was developed a MATLAB code and a SIMULINK model. The mathscript code is presented below, with a Pade approximation to represent the time delay. The polynomial ratio used at the next code represents a delay of 3 seconds with the ratio of two second order polynomials. The block association was developed through the use of the association commands *series* and *feedback*.

Representing the Smith Predictor in a MATLAB code:

```
% Smith Predictor

clc
clear all
close all

s=tf('s')

% Delay with Pade aproximation
[num_d,den_d]=pade(3,2)

% PI Control System
Kp=2;
Ti=15;
G=Kp*(1+(1/(Ti*s)));

H=tf(num_d,den_d)
Gc=feedback(G,series((1-H),(0.26/(23*s+1))))

CL=feedback(series(Gc,series(tf(num_d,den_d),0.26/(23*s+1))),1)

figure(1)
step(CL,200)
grid
```

It is possible to see that the association G$_c$ represents the control algorithm, where G is the Proportional Integral controller designed to the plant without delay. The system designed with SIMULINK model is presented at figure 9.

At the next figure the step response obtained at the end of the program. It is possible to see that the stationary error is equal to zero and that the control parameters could be adjusted to obtain a small overshoot.

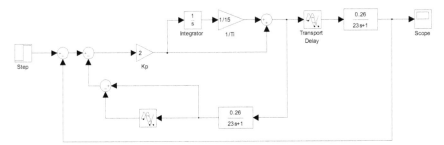

Figure 9. Smith Predictor in SIMULINK model.

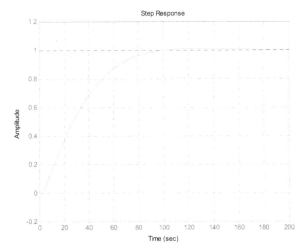

Figure 10. Closed loop system response.

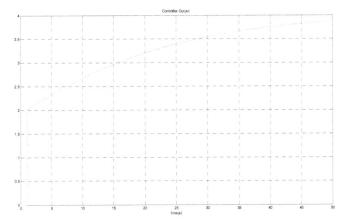

Figure 11. Controller output.

The output of the controller must be verified after the control system design to avoid the saturation of the actuators.

4.2. Digital control design

The control algorithm designed through the Smith Predictor may be described in a digital form, using the Z-Transform representation. The MATLAB script code below represents this transfer function.

```
% Digital Smith Predictor

clc
clear all
close all

s=tf('s')

Kp=2;
Ti=15;
G=Kp*(1+(1/(Ti*s)));

T=0.1;

Gz=c2d(G,T,'tustin')

n=3/T;

z=tf('z',0.1)

Hz=c2d(0.26/(26*s+1),T,'tustin')
Gcz=feedback(Gz,series(Hz,1-z^(-n))
```

The G transfer function represents the Proportional Integral algorithm and Gz is its discrete form using the Bilinear (Tustin) approximation. The sample time was adjusted in 0.1 s, since the dimension of time delay is about 30 times greater than this value. The time delay verified at the system may be easily modelled measuring how many samples the system measure along the total time delay. This measurement is represented at n=3/T.

The digital controller designed is represented by:

Transfer function:

$$2.007 z^{32} - 3.992 z^{31} + 1.986 z^{30}$$

$$1.001 z^{32} - 1.996 z^{31} + 0.9952 z^{30} - 0.001001 z^2 - 6.654e\text{-}006 z + 0.0009948$$

Sampling time: 0.1

The result presented above may be used to generate the difference equation:

$$u(k) = 2.007e(k) - 3.992e(k-1) + 1.986e(k-2) + 1.996u(k-1) - 0.9952u(k-2) + ...$$
$$...0.001u(k-30) + 0.000006u(k-31) - 0.00099u(k-32) \tag{12}$$

This equation implements the control algorithm at the digital system. The control algorithm designed to the temperature plant may also be described in a digital form, using the Z-Transform representation. At the next mathscript code this design procedure was applied, but at this case the sample frequency was adjusted to 1Hz, since the time response of the temperature system is very larger than the pressure system.

```
% Digital Smith Predictor - Temperature

G=Kp*(1+(1/(Ti*s)));

T=1;

Gz=c2d(G,T,'tustin')

n=85/T;

z=tf('z',T)

Hz=c2d(-0.133/(174*s+1),T,'tustin')
Gcz=feedback(Gz,series(Hz,1-z^(-n)))
```

Better results also were obtained using the Smith Predictor structure applied to the temperature loop control.

5. Conclusion

The analyses of two closed loops at a distillation process were presented at this chapter. The design specification presented at the references was attended through the use of an exhaustive search algorithm to obtain the best response according to the performance indices Integral Absolute Error (IAE). MATLAB code used to apply this algorithm is effective and generated a better response than that presented at references. Using MATLAB and SIMULINK it was designed a Smith Predictor algorithm and an enhanced control system was obtained. The MATLAB toolboxes used to analyse the control system was very useful to enhance the control system design. The digital representation of the control system was calculated with digital control systems commands.

Author details

A.B. Campo
Instituto Federal de Educação, Ciência e Tecnologia de São Paulo, Brazil

Acknowledgement

The author would like to thanks Instituto Federal de Educação, Ciência e Tecnologia de São Paulo for the MATLAB license and hardware resources used at the development of this work.

6. References

Alfaro, V. M., Vilanova, R. Arrieta O. Two-Degree-of-Freedom PI/PID Tuning Approach for smooth Control on Cascade Control Systems, *Proceedings of the 47th IEEE Conference on Decision and Control Cancun*, Mexico, Dec. 9-11, 2008.

Ang, K.H., Chong G. LI, Yun PID Control System Analysis, Design, and Technology, In: *IEEE Transactions on Control Systems Technology*, vol. 13, no. 4, july, 2005.

Åström, K.J. , Hägglund, T. (1995) *PID controllers Setting the standard for automation* 2nd Edition, 343 p., International Society for Measurement and Control.

Åström, K. J. , Hägglund, T. (1995) *PID Controllers: Theory, Design, and Tuning*, 2nd Edition ISBN 978-1-55617-516-9.

Cao, Yao. (January 2008). Learning PID Tuning III: Performance Index Optimization, In: *MATLAB CENTRAL File Exchange*, 08.04.2012, Available from http://www.mathworks.com/matlabcentral/fileexchange/18674-learning-pid-tuning-iii-performance-index-optimization

Mannini, P. ; Mello, V.F.; Santos, D.S.; Araújo, G.C.; Campo, A.B (2012) Projeto de controle PID em uma coluna de destilação de álcool, *Revista Sinergia* (submitted).

Mansour,T. (2011) *PID Control, Implementation and Tuning*, 238 p., InTech, ISBN 978-953-307-166-4, Rijeka, Croatia.

Ogata, K. (2009) *Modern Control Engineering*, 912p., 5nd. Edition, Prentice Hall ISBN-13: 978-0136156734,

Seborg, D.E.; Edgar, T.F., Mellichamp, D.A. *Process Dynamics and Control*, John Wiley & Sons, Singapore, 717p., 1989.

Santos, J.C. dos S.; Santos, R.P. dos; Salles, J.L.F. *Redução da Variabilidade do Teor Alcoólico na Indústria Sucroalcooleira*, ISA Show, Brazil, 2010.

Yurkevich, V. D. (2011) *Advances in PID Control*, InTech, ISBN 978-953-307-267-8, Rijeka, Croatia.

Chapter 3

Post Processing of Results of EM Field Simulators

Tomas Vydra and Daniel Havelka

Additional information is available at the end of the chapter

1. Introduction

In this chapter we shall focus on the needs that many researchers, scientists and even students have very often. When using commercial simulation software for numerical simulation of electromagnetic field we frequently encounter many insufficiencies which those software products have. Usually, main aim of computational software developers is to optimize and refine so called core of these programmes – EM field solver. After that CAD (Computer Assisted Design) and post processing parts of EM simulators are dealt with. Mainly this can be an issue with newer, short-time in development products but one's own post processing using Matlab can be greatly beneficial even when using well established simulators of EM field. This is largely due to its flexibility which cannot be overcome by any EM field simulator.

Throughout this chapter we will show you many ways of post processing which we use in our research of EM field in industrial and medical applications (Vrba et al., 2008; Vydra et al., 2011) and in primary research of EM field around living cells and structures inside cell bodies (Cifra et al., 2011; Havelka et al., 2011).

We hope that this chapter will aid many researchers and students in the vast field of EM research. Here, we present our knowledge and tips which we have gathered through our studies and our research.

1.1. Technical introduction

Generally, rough results we obtain using simulators of electromagnetic field - or from analytical solution of systems described by discrete elements - are in the form of complex vector components of intensity of electric and magnetic field (i.e. time dependent – periodical – components in the directions of coordinate axes). We process these results using Matlab and interpret them to draw conclusions. In this chapter we would like to present basic processing of rough data, calculation of specific absorption rate and other parameters in particular regions of simulation domain, visualization of results in many ways (pcolor, slices, histograms, multiple iso-surface, surf interpretation on various shapes according to specific task etc.). We will provide detailed examples with practical applications and explanation of advantages provided by presented solutions.

2. Rough results from EM field simulator

As mentioned above, in this chapter we suppose that we have obtained rough data from any numerical simulator of EM field and now we want to interpret them. First of all we should look at how the structure of this data looks like. To get the full understanding we shall briefly go through some EM field basics.

2.1. EM field basics

Electromagnetic Field can be described using well known Maxwell's equations (for more information on Maxwell's equations please refer to any book dealing with EM field theory).

$$\left.\begin{array}{l} \oiint DdS = Q \\ \oiint BdS = 0 \\ \oint Edl = -\dfrac{d\phi}{dt} \\ \oint Hdl = I_0 + I_c \end{array}\right\} \qquad (1)$$

Simply by solving those equations EM field can be completely described at all points of space and time. This leads us to complete description of EM field using only phasors of intensity of electric and magnetic field E and H (or D and B where $D = \varepsilon E$ and $B = \mu H$). This means that output of conventional commercial simulator is in the form of time dependent vectors that have components in axis x, y and z. These vectors are defined for each part of computational domain (e.g. when using FDTD (Thomas et. al., 1994), vectors are defined for each voxel – block discretizing computational domain).

We can see that this type of data can be extracted in form of matrices (multi-dimensional, e.g. 4D). Now, we shall look closer at those matrices.

2.2. Data structure

As we mentioned in previous chapter, results from simulators of EM field are represented as matrices, which directly predestines them to be processed in Matlab, which is the perfect tool for matrix operations.

There is a sample of data obtained from simulation in the following table. It depicts x-component of vector of intensity of electric field [V/m] in y-axis section in a part of some model.

X/Z [mm]	1	2	3	4	5	6	7	8	9	10
1	10	10	11	12	13	14	12	9	8	7
2	10	10	11	12	13	14	11	10	9	8
3	11	11	11	12	13	14	13	11	10	9
4	12	12	12	12	13	14	13	12	11	10
5	13	13	13	12	13	14	12	12	12	11
6	14	14	13	13	13	14	13	13	13	12
7	13	14	13	13	13	14	14	14	14	12
8	13	14	14	14	14	14	15	15	14	13
9	13	13	13	14	15	15	16	15	14	13
10	12	13	13	14	14	15	15	15	14	13

Table 1. X-component of vector of intensity of electric field [V/m]

Following graphical representation can help us shed some more light on the structure of data we obtained. These data are represented as four dimensional matrices (for phasors *E* and *H* separately) depicting whole computational domain and they are time dependent.

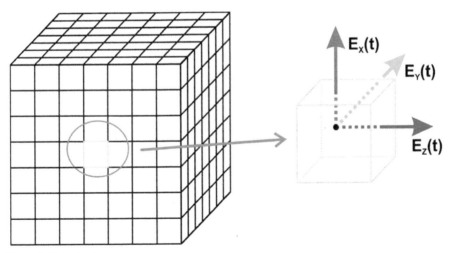

Figure 1. Data structure

Generally we can describe phasors as follows.

$$\widehat{V}_{(x,y,z,t)} = V_{(x,y,z)}e^{j\omega t} \tag{2}$$

Note: It may be necessary to convert data to suitable matrix form (e.g. rough data are in the form of a row vector with axial information for each element). We will look into it in the chapter 3.

Now that we know what our data source looks like we can simply process it to view the results and highlight some of their aspects according to our needs (see Table 2. for axial information).

```
73 -    actualAxisX(1) = loadedVectorX(1);
74 -    for a = (2:length(loadedVectorX))
75 -        if loadedVectorX(a) == loadedVectorX(1)
76 -            break;
77 -        else
78 -            actualAxis(a) = loadedVector(a);
79 -        end;
80 -    end;
81
82 -    d = 2;
83 -    actualAxisY(1) = loadedVectorY(1);
84 -    for b = (2:length(loadedVectorY)-1)
85 -        if loadedVectorY(b+1) ~= loadedVectorY(b)
86 -            actualAxis(d) = loadedVector(b+1);
87 -            d = d + 1;
88 -        else
89 -            if loadedVector(b+1) == loadedVector(1)
90 -                break;
91 -            end;
92 -        end;
93 -    end;
94
95 -    e = 2;
96 -    actualAxisZ(1) = loadedVectorZ(1);
97 -    for c = (2:(length(loadedVectorZ)-1))
98 -        if loadedVectorZ(c+1) ~= loadedVectorZ(c)
99 -            actualAxisZ(e) = loadedVectorZ(c+1);
100 -           e = e + 1;
101 -       end;
102        end;
```

Figure 2. Extraction of Axes (in our example)

3. Viewing the results

In this section we are going to show some examples of how obtained data can be viewed, how to interpret those results, what type of projection should we use etc. We shall illustrate this on some practical examples of EM field applications.

3.1. Basic transformation of rough data

As mentioned above we might obtain rough data in the form of a row vector. Let us illustrate this in this simple example. Our computational domain is 2 by 2 by 2 thus obtained row vector (x-component, apmlitude) has 8 elements. See Table 2.

x axis	1	2	1	2	1	2	1	2
y axis	1	1	2	2	1	1	2	2
z axis	1	1	1	1	2	2	2	2
Vector of values	8	6	5	2	5	6	8	9

Table 2. Amplitude of x-component of intensity of electric field [V/m]

From this we can extract axis. As long as we do not know the length of each axis we need to utilize this method to find actual axial data (see Figure 2.).

Note that actual axis arrangement can be different in your case (e.g. x and y axis arrangement may be commuted). Thus it is vital to get familiar with axial arrangement in your exporter from EM field simulator.

Furthermore, `actualAxis` vectors are underlined because they are growing on every loop iteration. Since axial vectors are not usually very long, this poses only mild concern. They cannot be preallocated because we generally do not know their actual length. If you are expecting very long axial vectors you may consider preallocating them safely longer than your expectations and then just using part of them which is non-zero (you may select this part of a vector using `find` – please refer to Matlab documentation).

Now that we know the length of each axial vector we may sort the vector of exported values and transform it to a matrix which will better represent three dimensional nature of our computational domain and will allow us to plot data with axial information. In this case we can very well utilize `reshape` which is built in Matlab.

MATRIX = reshape(vector_of_values,lenght(X),lenght(Y),lenght(Z))

Thanks to this process we now have every component of each vector (i.e. *E* and *H*) represented as three dimensional matrix and we can utilize it further.

3.2. Basic plotting of data

First of all, we need to bear in mind that we have time-dependent data. The most basic process is to plot actual situation (distribution of intensity of electric or magnetic) at a given time, or amplitude of vector. (In some applications we may need to plot just one component of this vector. This is even simpler because then we can disregard following method.)

Phasor of intensity of electric or magnetic field can be represented by modulus and phase or real and imaginary part. We need to merge all the components of the vector and obtain real and imaginary part. This can be simply done (i.e. vector adding component matrices together). Then we have one matrix of complex numbers. We can choose specific time in which we need EM field to be plotted simply by adding $<0,2\pi>$ to the phase of each vector and then we can plot real and imaginary modulus of the vector in specified time. Or we take just the amplitude of vectors and plot them.

It is very usual to plot RMS (i.e. Root Mean Square) value of vectors which is defined as follows.

$$RMS|E| = \frac{|E|}{\sqrt{2}}$$

(3)

This can be again obtained very simply from amplitude of intensity of electric field. (Note that this same procedure can be used also in the case of intensity of magnetic field H, usually in applications involving heating and/or drying we deal only with intensity of electric field E, because it is the source of heat generation in exposed samples.)

Now that we have three dimensional matrix of values of $RMS|E|$ we can plot it to see what our results look like. In the following section there is an example we prepared to illustrate how the results can be viewed and interpreted.

3.2.1. Example of basic data plotting

In this section we shall extract data from a simulation which has setup according to the Figure 3. Please note that this is just an example without any practical use, it serves only as an illustration.

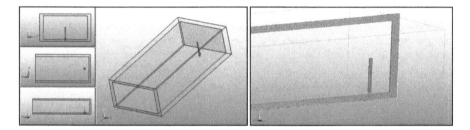

Figure 3. Model Setup and Its Voxel Representation (waveguide section with excitation probe at 2.45 GHz, voxels shown in section)

We simulated simple section of a waveguide (inner dimensions 100x50x200 mm) with one side shorted (there is an excitation probe in form of a cylinder in the distance of 17 mm from the shorted end) and the other side open (absorbing boundary condition – absorbs 99.9% of incident power). We extracted the data and plotted them using Matlab.

As you can see (Fig 4ab.) we used several colormaps which enable us to highlight different aspects in our results interpretation. Sometimes it is needed to have contrast colormap (jet, lines – for more information see Product Help of Matlab), at other circumstances you may need to use fine and moderate colormaps (hot, gray, bone, pink – for more information see Product Help of Matlab). In the fourth graph in Fig. 4 we used different shading – faceted. This enables us to highlight structure of computational grid. In many commercial simulators of EM field parts of a model need to be meshed finer than others (e.g. in our case the excitation probe needs to be meshed four times more than the rest of the waveguide to be voxeled sufficiently). In other examples we used shading interp to get more clear view.

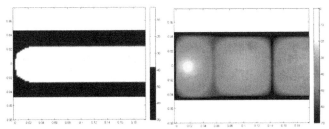

a - Interpretation of Extracted Data (Y-plane, middle section of the waveguide) [dB]

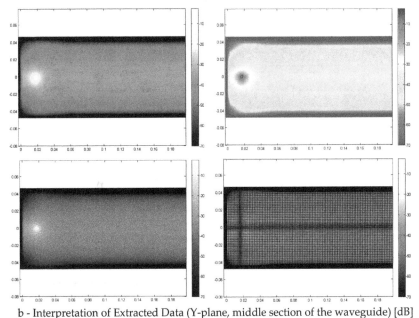

b - Interpretation of Extracted Data (Y-plane, middle section of the waveguide) [dB]

Figure 4. a - (*RMS*|*E*| colormap-Custom, real modulus E in phase 0° colormap-Hot)
b - (from left upper corner to right lower corner: *RMS*|*E*| colormap-Hot, *RMS*|*E*| colormap-Jet,
RMS|*E*| colormap-Gray, *RMS*|*E*| shading faceted)

We can also utilize custom colormaps. This can be exceptionally beneficial in applications where we need to find out where values are at some critical level or higher. We illustrated this feature in the first image in Fig. 4a. In Fig. 5. there is an Colormap Editor which can be accessed through: Figure – Edit – Figure Properties – Colormap pull-down menu – Custom.

In our example we set segment in the middle to black colour and segment next to it to white colour. This resulted in the graph as seen in Fig. 4a. For more information on colormaps please refer to the Product Help of Matlab.

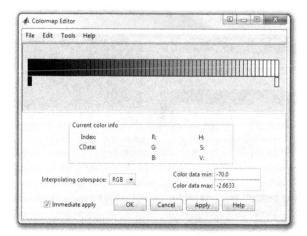

Figure 5. Colormap Editor Window

Furthermore, we illustrated how real modulus of vector of intensity of electric field at phase 0° is interpreted using Matlab (second image in Fig. 4a.). This is the most basic interpretation of obtained data we can do.

Note that this kind of results interpretation is much more flexible than the interpretation allowed by post processing tools in commercial EM simulators. In the following example we shall show how to work with time dependency of phasors. Since the results of EM field simulator are extracted when the steady state is reached time dependency is reduced to angle of phasors depicting the field of vectors. Through the following method we can alter phase of those phasors and show real part and imaginary part through one period. The results can be seen in Fig. 6. Figure 7. shows example of data processing to achieve this.

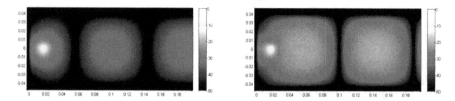

Figure 6. Phase Shifted Data – real part of vector E [dB] (left phase = 0°, right phase = 90°)

Note: In many EM field simulators you may encounter various errors. Pay special attention to the data structure of your exported data since it may not be useful in the way we have shown here (e.g. real and imaginary parts are exported as absolute values so the vital information about phase is lost).

Note: In the part of the script (Fig. 7.) where lowerThan variable is used we are changing the range of values. Since there are parts of model where values of intensity of electric or magnetic field are very near to zero, minimum of these values in dB would be around -400 dB. This renders produced images useless (value range is huge but most of the relevant values are in the region <-50,0>). Using function find we identify indexes of elements with values lower than -50 dB and we replace those elements with value -50 dB. For more information on function find please refer to the Product Help of Matlab.

Note: In this example we use function subaxis which has similar usage as function subplot but allows users to set the layout of plots in the figure more accurately (options Padding, Spacing, Margin etc.). For more information on subaxis please see internet documentation.

3.2.2. Treatment efficiency analysis

In the following example we will go through one of many useful applications of EM simulators today – evaluation of hyperthermia cancer treatment. Generally, hyperthermia is a method through which tissue is overheated (usually using microwave energy) and cells die (principle of this method is that energy is focused into the cancerous tissue which is less perfused and thus it is more heated – temperature in treated area rises above levels that trigger cell apoptosis). For more information on microwave hyperthermia see for example (Vrba & Oppl., 2008).

Model of simulated experiment can be seen in Figure 8. In this example we use waveguide applicator which is fed by coaxial line ending in protruding inner wire which is located near the shorted end of the waveguide section. There is a horn aperture which helps focus microwave energy to the desired area.

Relatively complex and complicated structure of human body is replaced with so called "phantom" that represents simple muscle tissue. In the model there is a tumor located 1 cm below the surface of phantom. This tumor has the same dielectric parameters as the surrounding muscle tissue (usually the only difference in simulations between muscle tissue and tumorous tissue is in their perfusion, heat transfer rate and heat generation rate – generated heat in tumorous tissue is usually transferred slower than in physiological surrounding tissue).

Additionally there is a water bolus which serves as a coolant body protecting the surface tissue of patient and moving the maximum of temperature to the lower layers. In this example we use source at 434 MHz and the applicator is filled with water (required dimensions of the applicator are effectively lower and impedance matching between waveguide-bolus and body are much better). For more information on waveguide hyperthermia applicators please refer to (Vera et al., 2006).

In this simulation we again extract rough data from EM simulator and we process them further using Matlab. We again have intensity of electric and magnetic field defined in every element of the model. For effective analysis of the treatment we need to evaluate SAR (Specific Absorption Ratio) which describes how much power is absorbed in a weight unit [W/kg]. For more information on SAR see http://www.ets-lindgren.com/pdf/sar_lo.pdf.

```
86
87
88        % In previous process we separated only one slice from the 3D matrices
89 -      complexMatrix = exportedRealPart + 1i.*exportedImaginaryPart;
90 -      phi = [0,pi/2]; % variable phase shift
91 -      cMatrixDimensions = size(complexMatrix);
92
93 -      logMatrix = zeros(cMatrixDimensions(1),cMatrixDimensions(2),length(phi));
94
95 -   ⊟for k = (1:length(phi))
96 -          phaseShiftedMatrix = complexMatrix.*exp(1j.*phi(k));
97
98 -          realMatrix = real(phaseShiftedMatrix);
99
100 -         hValue = max(max(abs(realMatrix)));
101
102 -         logMatrix(:,:,k) = 20.*log10(abs(realMatrix)./hValue);
103
104 -         lowerThan = find(logMatrix < -50);
105 -         logMatrix(lowerThan) = -50;
106 -    end;
107
108 -   d=figure(k); clf;
109 -   subaxis(1,2,1,'Padding',0.001,'Spacing',0.001,'Margin',0.03); hold on;
110 -   pcolor(osaY,osaX,logMatrix(:,:,1));
111 -   colormap(hot);
112 -   shading interp;
113 -   axis image;
114 -   colorbar;
115 -   subaxis(1,2,2,'Padding',0.001,'Spacing',0.001,'Margin',0.03); hold on;
116 -   pcolor(osaY,osaX,logMatrix(:,:,2));
117 -   colormap(hot);
118 -   shading interp;
119 -   axis image;
120 -   colorbar;
121
```

Figure 7. Method of phase shifting results

To determine how SAR is distributed we need to use this formula.

$$SAR = \frac{\sigma}{2\rho}|E|^2 \qquad (4)$$

As we see, in this case we can very well utilize $RMS|E|$. From formula (3) we can say that SAR is defined by following equation.

$$SAR = \frac{\sigma}{\rho}RMS|E|^2 \qquad (5)$$

SAR is thus depending on RMS value of intensity of electric field, on conductivity of a material and on its density. We need to obtain those values somehow. In our case whole phantom has homogeneous density and electric conductivity thus we can only mask matrix of $RMS|E|$ and multiply each element by coefficient produced by ratio of σ and ϱ.

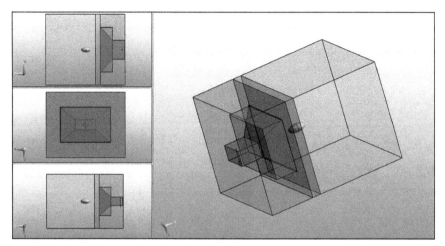

Figure 8. Model of microwave hyperthermia at 434 MHz

Note: There are other options how to do that. For example some EM simulator allow users to export matrix of dielectric parameters of a model (this will produce similar matrix to our masking matrix).

Now we should look into how to produce masking matrix efficiently. From our model we know that every element of the voxelized model is phantom if its value of y axis is higher than 120 mm (we can find out this in CAD part of EM simulator). We can prepare our three dimensional matrix of $RMS|E|$ according to previous sections. We also have actual axis of this matrix which we obtained from exported file as well. We simply need to identify which element is at the 120 mm value and then we shall mask the elements with lower value of y axis.

An elegant way to find the index at y axis of element which has the value nearest to 120 mm (note that the value is not usually exactly 120 so if we looked for the exact match we would probably fail) is to use function min. Example of this method is as follows.

```
lookFor = 120;
[min_difference, array_position] = min(abs(araay-lookFor));
% Minimal difference shows us the difference between the closest element
% and our looked for value. Array position then indicates the position of
% such element.
```

Figure 9. Example of finding the closest element position

In this example, we can illustrate one other useful feature of Matlab processing of EM simulator results. We can instantly normalize obtained results. Usually it is possible to extract actual power in the source which was simulated (e.g. 0.002496 W) and we can utilize this to obtain normalization coefficient. Power normalization coefficient is given by the following formula.

```
if min_difference > 0
    values(:,((position-1):-1:1),:) = 0;
    values(:,(position:length(actualAxisY)),:)...
    = (values(:,(position:length(actualAxisY)),:)).^2.*sigma./rho;
else
    values(:,((position+1):-1:1),:) = 0;
    values(:,(position:length(actualAxisY)),:)...
    = (values(:,(position:length(actualAxisY)),:)).^2.*sigma./rho;
end;
```

Figure 10. Covering Field of $RMS|E|$ with Mask

$$coef\, f_{power} = \frac{Power\, to\, which\, we\, want\, to\, normalize}{Actual\, Simulated\, Power} \tag{6}$$

Since this is the coefficient of power ratio we need to use coefficient of intensity of electric field ratio which is the square root of coefficient of power (see the equation below).

$$coef\, f_{power} \approx \frac{E^2_{norm}}{E^2_{acctual}} \Rightarrow coef\, f_E = \sqrt{coef\, f_{power}} \tag{7}$$

Simply by multiplying the matrix of data by this coefficient we obtain normalized data to the desired value of delivered power.

Now we can show several interpretations of results we obtained (Z section in the middle of the model). Thanks to Matlab's flexibility and versatility we can highlight the results in the way that is far more efficient than by using post processing of the EM field simulator. In the following figures we show intensity of electric field and SAR in the treated area.

As you can see in figure 11. each colour scheme highlights different thing (as for the first three). In the fourth graph we used custom colormap to show some kind of a critical zone. In this example we expected that higher values of SAR than 1000 W/kg are considered to be dangerous in some regions (note that these critical limits differ significantly in every application – many factors contribute, e.g. vital or sensitive organs near the treated area etc.) and thus we highlighted the zone with higher values using bright red colour. This may be very important but commercial simulation software generally omits such option.

It may be also very useful to show obtained data only in the region of the tumour or to show values in form of several slices, semi-transparent layers or iso-surface view. Now we shall show how to prepare masking matrix for some simple geometrical objects representing tumours. For more information on the mentioned advanced techniques of results representation please see section 4. Advanced Viewing Techniques.

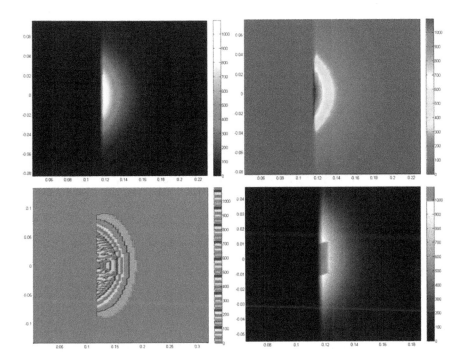

Figure 11. SAR [W/kg] in Different Colour Schemes (from left upper corner to right lower corner: hot, jet, lines, custom)

3.2.3. Preparation of masking matrix

Very simple masking (i.e. when the region that needs to be masked is in the form of a cuboid) was shown in previous section. Now we should look into masking regions round in shape (i.e. spheres, ellipsoids and other common shapes that parts of model can be represented by).

Spheres are case of ellipsoid and we shall treat them as such. So our main aim now is to mask region generally in ellipsoidal form. Equation defining an ellipsoid (with its origin at x_c, y_c, z_c) in the three dimensional coordinate system is shown below.

$$\frac{(x-x_c)^2}{a^2} + \frac{(y-y_c)^2}{b^2} + \frac{(z-z_c)^2}{c^2} \leq 1 \tag{8}$$

The graphical representation of a general ellipsoid can be seen in figure 12. There we can see that a, b and c are semi-principal axes of ellipsoid and define its dimensions.

Albeit there is a built-in function designed to generate ellipsoid (see the Product Help of Matlab) we shall show you an easy way which allows you to generate desired masking matrix (e.g. with values 0 or 1).

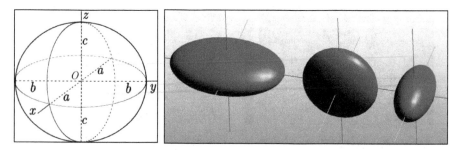

Figure 12. Representation of Ellipsoid (from left: scheme, tri-axial, oblate, prolate)

As you can see in Fig. 13. we simply utilized the formula representing ellipsoid and all elements whose coordinates meet the given restrictions are filled with ones. The other elements remain zero. Constants `elementsX`, `elementsY` or `elementsZ` define the length of axis of computational domain (i.e. `actualAxisX` and so on). Variables `xc`, `yc` and `zc` define centre of our ellipsoid.

```
85 -        maskingMatrix = zeros(elementsX,elementsY,elementsZ);
86          % Note that the size of a maskingMatrix will be the same as the size of
87          % matrix containing the results. We can use this to our advantage and
88          % define maskingMatrix using size[resultsMatrix].
89 -        for x = (1:elementsX)
90 -            for y = (1:elementsY)
91 -                for z = (1:elementsZ)
92 -                    if (((actualAxisX(x)-xc)^2/a^2)+...
93                             ((actualAxisY(y)-yc)^2/b^2)+...
94                             ((actualAxisZ(z)-zc)^2/c^2)) <= 1;
95 -                        maskingMatrix(x,y,z) = 1;
96 -                    end;
97 -                end;
98 -            end;
99 -        end;
```

Figure 13. Defining Ellipsoid in the Masking Matrix

Now we can simply use generated masking matrix and multiply every element of result matrix by according element of masking matrix. Then we can look how our results are interpreted in detailed view in the tumour.

From masked matrix of SAR we can also easily extract total power radiated to the tumorous region. Total power lost in the healthy tissue is than given by the difference between total power (in the case of perfectly matched source) and power lost in the tumour.

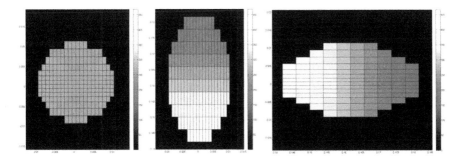

Figure 14. SAR [W/kg] in Tumour (from left: Y-slice, X-slice, Z-slice)

Note: In some cases it might be beneficial to set the colorbar range the same in all pictures (as shown in Fig. 14.). The simplest way to do this is to set value of [1,1] element of displayed matrix (i.e. a slice) to the maximum value of the whole three dimensional matrix (if needed, the minimum value should be set to element [max,max] of displayed matrix).

Additional information that we can obtain from masked result matrix is total absorbed power in the tumour. Since we know the dimensions of the tumour we can easily calculate its volume and use following formula.

$$P_{absorbed} = Volume \sum_{all\,voxels} RMS|E|^2 \sigma \tag{9}$$

The volume of standard ellipsoid is given as follows.

$$V = \frac{3}{4}\pi abc \tag{10}$$

For example in our case tumour has volume only 8.37766e-6 m^3. Information on total absorbed power may be very efficient way of preliminary evaluation for the treatment planning. Through this method we can determine power lost in any part of a simulated model. There may be some intricate volumes which are not as easily described as ellipsoid. Then we need to export their volume or masking matrix from the EM simulator (if possible).

We can determine the volume of such complicated shapes by summing elementary volumes of voxels representing those shapes. This may be unnecessary in some more advanced EM field simulators since they allow us to export model data in many suitable forms for Matlab processing. But the method presented in the following text is universal and can serve for better understanding of the model, its grid and working principals of EM simulations.

First of all we need to define which voxels are occupied by the model we want to evaluate. For this example we shall use our previously generated ellipsoid. As you can see in Fig. 14. generally grid of a simulation does not have to be symmetrical (i.e. voxels are not cubes but they are in the form of general cuboids). This means that each element may be representing different volume. We have our matrix of zeros and ones which we generated in Fig. 13. Now we need to apply this matrix to the actual coordinate system.

We can use built-in function `meshgrid` to produce three dimensional matrices which contain coordinates for specified element (for more information on function `meshgrid` please refer to the Product Help of Matlab). Now we can easily determine exact coordinates of elements occupied by our model (see Fig. 15.).

```
 7 -     oldValue = 1;
 8 -     for k = 1:length(actualAxisZ)
 9 -         [D,E] = find(valuesMasked(:,:,k) > 0);
10 -         if isempty(D) == 0
11 -             C(oldValue:(oldValue + length(D) - 1)) = k;
12 -             oldValue = oldValue + length(D);
13 -         end;
14 -         if k == 1
15 -             A = D';
16 -             B = E';
17 -         else
18 -             A = [A D'];
19 -             B = [B E'];
20 -         end;
21 -     end;
22
23 -     completeVolume = abs(actualAxisX(A + 1) - actualAxisX(A)).*...
24             abs(actualAxisY(B + 1) - actualAxisY(B)).*...
25             abs(actualAxisZ(C + 1) - actualAxisZ(C));
26
27 -     sum(completeVolume)
```

Figure 15. Determination of Coordinates of Model Elements

At this moment we need to get better understanding of how models are defined. Since the values (in this case ones) are located in the nodes of the grid not in the centers we need to determine how the model actually looks like. See the following figure for better understanding (2D-plane is used to illustrate).

As you can see there will be an error caused by this node to cell transformation. When the simulation grid is defined appropriately (i.e. it is fine enough) the error will be only marginal. If such error is unacceptable more advanced techniques of node to cell transformation should be used. But for purposes of this example this method is more than sufficient. For example, volume of previously defined ellipsoid determined voxel by voxel is $8.5302e-6$ m^3. This means that the relative error is 1.8 % (and this error includes error caused by voxelization itself – this means that node to cell transformation really brings only marginal error in simulations with fine grid).

In the Fig. 16. you can see that node to cell transformation can be done in a few (precisely 8) ways. We can easily determine which way is the most precise (i.e. [(A+1) – A] or [(A-1) – A] and its combinations with B and C). Since our model is voxelized symmetrically there is almost no difference between volumes computed accordingly to various node to cell transformations (ranging between 8.5302e-6 and 8.5304e-6).

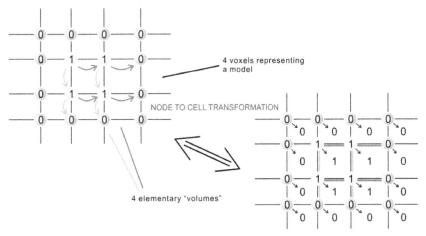

Figure 16. Actual Model Dimensions

4. Advanced viewing techniques

This section deals with some examples of advanced viewing of results that we have found useful during our work. As you have noticed, up to this point we have represented 3D results only in 2D graphs. This is because usually these 2D representations are clearer and easier to interpret. But for overviewing or demonstrational purposes we might need to show whole situation in 3D. For doing this we shall use multiple sections of a computational domain (slice or surf) and iso-surfaces.

4.1. Multiple layer viewing

We can display results in multiple 2D sections with variable transparency. This method of results visualization can give us much better overview of how a situation looks like.

It can be also beneficial to use surface view as semi-transparent layers to view results in semi-masked way. Through this we can highlight some regions of model without completely blocking visual output from other regions. For example, in our case, we can use one surface view of $RMS|E|$ in agar phantom and semi-mask it with alphamap of tumour (values 1) and the rest of tissue (values 0.5).

Figure 19. shows us how this graph is plotted and how transparencyMatrix is prepared.

Note that when using this type of transparency mapping maximum and minimum values must be present in transparencyMatrix (i.e. one edge of transparencyMatrix is set to 0 to denote the minimum value of transparency).

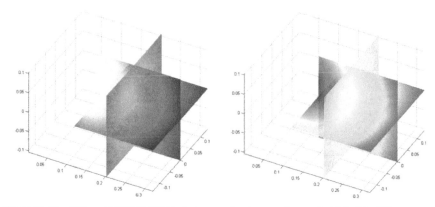

Figure 17. Sliced View of $RMS|E|$ [dB] (only in agar phantom, colormap hot, jet, alpha 0.7)

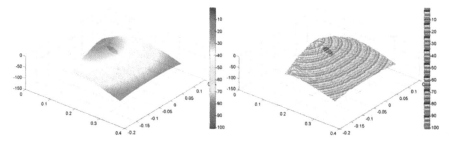

Figure 18. Surface View of RMS|E| in [dB] (transparency of tumour region set to 1 – opaque, transparency of other regions set to 0.5 – semi-transparent; colormap – jet and lines)

Through this method we can produce much more intricate visualizations of results which are unseen in commercial EM simulators. For example we can mask results in uninteresting regions (immediate vicinity of power source etc.) almost entirely, semi-mask results in exposed tissue and left results in tumour unmasked, vital organs and other key regions of simulation domain. Note that masking results with transparency matrix does not alter presented values.

This may pose a problem when values around a power source are extreme and render the rest of results unclear. For this purpose you may consider utilizing simmilar approach as presented in Figure 7. Instead of finding values lower than some value you may find values higher than some reasonable value and lower all higher values to this level.

Many more possibilities are offered thanks to post processing of EM results in Matlab. As mentioned before, the greatest advantage is that it is extremely flexible and can meet very specific requirements which can arrise with various applications of EM field. In the following section we shall demonstrate some results obtained during our primary research of EM field of microtubules (nanostructures in living cells which serve as a crude frame of a cell and have other important roles in life cycle of a cell).

```
104 —        transparencyMatrix = zeros(elementsX,elementsY,elementsZ);
105          % Note that the size of a transparencyMatrix will be the same as the
106          % size of matrix containing the results. We can use this to our
107          % advantage and define maskingMatrix using size[resultsMatrix].
108 —        for x = (1:elementsX)
109 —            for y = (1:elementsY)
110 —                for z = (1:elementsZ)
111 —                    if (((actualAxisX(x)-xc)^2/a^2)+...
112                          ((actualAxisY(y)-yc)^2/b^2)+...
113                          ((actualAxisZ(z)-zc)^2/c^2)) <= 1;
114 —                        transparencyMatrix(x,y,z) = 1;
115 —                    else
116 —                        transparencyMatrix(x,y,z) = 0.5;
117 —                    end;
118 —                end;
119 —            end;
120 —        end;
121
122 —        transparencyMatrix(length(actualAxisX),:,:) = 0;
123
124 —        figure(1);clf;
125 —        surf(actualAxisY(40:end),actualAxisX,valuesLog(:,40:end,51),...
126              'FaceAlpha','flat','AlphaDataMapping','scaled',...
127              'AlphaData',transparencyMatrix(:,40:end,51));
128 —        colorbar;
129 —        shading interp;
130 —        set(gca,'FontSize',14)
```

Figure 19. Fig. 19. Generation of Overalaying Transparency Matrix and Its Utilization

4.2. Iso-surface viewing

In this section we are going to show several results of EM field around microtubule. This structure is generally consisting of protofilaments which are polymerized tubulin heterodimers. Thirteen protofilaments bound together form a microtubule structure which resembles a long hollow tube (see Fig. 20).

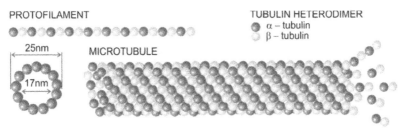

Figure 20. Microtubule Structure Visualization

Tubulin heterodimers (i.e. basic building block of microtubules) are highly polar structures and provided some form of external energy (movement of microtubules, mechanical vibrations etc.) they may produce EM field around themselves (Pohl, 1981; Fröhlich, 1978).

In our work EM field simulations of microtubule model were entirely conducted using Matlab. Tubulin heterodimers were represented as vibrating elementary electrical dipoles (EED) and EM field was determined for each of these EEDs. Combining the results led to unravelling the EM field produced by these complicated structures at whole (Havelka, 2009).

For the purpose of this text we shall look at visualization of these results we used to present obtained EM field. Because microtubules are symmetrical structures we have found out that representing its field by iso-surface view is very clear and easy to interpret.

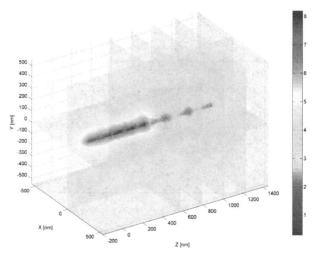

Figure 21. Sliced Semi-transparent View of Electric Field around Microtubule (see 4.1)

In the figure 23. you can see part of the code used to generate such visualization. More information on isosurface can be found in the Product Help of Matlab. In this particular example we wanted to view results in the form of several iso-surfaces. First of all we determined the range of data obtained through Matlab analysis of EM field around our sample microtubule.

Then we need to choose which values we want to be visualized as iso-surfaces (in this case, values range is extremely wide therefore we choose only exponents – 7, 5, 2). Then we need to find which positions at colour scale are lower than our actually viewed value (we generate the colour scale using function jet(length of colour scale)). Then we simply use function patch (to build 3D wire model of locations with desired values – i.e. 1e2, 1e5, 1e7) and we set its colour which we choose accordingly from our generated colour scheme.

Additionally you can choose lighting (particularly useful in this case is gouraud lighting which does not produce any glances on multiple iso-surfaces). It is also beneficial to use alpha which is lowered with each loop (to retain clarity of the visualization).

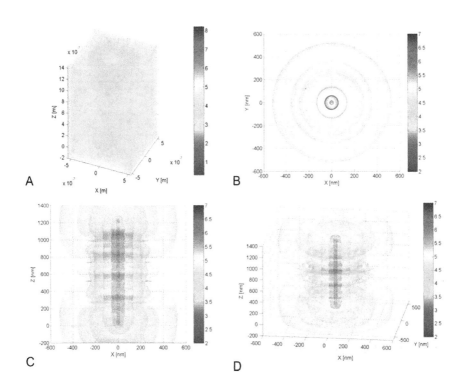

Figure 22. Iso-surface View of Electric Field around Microtubule [-] (A – rough data, B – iso-surface view from above, C – iso-surface view from enface, D – iso-surface view – general angle)

Last part is generating tiny triangle which is concealed in the middle of viewed data and contains the minimum and the maximum values which allows us to show colorbar appropriately for all the iso-surfaces .

5. Conclusion

In this work we have presented basic methods of how to process obtained rough data from commercial EM simulators or even process data from our own simulations done in Matlab. We show how Matlab processing can be greatly beneficial in highlighting results in many ways that are unseen in commercial EM simulators.

We present very simple way to modify data in the form suitable for further processing and then we illustrate how to view these data in ways highlighting specific aspects (i.e. values in specific regions (tumorous tissue), evaluation of treatment efficiency, utilization of Matlab in primary research, 3D viewing etc.). These innovative ways of combination of specialized software with researcher's versatile tool, such as Matlab is, yield in very productive and efficient way of scientific exploration of the vast field of electromagnetism.

```
2     max_E = log10(max(max(max(E_matrix)))); % Range of values in imported data
3     min_E = log10(min(min(min(E_matrix)))); % Range of values in imported data
4     ISOsurfaces = [7 5 2]; % Which values should be visualized
5     color_scale = 1000; % Refinement of colorbar
6    ⊟for u = 1:size(ISOsurfaces,2)
7
8        T_vp = find(ISOsurfaces(u) >=...
9                linspace(min(ISOsurfaces),max(ISOsurfaces),color_scale));
10       color_all = jet(color_scale);
11
12       figure(3);hold on
13         p = patch(isosurface...
14               (Xcoord*1e9,Ycoord*1e9,Zcoord*1e9,E_matrix,10^ISOsurfaces(u)));
15         set(p,'FaceColor',color_all(T_vp(1,end),:),'EdgeColor','none');
16
17         title({'Intensity of electric filed around model of microtubule';...
18                 'log_{10}(V/m)'});
19         xlabel('X [nm]'); ylabel('Y [nm]'); zlabel('Z [nm]');
20         grid on;
21         camlight; lighting gouraud
22         alpha(0.5 - 0.05*u)
23         hold on;
24         a = [1,1;0,0]*1e-9; b = [0,1;1,0]*1e-9; c = [0,0;0,0]*1e-9;
25         d = [max(ISOsurfaces) max(ISOsurfaces) ;...
26                 min(ISOsurfaces) min(ISOsurfaces)];
27         surf(a,b,c,d)
28         colorbar;
29    └ end;
```

Figure 23. Generation of Iso-surface View of EM Field around Microtubule

The results that are obtained in our research of EM field around living cell help us understand crucial facts about this part of our lives which has to be truly discovered yet. Matlab in this instance allows us to visualize result so we can support or on the other hand disapprove many theories (e.g. transportation of particles around microtubule via EM field).

Author details

Tomas Vydra and Daniel Havelka
Czech Technical University in Prague, FEE, Department of Electromagnetic Field, Czech Republic

Acknowledgement

This research is supported by the Grant Agency of the Czech Republic by project 102/08/H081: "Non Standard Applications of Physical Fields" and by CTU project SGS12/071/OHK3/1T/13: "Advanced techniques in the processing of industrial materials and biopolymers using electromagnetic field - multi-frequency processing ". Further it is supported also by research program MSM6840770012: "Transdisciplinary Research in the Area of Biomedical Engineering II" of the CTU in Prague, sponsored by the Ministry of Education, Youth and Sports of the Czech Republic.

6. References

Cifra, M.; Pokorný, J.; Havelka, D. & Kučera, O. (2010). Electric field generated by axial longitudinal vibration modes of microtubule, *BioSystems*, ISSN 0303-2647, vol.100, no.2 (May 2010), pp. 122-131, Oxford, GB

Fröhlich, H.; (1978). Coherent electric vibrations in biological systems and the cancer problem, *IEEE Transactions on Microwave Theory and Techniques*, Vol.26, No.8 (August 1978), pp. 613-618, ISSN 0018-9480

Havelka, D.; Cifra, M. (2009). Calculation of the Electromagnetic Field Around a Microtubule. *Acta Polytechnica*, Vol.49, No.2 (2009), pp. 58-63. ISSN 1210-2709.

Havelka, D.; Cifra, M.; Kučera, O.; Pokorný, J. & Vrba, J. (2011). High-frequency electric field and radiation characteristics of cellular microtubule network, *Journal of Theoretical Biology*, ISSN 0022-5193, vol. 286, no. 1, p. 31-40, London, GB

Pohl, H.A. (1981). Electrical oscillation and contact inhibition of reproduction in cells, Journal of Biological Physics, Vol.9, No.4 (1981), pp. 191-200, ISSN 0092-0606

Thomas, V.A.; Ling, K.; Jones, M.E.; Toland, B.; Lin, J. & Itoh, T. (1994). FDTF analysis of an active antenna, *IEEE Microwave Guided Wave Lett.*, Vol.4, No.9 (September 1994), pp. 296-298, ISSN 1051-8207

Vera, A.; Valentino, A.; Baez, A.; Trujillo, C.J.; Zepeda, H. & Leija, L. (2006). Rectangular Waveguide for Electromagnetic Oncology hyperthermia: Design, Construction and Characterization, *Proceedings of 3rd International Conference on Electrical and Electronics Engineering 2006*, pp. 1-4, ISBN 1-4244-0402-9, Veracruz, Mexico, September 6-8, 2006

Vrba, J.; Oppl, L.; & Vrba, D. (2008). Microwave Medical Imaging and Diagnostics, *Proceedings of EuMC 2008 38th European Microwave Conference*, pp. 408-411, ISBN 978-2-87487-006-4, Amsterdam, Netherlands, October 28-31, 2008

Vrba, J. & Oppl, L. (2008). Prospective Applications of Microwaves in Medicine, *Proceedings of COMITE 2008 14th Conference on Microwave Techniques*, pp. 1-4, ISBN 978-1-4244-2138-1, Prague, Czech Republic, April 23-24, 2008

Vydra, T.; Vorlicek, J. & Vrba, J. (2011). Measurement and analysis of microwave processing of biopolymers, *Proceedings of 21th International Conference Radioelektronika 2011*, pp. 1-4, ISBN 978-1-61284-325-4, Brno, Czech Republic, April 19-20, 2011

Chapter 4

Performances of the PCA Method in Electrical Machines Diagnosis Using Matlab

Jacques Fanjason Ramahaleomiarantsoa, Eric Jean Roy Sambatra, Nicolas Héraud and Jean Marie Razafimahenina

Additional information is available at the end of the chapter

1. Introduction

Nowadays, faults diagnosis is almost an inevitable step to be maintained in the optimal safety operating of every physical system. Electrical machines, main elements of every electromechanical system, are among the research topics of many academic and industrial laboratories because of the importance of their roles in the industrial process. Lots of technologies of these machines are old and well controlled. However, they remain the seat of several electrical and mechanical faults [1-4]. Thus, this article deals with faults detection of a wound rotor synchronous machine (WRIM) by the principal component analysis (PCA) method.

Several diagnostic methods have been proposed and used in the literature for the electrical machines diagnosis [1-4]. The PCA method, which showed his effectiveness in the fault detection and isolation (FDI), was implemented recently for the system diagnosis [5-8].

This work is then to prove the strength of PCA method in faults diagnosis of systems using WRIM as application device.

To proceed with, in the first, we propose an accurate analytical model of the WRIM without or in the presence of faults [1, 9]. This model provides the matrix data of several characteristic quantities of the machine. These data will be included as input variables of the PCA method.

Then, we present a complete approach of PCA method based on the study of residues [10]. Special attention has been paid for the choice of the number of principal components to be maintained [11, 12].

These models are then implemented in the Matlab software. Simulation results of several variables (stator and rotor currents, shaft rotational speed, electrical power, electromagnetic torque and other variables issued from mathematical transformations) of healthy and faulted WRIM are analyzed. Comparisons of simulation results with those of other diagnostic methods are performed to show the effectiveness and importance of the PCA method in fault diagnosis systems [9].

The following are the different steps of the approach:

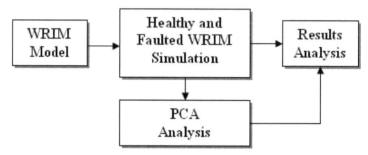

Figure 1. Synoptic diagram of the different steps of the data treatment

The Figure 1 shows that the proposed approach is divided in four blocs:

- WRIM modeling: mathematical equations calculation and simulation.
- Simulation :graph showing the output states of the system (healthy and faulted operation)
- Results Analysis: system diagnosis.
- PCA: data treatment.

2. WRIM modeling

In the process of faults survey and diagnosis, an accurate modeling of the machine is necessary. In this paper, three phases model based on magnetically coupled electrical circuits were chosen.

The aim of the modeling is to highlight the electrical faults influences on the different state variables of the WRIM. For that, some modeling assumptions given in the following section are necessary.

2.1. Modeling assumptions

In the proposed approach, we assumed that:

- the magnetic circuit is linear, and the relative permeability of iron is very large compared to the vacuum,
- the skin effect is neglected,

- hysteresis and eddy currents are neglected,
- the airgap thickness is uniform,
- magnetomotive force created by the stator and the rotor windings is sinusoidal distribution along the airgap,
- the stator and the rotor have the same number of turns in series per phase,
- the coils have the same properties,
- the WRIM stator and rotor coils are coupled in star configuration and connected to the considered balanced state grid.

2.2. Differential equation system of the WRIM

We note that the voltage vectors ([Vs], [VR]), the current vectors ([Is], [IR]) and the flux vectors ([Φs], [ΦR]) of the stator and rotor are respectively:

$$[V_S] = \begin{bmatrix} V_A \\ V_B \\ V_C \end{bmatrix} ; \quad [I_S] = \begin{bmatrix} I_A \\ I_B \\ I_C \end{bmatrix} ; \quad [\phi_S] = \begin{bmatrix} \phi_A \\ \phi_B \\ \phi_C \end{bmatrix}$$

$$[V_R] = \begin{bmatrix} V_a \\ V_b \\ V_c \end{bmatrix} ; \quad [I_R] = \begin{bmatrix} I_a \\ I_b \\ I_c \end{bmatrix} ; \quad [\phi_R] = \begin{bmatrix} \phi_a \\ \phi_b \\ \phi_c \end{bmatrix}$$

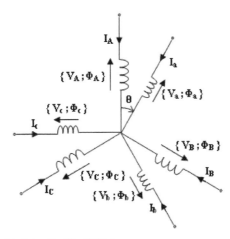

Figure 2. Equivalent electrical circuit of the WRIM

V_j, I_j and Φ_j (j : A, B, C for the stator phases and a, b, c, for the rotor phases) are respectively the voltages, the electrical currents and the magnetic flux of the stator and the rotor phases, θ is the angular position of the rotor relative to the stator.

The Figure 2 shows the equivalent electrical circuit of the WRIM. Each coil, for both stator and rotor, is modelised with a resistance and an inductance connected in series configuration (Figure 3).

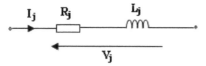

Figure 3. Equivalent electrical circuit of the WRIM coils

$$[V_S] = [R_S] [I_S] + \frac{d[\phi_S]}{dt} \tag{1}$$

$$[V_R] = [R_R] [I_R] + \frac{d[\phi_R]}{dt} \tag{2}$$

$$[\phi_S] = [L_S] [I_S] + [M_{SR}] [I_R] \tag{3}$$

$$[\phi_R] = [L_R] [I_R] + [M_{RS}] [I_S] \tag{4}$$

$[R_S]$ and $[R_R]$ are the resistance matrices, $[L_S]$ and $[L_R]$ the self inductance matrices, and $[M_{SR}]$ and $[M_{RS}]$ the mutual inductances matrix between the stator and the rotor coils.

With (3) and (4), (1) and (2) become:

$$[V_S] = [R_S] [I_S] + \frac{d\{[L_S] [I_S]\}}{dt} + \frac{d\{[M_{SR}] [I_R]\}}{dt} \tag{5}$$

$$[V_R] = [R_R] [I_R] + \frac{d\{[L_R] [I_R]\}}{dt} + \frac{d\{[M_{RS}] [I_S]\}}{dt} \tag{6}$$

By applying the fundamental principle of dynamics to the rotor, the mechanical motion equation is [13]:

$$J_t \frac{d\Omega}{dt} + f_v \Omega = C_{em} - C_r \tag{7}$$

$$\Omega = \frac{d\theta}{dt} \tag{8}$$

with:

$$C_{em} = \frac{1}{2} [I]^t * \frac{d([L])}{d\theta} * [I] \tag{9}$$

is the total inertia brought to the rotor shaft, the shaft rotational speed, $[I]=[I_A \ I_B \ I_C \ I_a \ I_b \ I_c]^t$ the current vectors, the viscous friction torque, the electromagnetic torque, the load torque, the angular position of the rotor relative to the stator and $[L]$ the inductance matrix of the machine.

Introducing the cyclic inductances of the stator and the rotor $L_{SC} = \dfrac{3}{2}L_S$ and $L_{RC} = \dfrac{3}{2}L_R$ (L_S is the self inductance of each phase of the stator and L_R is the self inductance of each phase of the rotor), the mutual inductances between the stator and the rotor coils M_{SR} and pole pair number p, the inductance matrix of the WRIM can be written as follow:

$$[L] = \begin{bmatrix} L_{SC} & 0 & 0 & M_{SR}f_1 & M_{SR}f_2 & M_{SR}f_3 \\ 0 & L_{SC} & 0 & M_{SR}f_3 & M_{SR}f_1 & M_{SR}f_2 \\ 0 & 0 & L_{SC} & M_{SR}f_2 & M_{SR}f_3 & M_{SR}f_1 \\ M_{SR}f_1 & M_{SR}f_3 & M_{SR}f_2 & L_{RC} & 0 & 0 \\ M_{SR}f_2 & M_{SR}f_1 & M_{SR}f_3 & 0 & L_{RC} & 0 \\ M_{SR}f_3 & M_{SR}f_2 & M_{SR}f_1 & 0 & 0 & L_{RC} \end{bmatrix} \tag{10}$$

$$f_1 = \cos(p\theta) \tag{11}$$

$$f_2 = \cos(p\theta + \frac{2\pi}{3}) \tag{12}$$

$$f_3 = \cos(p\theta - \frac{2\pi}{3}) \tag{13}$$

By choosing the stator and rotor currents, the shaft rotational speed and the angular position of the rotor relative to the stator as state variables, the differential equation system modeling the WRIM is given by:

$$[\dot{X}] = [A]^{-1}([U] - [B][X]) \tag{14}$$

with:

$$[X] = [I_A \ I_B \ I_C \ I_a \ I_b \ I_c \ \Omega \ \theta]^t$$

$$[A] = \begin{bmatrix} [L] & 0 & 0 \\ 0 & J_t & 0 \\ 0 & 0 & 1 \end{bmatrix}; \quad [U] = \begin{bmatrix} [V] \\ -C_r \\ 0 \end{bmatrix};$$

$$[V] = [V_A \ V_B \ V_C \ V_a \ V_b \ V_c]^t;$$

$$[B] = \begin{bmatrix} [R] + \Omega\dfrac{d[L]}{d\theta} & 0 & 0 \\ -\dfrac{1}{2}[I]^t \dfrac{d[L]}{d\theta} & f_v & 0 \\ 0 & -1 & 0 \end{bmatrix}$$

This model of the WRIM will be used to simulate both the healthy and the faulted configuration of the stator and the rotor.

2.3. WRIM faults

Despite the constant improvements on technical design of reliable machine, different types of faults still exist. The faults can be resulted by normal wear, poor design, poor assembly (misalignment), improper use or combination of these different causes.

Figure 4 and Figure 5 show the faults distribution carried out by a German company on industrial systems. The Figure 4 shows the faults of the low and medium power machines (50KW to 200KW), and the Figure 5 those of the high power machines (from 200KW) [1-2].

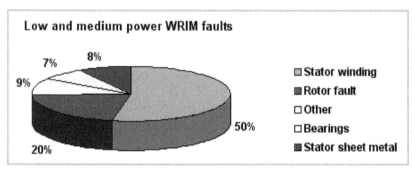

Figure 4. Low and medium power induction machines faults [1-2]

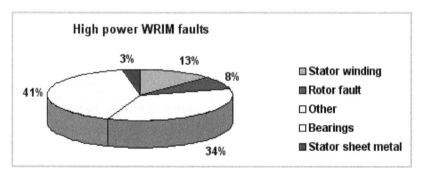

Figure 5. High power induction machines faults [1-2]

Figure 4 shows that the most encountered faults of the low and medium power on the induction machines are the stator faults and the Figure 5 shows that the faults due to mechanical defects give the highest percentage. The induction machine faults can be classified into four categories [2]:

The stator faults can be found on the coils or the breech. In most cases, the winding failure is caused by the inter-turns faults. These last grow and cause different faults between coils, between several phases or between phase and earth point before the deterioration of the machine [3]. The breech of electrical machines is built with insulated thin steel sheets in order to minimize the eddy currents for a greater operational efficiency. For the medium and great power machines, the core is compressed before the steel sheets emplacement to minimize the rolling sheets vibrations and to maximize the thermal conduction. The core problems are very low, only 1% if compared to winding problems [4].

The rotor faults can be bar breaks, coils faults or rotor eccentricities.

The bearings faults can be caused by a poor choice of materials during the manufacturing steps, the problems of rotation within the breech caused by damaged, chipped or cracked bearing and can create disturbance within the machines.

The other defaults might be caused by flange or shaft defaults. The faults created by the machine flange are generally caused during the manufacturing step.

2.4. Considered faults

The considered faults are on the resistance values which increase due to the rise of their temperature. In normal operation, a resistance value variation compared to its nominal value (in ambient temperature, 25°C) is a faulted machine due to machine overload or coils fault [1,9]. The resistance versus the temperature is expressed as:

$$R = R_0(1 + \alpha \Delta T) \tag{15}$$

R_0 is the resistance value at $T_0 = 25°C$, α the temperature coefficient of the resistance and ΔT the temperature variation.

3. PCA methodology

The PCA method is based on simple linear algebra. It can be used as exploring tool, analyzing data and models design. The PCA method is based on the transformation of the data space representation. The new space dimension is smaller than that the original space dimension. It is classified as without model method, [5] and it can be considered as full identification method of physical systems [6]. The PCA method allows providing directly the redundancy relations between the variables without identifying the state representation matrix of the system. This task is often difficult to achieve.

3.1. PCA method formulation

We note by $x_i(j) = [x_1\ x_2\ x_3\ ...x_m]$ the measurements vector. « i » represents the measurement variables that must be monitored ($i = 1$ to m) and « j » the number of measurements for each variable « m », $j = 1$ to N.

The measurements data matrix ($X_d \in R^{N*m}$) can be written as follows:

$$X_d = \begin{pmatrix} x_1(1) & \dots & x_m(1) \\ \dots & \dots & \dots \\ x_1(N) & \dots & x_m(N) \end{pmatrix} \tag{16}$$

The data matrix is described by a smallest new matrix, that is an orthogonal linear projection of a subspace of m dimension on a less dimension subspace l ($l<m$). The method consists in identifying the PCA model and it is based on two steps [10]:

- Determination on the eigenvalues and the eigenvectors of the covariance matrix R.
- Determination of the structure of the model, which consists in calculating the component number « l » to be retained in the PCA model.

3.2. Eigenvalues and eigenvectors determination

The first step is the data normalization. The variables must be centered and reduced. Then, the obtained normalized matrix is:

$$X = [X_1 \dots X_m] \tag{17}$$

And the covariance matrix R is given by:

$$R = \frac{1}{N-1} XX^T \tag{18}$$

By decomposing R, (17) can be expressed as:

$$R = P\Lambda P^T \tag{19}$$

With

$$PP^T = P^T P = I_m \tag{20}$$

Λ is the diagonal matrix of the eigenvectors of R and their eigenvalues are ordered in descending order with respect to magnitude values ($\lambda_1 \geq \lambda_2 \geq \dots \geq \lambda_m$).

The eigenvectors matrix P is expressed as:

$$P = [p_1, p_2, \dots, p_m] \tag{21}$$

p_i is the orthogonal eigenvectors corresponding to the eigenvalue λ_i. Then, the principal components matrix can be calculated using:

$$T = XP \tag{22}$$

$$T \in \mathfrak{R}^{N*m}$$

3.3. PCA model construction

To obtain the structure of the model, the components number « l » to be retained must be determined. This step is very important for PCA construction. The component number can be determined by using the following:

$$\left(\frac{\sum_{i=1}^{l} \lambda_i}{\sum_{k=1}^{m} \lambda_k}\right) * 100 \geq thc, l < m \tag{23}$$

Where "thc" is an user defined threshold expressed as percentage. Now, user should retain only the components number « l » which was associated in the first term of (23). By reordering the eigenvalues, the minimum numbers of components are retained while still reaching the minimum variance threshold [14].

By taking into account the number of components to be retained and by partitioning the principal component matrix T, the eigenvectors matrix P and the eigenvalues matrix Λ [12], the constructed PCA model is given by:

$$T = \left[T_p^{N*l} T_r^{N*(m-l)}\right] \tag{24}$$

$$P = \left[P_p^{N*l} P_r^{N*(m-l)}\right] \tag{25}$$

$$\Lambda = \begin{bmatrix} \Lambda^{l*l} & \cdots & 0 \\ \vdots & \ddots & \vdots \\ 0 & \cdots & \Lambda^{(m-l)(m-l)} \end{bmatrix} \tag{26}$$

T_p and T_r are respectively the principal and residual parts of T, P_p and P_r are respectively the principal and residual parts of P.

With this PCA model, the centered and reduced matrix X can be written as:

$$X = P_p T_p^T + P_r T_r^T \tag{27}$$

By considering:

$$X_p = P_p T_p^T = \sum_{i=1}^{l} P_i T_i^T \tag{28}$$

$$E = P_r T_r^T = \sum_{i=l+1}^{m} P_i T_i^T \tag{29}$$

The centered and reduced data matrix is given by:

$$X = X_p + E \tag{30}$$

X_p is the principal estimated matrix and E the residues matrix which represents information losses due to data matrix X reduction. It represents the difference between the exact and the approached representations of X. This matrix is associated with the lowest eigenvalues $\lambda_{l+1}, ..., \lambda_m$. Therefore, in this case, the data compression preserves all the best information that it conveys.

4. PCA method application on WRIM

4.1. Simulation conditions

Nine state variables (m=9) have been chosen to be monitored and 10000 measures (N=10000) during 4s are considered. The WRIM faults are introduced from the initial time (t=0s) to the final time (t=4s) of the different simulations. The machine is coupled to a mechanical load torque (10Nm) at t=2s. The considered faults are respectively, increases from 10% to 40% of the resistance value of both stator and rotor coils.

4.2. Choice of the number of principal components

The Figure 6 and the Figure 7 represent the residues variation of the WRIM stator current versus time and show impact of the « l » number in the diagnosis approach.

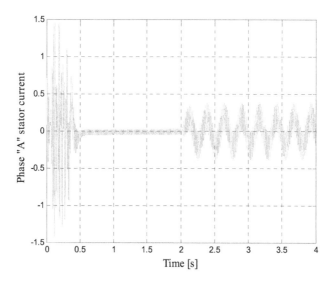

Figure 6. Stator current residue for $l = 5$

Figure 6 show that the chosen number of components is too high then the residual space dimension is reduced. Some faults are projected in the principal space and the stator current residues can not be detectable.

However, with the Figure 6, the number of components is well chosen. Faults can be detected and localized and the PCA model is well reconstructed.

Generally, the detection approach in the case of diagnosis based on analytical model is linked with the residues generation step. From these residues analysis, the decision making step must indicate if faults exist or not. The residues generation approach can be the state estimation approach or the parameter estimation approach.

The residue indicates the information losses given by the matrix dimension reduction of the state variables matrix data to be monitored. Indeed, a small residue means that the estimated value tends to approach the exact value in healthy operation case.

In our case, the eigenvalues corresponding to the number of the retained principal components represent 93% of the total sum of eigenvalues. Only 7% of the total represent the residues subspace. One can conclude that the PCA model has been well constructed.

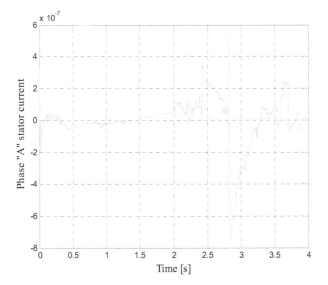

Figure 7. Stator current residue for $l = 6$

5. Simulation results

The different simulation results have been performed with respect to the simulation conditions mentioned earlier.

Figure 8 to Figure 13 and Figure 16 represent the real variations without PCA method, and Figure 14, Figure 15 and Figure 17 represent the residue variations with PCA application of the faulted WRIM state variables in considering the stator defaults.

With the WRIM state variables, other quantities obtained by their transformations have been calculated:

- quadrature axis and direct axis currents with Park transformation,
- α axis and β axis currents with Concordia transformation.

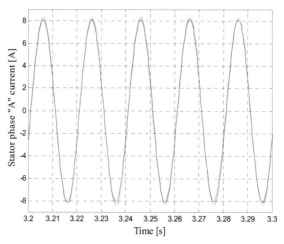

Figure 8. Real variations versus time of the stator current of the healthy and faulted WRIM

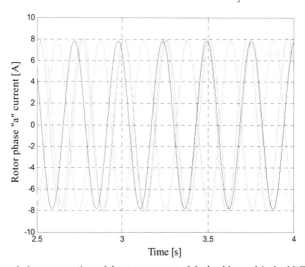

Figure 9. Real variations versus time of the rotor current of the healthy and faulted WRIM

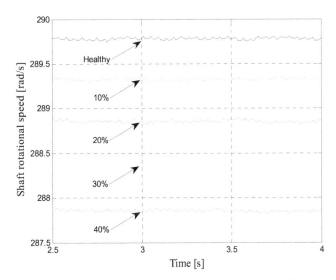

Figure 10. Real variations versus time of the shaft rotational speed of the healthy and faulted WRIM

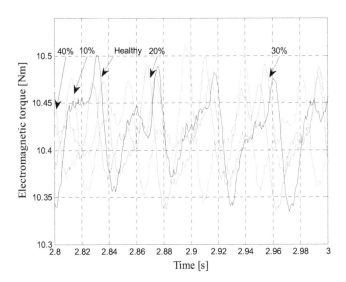

Figure 11. Real variations versus time of the electromagnetic torque of the healthy and faulted WRIM

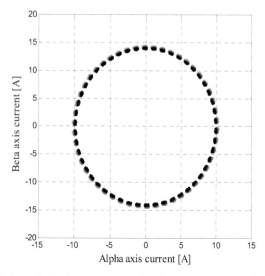

Figure 12. Real variations of β axis current versus the phase α axis current of the stator phase

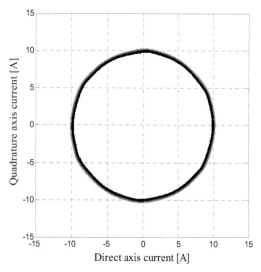

Figure 13. Real variations of the quadrature axis current versus the phase direct axis current of the stator phase

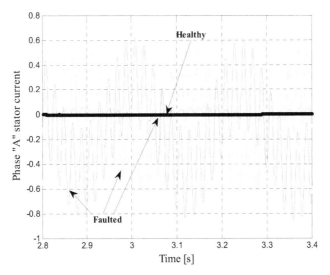

Figure 14. Variations of the stator phase "A" current residues versus time of the healthy and faulted WRIM

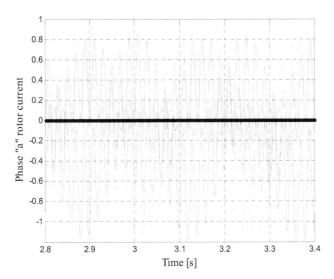

Figure 15. Variations of the rotor phase "a" current residues versus time of the healthy and faulted WRIM

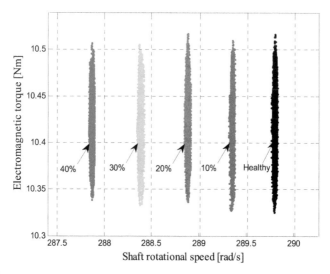

Figure 16. Real variations of electromagnetic torque versus the shaft rotational speed of the WRIM

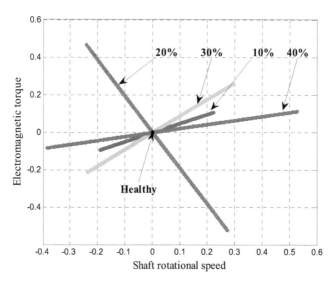

Figure 17. Variations of electromagnetic torque residues versus the shaft rotational speed residues of the WRIM

6. Discussion

Several types of representations are used in the signals processing domain, especially for the electrical machines diagnosis. We can mention the temporal representation (Figure 8 to Figure11, Figure 14 and Figure 15) and the signal frequency analysis. Although they have proved their efficiency, the state variable representations between them also show their advantages. They can be performed without mathematical transformation (Figure 16) and with mathematical transformation (Figure 12 and Figure 13).

The latter representation type and the temporal representation are confronted with the PCA method application results (Figure 14, Figure 15 and Figure 17). Only the simulation results with stator faults are presented because the global behavior of the state variables in both rotor and stator faults are almost similar.

For the temporal variations case, the rotor currents (Figure 9) and the shaft rotational speed (Figure 10) are the variables which produce the most information in presence of defaults. The defaults occur on the rotor current frequency and the shaft rotational speed magnitude.

The electromagnetic torque variations versus the shaft rotational speed also show clearly the WRIM operation zone in the presence of defaults (Figure 16). On the opposite, the representations with mathematical transformations (Figure 12 and Figure 13) do not provide significant information due to the fact that the stator currents remain almost unchanged in the presence of defaults (Figure 8).

With PCA method application, every representation type shows precisely the differences between healthy and faulted WRIM (Figure 14, Figure 15 and Figure 17). In the healthy case, residues are zero. When defaults appear, the residue representations have an effective value with an absolute value superior to zero.

In the figure 17, the healthy case is represented by a point situated on the coordinate origins. Therefore, one can show several right lines corresponding to the faulted cases. This behavior is due to the proportional characteristic of the considered faults.

PCA method proved to be very effective in electrical machines faults detection. This requires a good choice of the number of the principal components to be retained so that information contained in residues is relevant.

7. Implementation of the WRIM and the PCA models in the Matlab software

The differential equations system governing the WRIM is composed of linear differential equation which has the following form:

$$\frac{dy}{dt} = f(y) \tag{31}$$

Pre-programmed solvers are available in the Matlab software to solve easily this type of equation. These pre-programmed functions (ode45, ode113 ...) proposed by the software helped to solve correctly with scalable computation time by the number of data to be processed. We adopted "*ode45*", solver based on the Runge-Kutta 4, 5 numerical resolution method. After creating a function detailing the differential equation system, we have to use it in the chosen solver to calculate numerically the equations governing the WRIM.

The following extract lines of code illustrate the use of the pre-programmed function "*ode45*" (Figure 18):

```
Editor - D:\IST-D\Recherche\These\RAMAHALEOMIARANTSOA-Fanjason-Jacques\Book_
File   Edit   Text   Desktop   Window   Help

41
42   [t,Y] = ode45('Diff_Equa_WRIM', Time, Initial_Values, Options);
43
44   iA    =    Y(:,1);
45   iB    =    Y(:,2);
46   iC    =    Y(:,3);
47   ia    =    Y(:,4);
48   ib    =    Y(:,5);
49   ic    =    Y(:,6);
50   Omega =    Y(:,7);
51   Teta  =    Y(:,8);
52
```

Figure 18. Use of ode45 solver to solve the differential equations system of the WRIM

The differential equations system is established in the "*Diff_Equa_WRIM*" function.

One of the major strengths of Matlab is the matrix manipulation. With the amount of data in matrix form that we consider in this paper, this feature of the software allows us to treat easily and without complexity these data. Thus, for the ACP method, matrix manipulations are done by simple operations because all variables in Matlab are intrinsically represented by matrix forms. In addition, pre-programmed functions are available to perform some precise operations such as the descendant sorting with "*descend*" function.

And finally, Matlab offers a multitude of possibilities for graphic representations. At the end of the PCA process, the original data and those from the treatment are represented graphically. This allowed more comparative studies as well as quantitative and qualitative analysis of the entire device. A function was reserved to the automatic superposition of curves of the same variables for the different considered defaults.

To summarize, three major functions have been developed to carry out the approach:

• resolution of de differential equations system governing the WRIM,

- resolution of the PCA method,
- visualization of comparative curves.

We would like to note that each approach has been developed as a separate function, but our program runs automatically. These functions are executed automatically, one after the other, in another function.

8. Conclusion

PCA method based on residues analysis has been established and applied on WRIM diagnosis.

An accurate analytical model of the machine has been proposed and simulated to perform the healthy and faulted data for PCA approach need.

Several representations of nine state variables of the machine have been analyzed. For the temporal variation without PCA, the rotor current and the shaft rotational speed are the more affected by the considered fault type. The representations of the electromagnetic torque versus the shaft rotational speed in both with and without PCA approach show clearly the presence of defaults. Indeed, PCA method is interesting for all types of representation compared to some other signal processing types.

Simulation results show the efficiency of the detection but require a good choice of the number of principal components.

Author details

Jacques Fanjason Ramahaleomiarantsoa and Nicolas Héraud
Université de Corse, U.M.R. CNRS 6134 SPE, BP 52, Corte, France

Eric Jean Roy Sambatra
Institut Supérieur de Technologie, BP 509, Antsiranana, Madagascar

Jean Marie Razafimahenina
Ecole Supérieure Polytechnique, BP O, Antsiranana, Madagascar

Acknowledgement

This research was supported by MADES/SCAC Madagascar project. We are grateful for technical and financial support.

9. References

[1] Benbouzid M. E. H (2000) A Review of Induction Motors Signature Analysis as a Medium for Faults Detection, IEEE Transactions On Industrial Electronics, vol. 47, N° 5, pp. 984-993.

[2] Chia-Chou Y & al. (2008) A reconfigurable motor for experimental emulation of stator winding interturn and broken bar faults in polyphase induction machines, 01, IEEE transactions on energy conversion, vol.23, n°4. pp. 1005-1014.

[3] Sin M.L, Soong W.L, Ertugrul N (2003) Induction machine on-line condition monitoring and fault diagnosis – a survey, University of Adelaide.

[4] Negrea M.D (2006) Electromagnetic flux monitoring for detecting faults in electrical machines, PhD, Helsinki University of Technology, Department of Electrical and Communications Engineering, Laboratory of Electromechanics, TKK Dissertations 51, Espoo Finland.

[5] Liu L (2006) Robust fault detection and diagnosis for permanent magnet synchronous motors, PhD dissertation, College of Engineering, The Florida State University, USA.

[6] Benaïcha A, GuerfeL M, Bouguila N, Benothman K (2010) New PCA-based methodology for sensor fault detection and localization, 8th International Conference of Modeling and Simulation, MOSIM'10, "Evaluation and optimization of innovative production systems of goods and services", Hammamet, Tunisia.

[7] Ku W, Storer R.H, Georgakis C (1995) Disturbance detection and isolation by dynamic principal component analysis. Chemometrics and Intelligent Laboratory Systems, 30. pp. 179-196.

[8] Huang B (2001) Process identification based on last principal component analysis, Journal of Process Control, 11. pp. 19-33.

[9] Ramahaleomiarantsoa J. F, Héraud N, Sambatra E. J. R, Razafimahenina J. M (2011) Principal Components Analysis Method Application in Electrical Machines Diagnosis, ICINCO'08, Noordwykerhout, Pays Bas.

[10] Li W, Qin S.J (2001) Consistent dynamic pca based on errors-in-variables Subspace identification, Journal of Process Control, 11(6). pp. 661-678.

[11] Valle S, Weihua L, Qin S.J (1999) Selection of the number of principal components: The variance of the reconstruction error criterion with a comparison to other methods, Industrial and Engineering Chemistry Research, vol. 38. pp. 4389-4401.

[12] Benaïcha A, Mourot G, Guerfel M, Benothman K, Ragot J (2010) A new method for determining PCA models for system diagnosis, 18th Mediterranean Conference on Control & Automation Congress Palace Hotel, Marrakech, Morocco June 23-25. pp. 862-867.

[13] Wieczorek M, Rosołowski E (2010) Modelling of induction motor for simulation of internal faults, Modern Electric Power Systems, MEPS'10, paper P29, Wroclaw, Poland.

[14] Halligan R.G, Jagannathan S (2009) PCA Based Fault isolation and prognosis with application to Water Pump, paper1, thesis, Fault detection and prediction with application to rotating machinery, Missouri University of Science and Technology.

Chapter 5

Modelling and Characterization of Power Electronics Converters Using Matlab Tools

Sven Fagerstrom and Nagy Bengiamin

Additional information is available at the end of the chapter

1. Introduction

Advances in semiconductor technologies to produce high power devices have facilitated numerous applications where high power density is a key for practical and sophisticated solutions. Instead of being limited to the traditional low power electronics applications, high power devices opened a broad frontier for engineering design. These devices are now embedded in systems that span the full range from small electric motor drives to very high voltage transmission lines where hundreds of amperes are regulated while the devices are exposed to thousands of volts. Compared to the traditional rotating electric machine based (dynamic) energy conversion, these devices made static conversion from one form of electricity to another so seamless that employing a certain form of electric power (AC, DC, or a combination) has become an engineering design option rather than a forced solution. Application areas like in motor drives, fuel cells, solar panels, wind turbines, electric cars, and high speed transportation systems are only a few of the major beneficiaries of advances in power electronics. Emphases on energy conservation motivated the design for improved system efficiency where power electronics devices are utilized in their most desirable mode. These efforts resulted in increased portability of high power density systems and affected the design of the full range of power systems including those for small electronic equipment which are becoming more demanding on power for their ever increasing features and capabilities. Like all advanced engineering design applications, mathematical developments and supporting software tools for modeling, simulation and analysis are critical (Shaffer, 2007; Assi, 2011). In addition to introducing some of the fundamental concepts in power electronics and related applications, this chapter exploits the capabilities of Matlab and its associated SimPower and Simulink toolboxes as an effective relevant engineering tool.

When dealing with an alternating current, changing voltage levels, at the same frequency, is achieved simply by utilizing AC transformers where the principle of mutual induction exists between two magnetic coils with the proper turns-ratio. Mutual induction is possible due to the rate at which the magnetic lines cut the wires of the transformer coils and the produced electromotive force that is capable of producing current in closed electric loops. This fundamental concept is not applicable to DC voltage and current due to the absence of the alternating nature of the produced magnetic fields. Therefore, changing DC voltage from one level to another must be achieved using different methodologies. One possible methodology is to modulate DC voltages by switching them on and off at proper rates and durations such that the average produced voltage is controlled. The key concept here is to store energy then release it at the proper time with the proper rate needed for the desired load. Energy storage elements like inductors and capacitors facilitate this methodology. Therefore, a combination of energy storage elements and switching schemes provide the basic ingredients for the design of DC-DC conversion devices. Such devices are referred to as power electronic DC-DC converters. The modes of operation of these devices are dependent on the shape of the produced voltage waveform which is manipulated by the switching scheme and the size of the energy storage elements. Compared to AC transformers which usually exhibit linear characteristics for its most modes of operation, DC transformers (DC-DC converters) possess highly non-linear characteristics which require more intensive analysis and design schemes.

Optimization of power electronics systems' design and operation is important to accommodate the growing need for energy efficiency in portable electronic devices to extend their battery life and respond to their increasing functionality and features. These features demand more electric power while the devices must reduce in size and weight; i.e. increased energy density. DC-DC converters are embedded in numerous electronic equipment and they have become an integral part of many commercial and industrial products. These converters are employed to lower (buck) or raise (boost) DC voltage levels as needed by the application. Buck and boost converters are emphasized in this chapter for their different topologies and modes of operation. The presented methodologies facilitate analysis, characterization, and design of efficient DC-DC converters. Sufficient background and theoretical development are provided for completeness.

2. Static power converters

Static power converters can take numerous topologies which enable AC-AC, AC-DC, DC-AC, and DC-DC conversion. AC-AC converters vary in complexity from the crude chopping of the AC waveform in order to regulate the delivered average power like in light dimmers and electric stove burners to varying the produced frequency like in Variable Speed Drives (VSD) for AC motors. AC-DC converters usually utilize the simple rectifier bridge configuration. They are popular in windmill applications as a front stage before converting to AC for interface with the utility grid. This last stage employs the DC-AC converter which is also popular in applications like solar panels interface with the utility grid. In addition to the AC-DC converter, most household and commercial electronic equipment use DC-DC converters. These converters produce the multiple DC voltage levels necessary for the operation of the equipment. DC-DC converters are also critical for battery powered portable electronic devices where power density is high and efficiency of converters is critical to the charging cycle of the device.

2.1. AC-AC converter

Converting AC at the same frequency is most effectively achieved using induction transformers. This is particularly true for high frequency/low-power applications where the magnetic core is relatively small. Applications that require converting to different frequencies, however, can be achieved in several configurations. One configuration may utilize an intermediate stage of AC-DC back-to-back with DC-AC as is the case for wind energy conversion for example; assuming that the wind turbine is coupled to an AC electric generator. Cycloconverters (Rashid, 2004) on the other hand, don't require an intermediate stage as they utilize chopping techniques to shape the waveform directly. Conversion from three-phase to either single-phase or three-phase is usually possible with the proper control scheme. One crude application to regulate power at the same frequency using waveform chopping is that of the light-dimmer (Paul, 2001); used here to illustrate some of the basic concepts. Although light dimmers usually regulate power consumption without altering the fundamental frequency of the source, they provide a more economical solution compared to tap-changing induction type transformers.

Fig. 1 depicts the circuit configuration for a simple light dimmer where the primary power control device is the Triac whose gate firing device is the Diac (Skvarenina, 2002). The Diac is a fixed break-over voltage device compared to the Triac that permits a variable firing angle through its gate terminal. Compared to the Silicon Controlled rectifier (SCR) which is also gate controlled, the Triac permits device firing on the positive and negative half-cycles of the AC waveform. The SCR has a similar characteristic to that of a rectifier (unidirectional) but with an adjustable conduction angle (Rashid, 2004). Both devices are self-commutated, i.e. they turn off naturally at the zero crossings of the waveform. The triggering circuit for the Triac is comprised of R_1, R_2, and C where the potentiometer R_2 represents the adjustable resistor which is usually operated by the dial (or slide switch) on the operating plate of the light dimmer. The value of R_2 controls the conduction phase of the Triac. As the capacitor charges to a voltage higher than the break-over voltage of the Diac, a pulse is produced at the gate of the Triac to turn it on. In the conduction mode, the internal resistance of the Triac becomes small causing the flow of current through the light bulb. A higher value of R_2 elongates the charging time of C (longer time constant $\tau=C(R_1+R_2)$), causing a delayed triggering pulse and a shorter conduction period for the Triac. The average power transmitted to the light bulb becomes less, resulting in a dimmer light. The same logic works for both halves of the source's waveform cycle. This application will be analyzed using Matlab in Section 4 to demonstrate some of the capabilities of the SimPower and Simulink tool boxes.

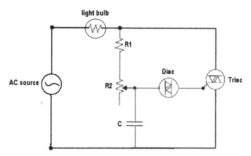

Figure 1. Light Dimmer Circuit

Several practical notes relative to the circuit in Fig. 1 are due,

1. While it may seem that the Diac is an unnecessary device in this application since the voltage of the capacitor may trigger the gate of the Triac directly, it must be noticed that Triacs are notorious for not firing symmetrically. Lack of symmetry in triggering at the same voltage level for both polarities of a full cycle produces unnecessary additional harmonics that negatively affect the efficiency of the circuit. The symmetrical characteristic if the Diac provides accurate timing that enhances the firing symmetry of the Triac.
2. One may use two SCRs back-to-back to implement the power control device in place of the Triac.
3. The firing time through the RC circuit is perfectly synchronized with the conduction cycle of the Triac because they are both powered by the same AC source.

2.2. DC-DC converter

Converting DC voltage to the proper levels from a single energy source that might be depleting, like in battery applications, requires employing energy storage elements (inductors) with associated power electronics devices. When switched ON-OFF at a certain rate, stored energy gets released to the load at the proper time to maintain the desired voltage level. Pulse-Width-Modulation (PWM) techniques are most popular in this application. Converters of this type are suited for boosting or bucking the source voltage; commonly known as switching power supplies. Since the current is DC and zero crossing is not one of the steady cyclic features like in AC circuits, self-commutation is not possible. Therefore, Gate-Turn-Off (GTO) devices are required (Skvarenina, 2002). These devices are turned off with a negative pulse on the gate terminal. MOSFETs and BJTs also provide a viable option in low power applications. Feedback loop methodologies are an integral part of DC-DC converters to regulate the load voltage, compensating for load variations and irregularities in the source voltage.

Current and voltage ripples, and high frequency harmonic distortion are common byproducts of switching techniques. Capacitors are usually employed to insure acceptable ripple content. Harmonics negatively affect the efficiency of the converter and produce losses in the form of heat. While the produced load current is regulated for a desired average value, the cyclic behavior produces current fluctuations in the energy storage elements. Operating at zero current for energy storage elements during part of the cycle results in a highly nonlinear characteristic, where the converter is known to be in its Discontinuous Conduction Mode (DCM). The Continuous Conduction Mode (CCM), however, insures nonzero current during the full cycle of switching (Rashid, 2004; Shaffer, 2007). Each mode of operation has certain implications on the ripples and harmonics content which affects the efficiency of the converter.

2.2.1. Buck converter

In low power applications, voltage bucking is usually achieved using voltage divider resistors. This simple solution is acceptable because the current is usually too small to cause significant losses in the resistors. Employing this approach in high power applications is unrealistic because the losses of the resistors may exceed the useful power consumed by the load; that is in addition to the associated heat dissipation issues that must be resolved to insure sufficient ventilation. The DC-DC converter provides a more practical solution in spite of its associated design complexities at times.

Bucking DC source voltages can be achieved using a topology like the one shown in Fig. 2. The energy storage element (L) is to be sized for the desired mode of operation (CCM or DCM). The power device (GTO in this case) switches On-OFF using PWM where the duty-ratio ($D=T_{on}/T$) determines the average load voltage; T is the time of one period of the switching frequency (f). The diode facilitates inductor current wheeling during the OFF time of the GTO. The capacitor is usually sized to reduce the load current ripples. The inherent inductor current ripples (usually in the range of about 30%) are then facilitated by the capacitor while blocking it from flowing through the load. Snubber circuits are installed across the power devices for protection and to minimize the stress on the device that may result from opening the circuit while the current cannot be stopped instantaneously due to the nature of the energy storage element. Current and voltage waveforms will be shown in Section 4 for illustration.

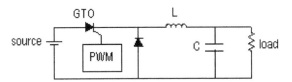

Figure 2. DC-DC Buck Converter

Design of the DC-DC converter centers around determining the size of the energy storage element (L) which achieves predetermined V_{source}, V_{load}, ΔV_{load} (load voltage ripple), and I_{ripple}. Knowing that $I_{ripple}=\Delta I_L$, $D=V_{load}/V_{source}$ assuming CCM, $T=1/f$, and $V_L=V_{source}-V_{load}$ during T_{on} (Rashid, 2004), Eq. (2) can be obtained.

Since,

$$V_L = L\frac{di_L}{dt} \tag{1}$$

therefore,

$$L = V_L\frac{\Delta T}{\Delta i_L}$$

$$= (V_{sourse} - V_{load}).(\frac{D}{f}).(\frac{1}{I_{ripple}}) \tag{2}$$

$$= (V_{load} - \frac{V_{load}^2}{V_{source}}).(\frac{1}{f.I_{ripple}})$$

Notice that L is charging during T_{on} only, which means that $\Delta T = D/f$. The calculated "L" is usually well above the minimum inductance needed to insure CCM in many applications. Only very light load conditions may force DCM.

The capacitor "C" is sized to reduce load current ripple while providing a pass for the inductor current ripples (I_{ripple}). It is worth noting that the inherent Effective Series Resistance (ESR) of the capacitor plays a major role in determining the size of the capacitor.

Since,

$$i_C = C\frac{dV_C}{dt} \tag{3}$$

but,

$$\Delta V_C = \Delta i_C(ESR + \frac{\Delta T}{C}) \text{ and } \Delta V_C = \Delta V_{load} \tag{4}$$

therefore,

$$C = \frac{\Delta i_C.\Delta T}{\Delta V_{load} - ESR.\Delta i_C}$$

$$= \frac{I_{ripple}.D}{f(\Delta V_{load} - ESR.I_{ripple})} \tag{5}$$

Eq. (5) shows that the capacitor's ESR rating can have a significant effect on the size of the capacitor knowing that the tolerated ΔV_{load} is usually small in sophisticated applications. Therefore, the ESR rating shouldn't be overlooked when selecting the capacitor. The Effective Series Inductance (ESL) rating of the capacitor is also relevant but it is usually considered for very high switching frequencies only (>1 MHz). By then, inductive effect of board tracings can start to be critical as well.

2.2.2. Boost converter

While bucking the source voltage for low power applications can be achieved with resistor voltage dividers (passive components), boosting the voltage requires active devices like Operations-Amplifiers (OpAmps). Power OpAmps are also available for low-voltage medium power (500 Watt) applications but they usually exhibit high power loss and they need active cooling (fans) in addition to passive cooling via heat sinks. OpAmps are also analog devices which are usually controlled with analog control voltages, while PWM controlled power devices can be easily interfaced with digital controllers. Real-time load voltage regulation is achieved most effectively with embedded digital controllers.

By rearranging the components of the buck converter as shown in Fig. 3, it becomes possible to boost the source voltage. The underlying principle of operation is in the fact that the polarity of the inductor (L) voltage reverses instantaneously when the rate of change in the inductor current (i_L) reverses pattern; i.e. di_L/dt changes sign. During the ON time (T_{on}) of the GTO, the inductor charges with its voltage taking the opposite polarity of the source. When the GTO turns OFF during T_{off}, the inductor current starts to drop and accordingly its polarity reverses direction to become in the same direction like the source. The load, then, becomes supported by V_{source} plus V_L which signifies the higher load voltage compared to the source voltage. The role of the capacitor is similar to that of the buck converter, that is to reduce the ripples of the load voltage as it supports the load voltage during T_{on} in this case. It must be noted that V_L is equal to $L(di_L/dt)$ which means that the inductor voltage can rise significantly if the current is allowed to change at a high rate, resulting in load voltages much higher than that of the source. The inductor, however, must be sized properly and allowed to charge enough by increasing the duty-ratio (D) of the PWM scheme such that it stores enough energy to feed the load during T_{off}. The ratio V_{load}/V_{source} is determined by $1/(1-D)$ which implies that V_{load} can rise well above V_{source} as the duty ratios gets closer to 100% (Rashid, 2004). The physical limit of the employed components is usually the determining factor for how high V_{load} may be attained.

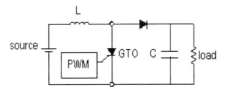

Figure 3. DC-DC Boost Converter

2.2.3. Buck-boost converter

Rearranging the components as shown in Fig. 4 provides the flexibility to buck or boost the source voltage by adjusting the duty-ratio (D) of the PWM. A 50% duty-ratio provides the load with the same source voltage while a lower duty-ratio bucks the voltage and a higher duty ratio boosts the voltage (Rashid, 2004). It was proven that V_{load}/V_{source} is determined by

D/(1-D). The orientation of the diode is such that the load current is blocked while the inductor is charging during T_{on}. During T_{off} the inductor releases its energy to the load through the diode loop resulting in an opposite voltage polarity compared to that of the buck or boost configurations. The size of the storage element (L) is critical to facilitating the boost mode. To insure CCM, the inductor must be of a certain minimum size (Rashid, 2004). Current and voltage waveforms will be shown in Section 4 for illustration.

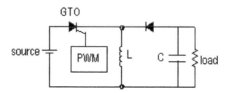

Figure 4. DC-DC Buck-Boost Converter

2.3. Voltage control

Control of switching power converters requires modulating the width of the pulse provided to the power devices' gate, based on feedback from the load voltage and the inductor's current. Fig. 5 illustrates the basic components of an analog control scheme; where the output voltage provides the desired feedback. This scheme is identified as the "voltage-mode" control. The low-pass filter (R_3, C_3) of the error amplifier along with R_1 provide feedback gain and reduce harmonics. The PWM hardware can be a typical controllable IC and the Schmitt-trigger is to produce sharp edges for the power device's gate. Needed high gate current usually requires current amplification as well.

The compensator can be implemented with Op-Amps to realize desired dynamic characteristics for voltage recovery and regulation. Traditional compensators like PID, lead-lag, and Sliding Mode Control (SMC) are all applicable. Digital control, however, provides flexibility in implementing sophisticated control schemes and mixed mode operations to achieve power saving and to possibly automatic controller tuning. Digital schemes also reduce magnetic interference effects which would most probably exist in applications that require DC-DC power conversion. Digital Signal Processors (DSPs), microcontrollers, and Field Programmable Gate Arrays (FPGAs) together with the Analog-to-Digital Converter (ADC) are widely used to implement digital controllers. However, high-speed high-resolution ADCs are expensive and they are not easy to consolidate into an integrated circuit.

Design of the compensator requires transient analysis and solving the differential equations that describe each waveform. Retaining the instantaneous detailed characteristic of the circuit requires analysis of each mode of the switching cycle. This level of detail is usually not necessary for the design of the compensator. Averaging over a number of switching cycles provides viable approximate models (Forsyth & Mollov, 1998) which simplify the compensator design significantly. In this technique, the state equations for the RC circuit are written for both modes of the converter (ON and OFF). A combined state equations model is then formed using the weighted average of the state matrices of the ON and OFF models according to the duty ratio (D). The produced model is a set of two linear time-variant state equations which ignore ripple components. The time-variant effect is due to the presence of the control variable "D(t)" (varying duty-ratio) in the state matrices rather than being part of the input control variables vector. Since solving time-variant equations is difficult, further simplifications are required. Linearization techniques are then employed for specific operating conditions, resulting in small-signal state-space models (Johansson, 2004). These models facilitate frequency and time domain design methodologies.

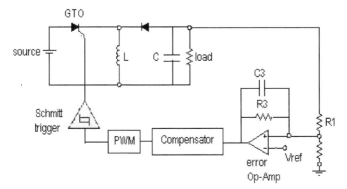

Figure 5. Voltage Control of Buck-Boost Converter

In addition to the above explained voltage-mode control scheme, current-mode control can also be achieved by sensing the current of the switching power device or the energy storage element and integrating it into the main voltage control loop (Johansson, 2004). In this scheme, the output of the voltage compensator acts are the reference voltage for the current feedback loop which controls the PWM and adjusts the gate pulse for the power device. This scheme usually improves the stability of the converter in high performance applications. Controlling the peak inductor current is one of the popular schemes employed. Current sensing can also be used to determine when to switch between CCM and DCM which facilitates implementing high efficiency schemes for operation.

2.4. Power saving and improved efficiency

Minimization of DC-DC converter power losses is important to accommodate the growing need for a longer battery life and reduced size and weight of portable electronic devices. Power losses are usually dependent on the type of power devices and their conduction losses, the effective series resistance of inductors and capacitors, mode of operation of the converter, switching scheme, and the switching frequency. While diodes are simple in their use, they may reduce the efficiency of the converter due to their high losses in certain modes of operation. The same function of a diode can be achieved by using a switching power device similar to the main energy transfer device of the converter (e.g. GTO or MOSFET).

This will require applying switching logic to multiple devices in the same converter. Synchronizing the switching of the devices introduces an additional control challenge and the converter topology is therefore referred to as the "synchronous" topology. The diode topology is then called "asynchronous". A detailed characterization of power losses in DC-DC converters is offered by Gildersleeve, et.al., (2002).

Various techniques were proposed in the literature to reduce power losses in DC-DC converters, including soft-switching (Zhou & Rincon-Mora, 2006), synchronous rectification (Djekic & Brkovic, 1997; Arbetter et al., 1995), mode hopping between CCM and DCM (Wang et al., 1997), Zero-Voltage Switching (Stratakos, 1998), mixed synchronous-asynchronous control (Saggini et al., 2007), variable switching frequency (Djekic & Brkovic, 1997; Arbetter et al., 1995), and Hybrid Mode Hopping combined with variable frequency (Wang et al., 1997). These techniques are summarized and compared by Zhou (2003). Djekic et al. (1997) compared synchronous and asynchronous rectification buck converters for efficiency at various loads and switching frequencies. This work was extended to the buck-boost converter recently (Fagerstrom & Bengiamin, 2011). The methodologies herein build on that latest work.

The basic asynchronous and synchronous converter topologies are given in Figs. 6.a and 6.b, respectively. Table 1 lists the sources of losses considered assuming a MOS switching device.

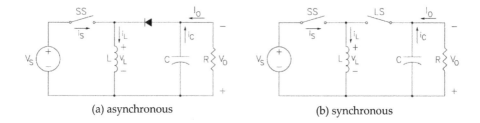

(a) asynchronous   (b) synchronous

Figure 6. Buck-Boost Converter Architecture

Synchronous	Asynchronous
PMOS Conduction	PMOS Conduction
PMOS Switching	PMOS Switching
PMOS Gate Drive	PMOS Gate Drive
NMOS Conduction	Diode Conduction
NMOS Switching	Diode Leakage
NMOS Gate Drive	Diode Junction Capacitance
NMOS Body Diode	
Dead Time	

Table 1. Buck-Boost Converter Losses Considered

Extensive lists of DC-DC converter losses may be found in Zhou, S. (2003) and Djeki, O. & Brkovic, M. (1974). Buck-boost converter losses considered in this work are given in Table 1, as itemized and developed analytically in the following subsections. The PMOS is used for the Source Switch (SS) and NMOS is used for the Load Switch (LS), respectively.

a.   PMOS Source Switch Conduction Loss

When the PMOS transistor is in forward conduction there is a resistive loss in accordance with Eq.(6). PMOS conduction loss is associated with both asynchronous and synchronous converters (Gildersleeve et al, 2002; Klien, J., 2006).

$$\text{PMOS Conduction Loss} \triangleq SScL = I_{SS}^2 R_{DS} D \tag{6}$$

Where, I_{SS}=PMOS current (Amp) R_{DS}=PMOS forward conduction ON resistance (Ohm), D=duty ratio

b.   PMOS Source Switch Switching Loss

During the transition of voltage rising or falling between the maximum and minimum steady-state values across either switch, and similarly the rise or fall transition of current through the same switch, losses occur. Much work has been done in an effort to correctly model this behavior (Klein, 2006; Xiong et al, 2009), without a highly accurate model still as yet developed. A combination of the work of Klein, (2006) and Xiong et al, (2009) are presented here to develop the switch model loss. The development starts with the following power loss equation.

$$P_{SW} = \frac{1}{2} I_{SW} V_{SW} f_s \left(t_{s(off)} + t_{s(on)} \right) \tag{7}$$

Where, P_{SW}=MOSFET switching loss power (Watt), I_{SW}=current through MOSFET (Amp), V_{SW}=drain to source voltage across the MOSFET, f_s=switching frequency (Hertz), $t_{s(off)}$=MOSFET switching time transitioning off, $t_{s(on)}$=MOSFET switching time transitioning on. All parameters of Eq. (7) are readily measurable in a physical circuit except the switching time terms t_{off} and t_{on} which are developed in the following equations.

$$t_{s(on)} = \frac{Q_{G(SW)}}{I_{Driver(L-H)}} \tag{8}$$

$$t_{s(off)} = \frac{Q_{G(SW)}}{I_{Driver(H-L)}} \tag{9}$$

$$I_{Driver(L-H)} = \frac{V_{DD} - V_{SP}}{R_{Driver(Pull-up)} + R_G} \tag{10}$$

$$I_{Driver(H\text{-}L)} = \frac{V_{SP}}{R_{Driver(Pull\text{-}up)} + R_G} \tag{11}$$

$$V_{SP} \approx V_G + \frac{I_{SW}}{G_m} \tag{12}$$

Where, $Q_{G(SW)}$=MOSFET switching-point gate charge (Coulomb), $I_{Driver(L\text{-}H)}$=MOSFET gate current while switching on (Amp), $I_{Driver(H\text{-}L)}$=MOSFET gate current while switching off, V_{DD}=gate drive controller voltage, V_{SP}=MOSFET gate voltage at switching point, $R_{Driver(Pull\text{-}up)}$=gate drive controller internal resistance, R_G=MOSFET gate resistance, V_G=MOSFET gate switching voltage, G_m=MOSFET transconductance.

Combining Eqs. (7) through (12) gives the combined switching loss Eq. (13).

$$P_{sw} = \frac{1}{2}I_{SW}V_{SW}f_s Q_{G(SW)}G_m\left(R_{Driver(Pull\text{-}up)} + R_G\right)\left(\frac{1}{V_G G_m + I_{SW}} + \frac{1}{V_{DD}G_m - V_G G_m - I_{SW}}\right) \tag{13}$$

c.   PMOS Source Switch Gate Drive Loss

Gate drive loss accounts for the energy dissipated by the MOSFET to drive the gate for the switching operation. The loss equation is given in Eq. (14). PMOS gate drive loss is associated with both converters.

$$\text{PMOS Gate Drive Loss} \triangleq gdL = Q_{G(SW)}V_G f_s \tag{14}$$

d.   NMOS Load Switch Conduction Loss

Load switch conduction loss is similar to that of the source switch shown in Eq. (6), differing by the (1-D) factor as this loss occurs during the latter portion of the switching period. This loss is represented in Eq. (15). NMOS conduction loss is associated with only the synchronous converter.

$$\text{NMOS Conduction Loss} \triangleq LScL = I_{LS}^2 R_{DS}\left(1\text{-}D\right) \tag{15}$$

Where, I_{LS}=load switch drain to source voltage.

e.   NMOS Load Switch Switching Loss

The load switch MOSFET switching loss is calculated with the same model as the source switch shown in Eq. (14). NMOS switching loss is associated with only the synchronous converter.

f.   NMOS Load Switch Gate Drive Loss

NMOS gate drive loss is accounted for by simply doubling the gate drive loss Eq. (15) for the synchronous case. NMOS gate drive loss is associated with only the synchronous converter.

g.   NMOS Load Switch Body Diode Loss

The load switch body diode loss occurs only in the load switch due to the reverse bias during the ON portion of the period (Djekic et al., 1997). The reverse-bias voltage and leakage current dissipate power according to the equation shown in Eq. (16). NMOS body diode loss is associated with only the synchronous converter.

$$\text{NMOS Body Diode Loss} \triangleq \text{LSbdL} = i_{\text{leakage}} V_{\text{LS}} D \tag{16}$$

Where, $i_{leakage}$=reverse bias leakage current, V_{LS}=load switch drain to source voltage.

h.   Synchronous Switching Dead-Time Loss

Dead-time loss occurs through the load switch when neither transistor is on as the load switch is in forward conduction (Klien, 2006). A period of dead-time must exist to prevent current "shoot-through" whereby current flows through both switches simultaneously to the load. The value of t_{dead} is assumed to be 60 ns as is typical for DC-DC converter controllers (Djekic & Brkovic, 1997). The dead-time loss representation is shown in Eq. (17). Synchronous switching dead-time loss is associated with only the synchronous converter.

$$\text{Dead-Time Loss} \triangleq \text{deadL} = I_{\text{load}} V_{\text{LS}} f_s t_{\text{dead}} \tag{17}$$

Where, I_{load}=load current, t_{dead}=time where both switches are off.

i.   Diode Conduction Loss

Diode forward conduction losses are found with the equation shown in Eq. (18). Diode conduction loss is associated with only the asynchronous converter.

$$\text{Diode Conduction Loss} \triangleq \text{DcL} = I_D V_f (1\text{-}D) \tag{18}$$

Where, I_D=current through diode, V_f=diode forward voltage.

j.   Diode Reverse Bias Loss

During the portion of the period d, the diode has a reverse bias across it. There is a certain amount of leakage current under this condition that is listed by the manufacturer on the data sheet. This value is used to calculate diode reverse bias leakage loss in Eq. (19). Diode reverse bias loss is associated with only the asynchronous converter.

$$\text{Diode Reverse Bias Loss} \triangleq DrbL = V_D i_{leakage} D \tag{19}$$

Where, V_D=voltage across diode.

k.   Diode Junction Capacitance Loss

Diodes have a certain capacitance associated with changing voltages across them (Klein, J., 2006). The charging and discharging of this capacitance creates a power loss as modeled by Eq. (20). Diode junction capacitance loss is associated with only the asynchronous converter.

$$\text{Diode Capacitive Loss} \triangleq \text{DcapL} = \frac{CV_D^2 f_s}{2} \qquad (20)$$

3. Matlab capabilities

The Matlab simulation platform (by MathWorks, Inc.) offers a versatile and robust option in design and simulation of power electronic converter systems. Matlab is matrix based, offering diverse options in data manipulation, preparation, and presentation. Simulink, a sub-program of Matlab included in the standard software package, offers a relatively high-level programming language utilizing drag-and-drop function blocks that mask embedded functions. These icons can be incorporated into yet larger models and again masked into new system blocks. This modular block-symbol based modeling system allows ease of construction and programming of large complex systems while maintaining the ability to edit and control internal systems all the way down to the most base-level functions.

The power electronic system designer upon starting Simulink, then, is entering the design process at the phase of assembly of power electronic, measurement, and signal routing components into larger more complex systems to accomplish a desired task. The designer may from time to time wish to delve into base Simulink models to change component characteristics and behavior, add base-level monitoring of characteristics, change signal routing, confirm calculation methods, or even develop system models from scratch.

This section is intended for the Matlab user who possesses basic workspace programming knowledge. Many resources are available to learn or refresh on Matlab workspace programming, including the help files included with the Matlab software. Matlab help files are an invaluable resource in workspace and Simulink programming and are recommended for perusal.

3.1. SimPowerSystems toolbox

Simulink provides a rich suite of toolboxes applicable to wide areas in engineering applications. The power electronics devices discussed in this chapter are simulated using "SimPowerSystems", a versatile toolbox for modeling electro-mechanical systems. In addition to popular power electronics devices, this toolbox provides a wide range of simulation apparatuses such as transformers, rotating machines, hydraulic turbine & governor, and wind turbines, as well as basic electric circuit components. Detailed characteristic parameters can be configured for these components to represent typical performance scenarios. To monitor the performance of constructed models, a host of measurement blocks are available for discreet, continuous, and phasor based measurements. Relevant variables like active & reactive power, total harmonic distortion, and power factor can be monitored with ease. Custom functions can also be set up with simple manipulations. Since this chapter deals with power electronics applications, attention is focused on the Power Electronics block-set which includes several power electronics semiconductor simulation blocks relevant to industry, Table 2. Devices shown in Table 2 are modeled into systems with other standard Simulink and SimPower devices, some of which are presented in Table 3.

Type	Schematic Symbol	SimPower Device	Commutation	Characteristics	Typ. Application
SCR		Thyristor	Line	Pass current in one direction, active control	Simple power control circuits, overcurrent protection circuits (crowbar)
DIAC		Opposing Diodes	Line	Pass current in both directions, A/C waveforms, passive control (forward voltage)	Light dimmer, symmetrical firing of TRIACs
GTO		Gto	Forced	High power applications, active control, extended switch-off time (tail-time)	HVDC Systems, applications with low switching frequencies
Diode		Diode	Line	Pass current in one direction, passive control (forward voltage)	Rectifier, protection circuitry (free-wheel)
IGBT		IGBT	Forced	Fast switching, medium or high power applications	Electric Heater, audio amplifier
MOSFET		Mosfet	Forced	Low power capablities	Signal amplifier, electronic switching

Table 2. SimPower Power Electronics Models

3.2. Simulation parameters and data presentation

For proper numerical computations Matlab provides various simulation options including the specific numerical method (solver), the allowed tolerance, and mode of computation. Since some numerical methods are more computationally intensive than others, the user may choose a less intensive method for simulations that don't require solving highly nonlinear differential equations, for example. This improves the efficiency of the simulation and accelerates obtaining results. Some trial and error may be necessary to achieve a successful simulation. However, the default simulation options can typically be used for most simulations. If the simulation takes too long to execute or the computed data is incomplete, is at an unacceptable resolution, or has errors, it will be necessary to change simulation parameters. Highly complex simulations may require some time invested in finding the correct solver for the application in order to achieve a good balance between accuracy and computation times. The Configuration Parameters dialog box is found under the Simulation tab in Simulink, Fig. 7. Usually the best choice is to leave these set to "auto" to allow Simulink to determine simulation parameters automatically, based on the model.

SimPower Device	Notes	SimPower Device	Notes	SimPower Device	Notes
Parallel RLC Branch	Can be reduced to any combination of R, L, C	Display	Numerical readout in a variety of formats	From, Goto	Signal routing tags for complex models to avoid confusing model interconnections
Ground	Constant zero voltage reference	RMS	Similar functions available such as mean, THD, fourier, active power, etc.	Demux, Mux	Multiplexers, settable number of inputs/outputs
AC Voltage Source	Programmable source, DC, current, battery, etc. also available	Gain	Multiply input by constants, functions, or variables	Current, Voltage Measurements	Impedance, multimeter, 3-phase, etc. also available
Math Function	Other fxns: log, exp, square, power, conjugate, etc.	Logical Operator	Configurable as OR, NAND, NOR, XOR, NXOR, NOT	Rational Operator	Compare 2 signals rationally: greater, less, equal, etc.
Constant	Constant value independent of all variables	Integrator	Transfer functions also available	Saturation	Model effects of saturation
Scope	Used to view waveforms	Sine Wave	Other sources such as step, ramp, pulse, stair, etc.	First order hold	An array of discreet-time functions available

Table 3. Common SimPower Power Electronics Models

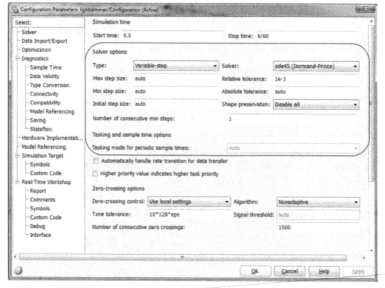

Figure 7. Configuration Parameters Dialog Box

The solvers are categorized into two general types: Fixed step, and Variable step. Fixed step simulations evaluate in user-set time steps that are constant throughout simulation. Variable step solvers dynamically change the simulation step size to optimize simulation time vs. accuracy. Therefore, the goal in choosing the solver is to find the least computationally intensive method that yields the level of accuracy required. Solver types are summarized in Table 4.

Step		Solver Type	Order of Accuracy	Method	Trial Order	Notes
		Discrete				Settable maximum step size
		ode45	Fifth, Medium	Runge-Kutta	1	Default
		ode23	Low	cubic Hermite interpolation	2	
		ode113	Low to High	Adams-Bashforth-Moulton PECE		Models with stringent error tolerances or computationally intensive
	Variable (continuous)	ode15s	Variable order (1-5), Medium to Low	Numerical Differentiation	3	Try if ode45 fails, limit order to 2 initially, and increase as needed
		ode23s	Second, Low	Modified Rosenbrock	4	Try if ode15s is not effective
		ode23t	Low	Trapezoidal rule with "free" interpolant	5	Try if ode15s is not effective
		ode23tb	Second, Low	TR-BDF2, trapezoidal with second order backward differentiation	5	Try if ode15s is not effective
		Discrete				Settable fixed step size
		ode1	First	Euler's Method		
		ode2	Second	Heun's Method		No error control, accuracy & simulation time depend on step size, small steps yield higher accuracy and higher simulation time, and vice-versa
	Fixed (discreet)	ode3	Third	Bogacki-Shampine		
		ode4	Fourth	Runge-Kutta RK4		
		ode5	Fifth	Dormand-Prince RK5		
		ode8	Eighth	Dormand Prince RK8		
		ode14x	Variable	Newton's method/ extrapolation		Settable Jacobian method, Newton's iterations, extrapolation order

Table 4. Solver Types

3.3. Configuration of SimPowerSystems blocks

Simulation of any SimPower circuit involves parameter configuration within model blocks after circuit is constructed. This is achieved by double-clicking on the circuit block to reveal block parameters. Table 5 shows the possible block configuration parameters for common SimPower power electronic devices. A user may also elect to use typical values provided by default.

Abbreviation	Parameter	SCR (Thyristor)	Diode	GTO	IGBT	Mosfet
Ron	Conduction resistance	X	X	X	X	X
Lon	Conduction capacitance	X	X	X	X	X
Vf	Forward voltage drop	X	X	X	X	X
Ic	Initial current	X	X	X	X	X
Rs	Snubber resistance	X*	X*	X*	X*	X*
Cs	Snubber capacitance	X*	X*	X*	X*	X*
Il	Latching current	X				
Tq	Turn-off Time	X				
Tf	Current 10% fall-time			X	X	
Tt	Current tail-time			X	X	
Rd	Internal diode resistance					X

* set Rs=inf or Cs=0 to eliminate snubber, or Cs=inf for resistive snubber

Table 5. SimPowerSystems Block Configuration Parameters

The parameters of Table 5 can be classified according to the following: R_{on}, L_{on}, V_f are applicable during forward conduction of current, current 10% fall time and current tail time are applicable during shut-off, and snubber resistance and snubber capacitance affect the circuit during the OFF condition.

The definitions of R_{on}, L_{on}, and V_f are evident by inspection of the typical power electronic device circuit diagram shown in Fig. 8.

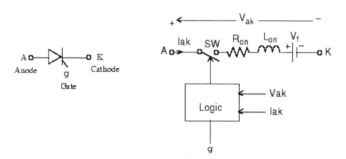

Figure 8. Example SimPower Power Electronic Device Equivalent Circuit

Initial current is the amount of current in amperes flowing through device at the start of simulation. Snubber resistance and capacitance (Rs and Cs) are self-evident for snubber circuits. Latching current (Il) is defined as the amount of current required for thyristor to become self-commutated. Turn-off time (Tq) is defined as the minimum amount of time required for the voltage across anode and cathode to be zero or less to avoid the device automatically turning on again when a forward voltage is seen. Current fall-time and tail time are explained in waveform shown in Fig. 9 (from Matlab help file).

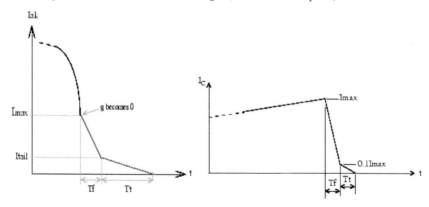

Figure 9. SimPower GTO and IGBT Fall-Time and Tail-Time Waveform, Respectively

Internal diode resistance of the MOSFET (Rd) is explained in Fig. 10.

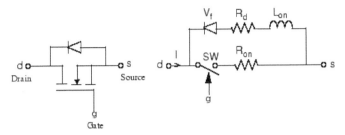

Figure 10. SimPower MOSFET Equivalent Circuit

4. Simulation, analysis, and design

A Matlab script file can accompany simulations performed in the Simulink environment. Script files provide ease in defining and computing variables from a single location which allows the model to be general and applicable to many different cases as well as maintain uniformity in plotting and results presentation. If modification of parameters is desired, the changes are easily accomplished by changing the numbers in the workspace and repeating the simulation. This general-modeling functionality is a distinct advantage of Matlab over Multisim.

Simulink offers a simple and versatile platform for equation modeling. Practically any equation can be implemented in Simulink following an easy and direct method. Consider Eq. (1), the inductor voltage as a function of inductor current – these are the input and output variables of what can be implemented as a small subsystem in Simulink. The first modeling step can be to introduce variable routing tags for each input and output variable as shown in Fig. 11 (a). Next, consider the intermediate mathematics of the function. It is observed that the equation involves multiplication by a constant and a derivative – therefore drag these function blocks into the Simulink workspace and connect appropriately, Fig. 11 (b). For example Eq. (1) is simulated as in Fig. 11 (b). Following the signal step-by-step as shown in Fig. 11 (c) reveals that the subsystem output is the voltage of the inductor based on the input current to the inductor. The equation is therefore successfully modeled. It is well to mention that the model shown in Fig. 11 is an analytical exercise only; physically implementing the model shown is not recommended as the differentiator will amplify noise in a real system.

As an exercise to bring together the concepts discussed of blocks performing functions based on embedded subsystems and equation modeling, consider the non-linear signal created with the Matlab program shown in Fig. 12.

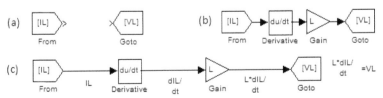

Figure 11. Equation Modeling: Inductor Voltage as a Function of Current

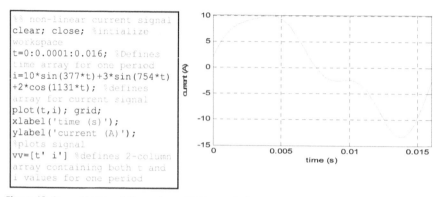

Figure 12. Sinusoidal Signal Generation with Harmonic Content

The signal shown in Fig. 12 can be imported into the Simulink model with the "From Workspace" block and evaluated for total harmonic distortion (21) as shown in Fig. 13.

$$THD = \frac{I_{Harmonic}}{I_{1_{RMS}}} = \frac{\sqrt{I^2_{RMS} - I^2_{1_{RMS}}}}{I_{1_{RMS}}} \tag{21}$$

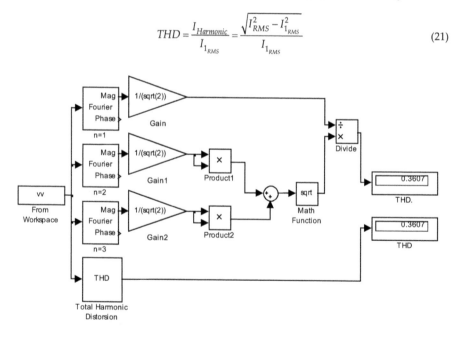

Figure 13. Total Harmonic Distortion Analysis of Signal with Harmonic Content

Compare the top three forward paths of the block diagram in Fig. 13 to Eq. (21). It can be seen that the signal has been successfully evaluated for Total Harmonic Distortion (THD) of the given signal (neglecting harmonic content beyond the 3rd). Now consider the fourth forward path of the block diagram and compare the THD measurement blocks at the right – the results are identical illustrating the embedded mathematical functionality contained in Simulink blocks. To explore further, right-click on the Simulink THD block, choose "Look Under Mask", and compare mathematical functionality.

Applying the same modeling techniques shown in the THD example in an effort to aid in optimization of power electronic converters and to exemplify the block modeling concepts discussed, the loss equations introduced in section 2.4 have been modeled in Simulink (Fig. 14) for the buck-boost converter and combined into a Simulink model block (Fig. 15). The Buck-Boost Converter Power & Efficiency block is used in section 4.3 for converter optimization.

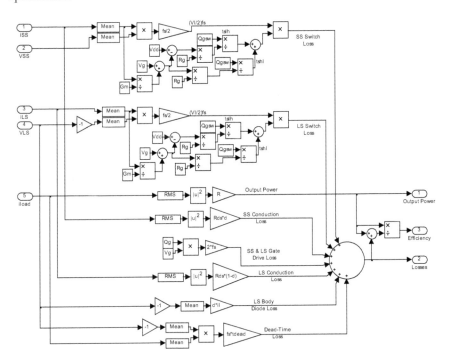

Figure 14. Buck-Boost Power & Efficiency Block Embedded Calculations

4.1. Light dimmer

Consider the light dimmer circuit introduced in section 2.1. A good first step in simulation of this circuit is to understand the range of available output voltage and power as controlled by varying the potentiometer R2. As R2 is adjusted between its minimum and maximum resistance values, Matlab can be used to plot the waveforms to illustrate the output characteristics of the circuit. The light dimmer TRIAC is self-commutating as introduced in section 2.1. This behavior in general is plotted as shown in Fig. 16, where alpha represents the firing angle of the TRIAC in the supplied waveform.

To find the output power of the light dimmer circuit, the light dimmer voltage waveform shown in Fig. 16 can be evaluated for RMS current over one-half period (as negative portion of waveform is symmetrical) giving,

$$I_{RMS} = \sqrt{\frac{1}{\pi}\int_\alpha^\pi \frac{V_m^2}{R^2}\sin^2(\theta)d\theta} = \frac{V_m}{R}\sqrt{1-\frac{\alpha}{\pi}+\frac{1}{2\pi}\sin(2\alpha)} \tag{22}$$

It follows that,

$$P(\alpha)=I_{RMS}^2 R = \frac{Vm^2}{2R}\left[1-\frac{\alpha}{\pi}+\frac{1}{2\pi}\sin(2\alpha)\right] \tag{23}$$

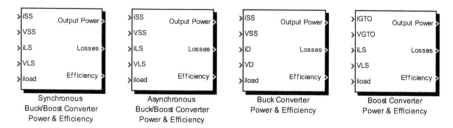

Figure 15. Developed DC/DC Converter Power & Efficiency Blocks – Buck, Boost, Buck-Boost

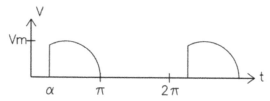

Figure 16. Self-Commutation at Firing Angle Alpha

and,

$$V(\alpha)=\sqrt{[P(\alpha)](R)} \tag{24}$$

where α = firing angle of TRIAC

The relationships shown in 23 and 24 can be plotted in the Matlab workspace as shown in Fig. 17, assuming a supply of 120V_RMS, 60 Hz, and light bulb impedance of 576Ω (purely resistive – inductive effects negligible).

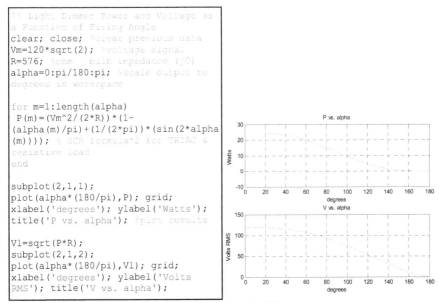

```
%% Light Dimmer Power and Voltage as
a Function of Firing Angle
clear; close; %clear previous data
Vm=120*sqrt(2); %voltage signal
R=576; %ohm  bulb impedance (j0)
alpha=0:pi/180:pi; %scale output to
degrees in workspace

for m=1:length(alpha)
 P(m)=(Vm^2/(2*R))*(1-
(alpha(m)/pi)+(1/(2*pi))*(sin(2*alpha
(m)))); % SCR formula*2 for TRIAC &
resistive load
end

subplot(2,1,1);
plot(alpha*(180/pi),P); grid;
xlabel('degrees'); ylabel('Watts');
title('P vs. alpha'); %plot results

Vl=sqrt(P*R);
subplot(2,1,2);
plot(alpha*(180/pi),Vl); grid;
xlabel('degrees'); ylabel('Volts
RMS'); title('V vs. alpha');
```

Figure 17. Power and Voltage as a Function of Firing Angle Alpha

Fig. 17 reveals power and voltage characteristics that can be expected from the light dimmer circuit. As expected, the power output is non-linear, i.e. proportional changes in potentiometer dial rotation do not result in proportional changes in lamp brightness. The graph also confirms the maximum voltage and power the lamp will experience for proper lamp sizing.

To examine light dimmer circuit behavior in more detail and observe waveforms, the circuit can be implemented in Simulink. The model can be constructed as shown in Fig. 18. Simulink blocks are added to the model simply by dragging-and-dropping from the Simulink Library Browser, while connections between blocks are accomplished by single-clicking and dragging to appropriate nodes. The blocks shown are color coded by type of block as organized within Simulink as follows: orange – SimPower sources, red – SimPower power electronic devices, magenta – SimPower elements, light blue – SimPower measurements devices, dark blue – standard Simulink blocks.

Some devices shown in Fig. 18 are identical to those introduced in Fig. 1, such as resistors and capacitors. The DIAC is represented by two diodes placed to conduct current in opposite directions (for AC) as diodes exhibit the same self-commutating behavior. The TRIAC is implemented using two thyristors to pass AC current in much the same way as the DIAC, the difference being the active control input at the gate. Thyristors are chosen in SimPower for their self-commutating behavior and representation of TRIAC characteristics. Double-click model blocks to set parameters according to those shown.

Note the block in Fig. 18 labeled "powergui" near the AC voltage source. This block automatically appears upon running a SimPower simulation, and is required. The powergui contains configuration functions such as initial states, machine initialization parameters, FFT analysis, and other useful tools, albeit none are utilized in this chapter.

The results of evaluating the light dimmer circuit in Simulink are shown in real time as the simulation progresses on the numerical readouts. After the simulation is completed, double-clicking on the "V$_{load}$" scope icon reveals a waveform similar to Fig. 19. The waveform of Fig. 19 shows the self-commutation behavior discussed earlier in that, once fired, the TRIAC passes current until the voltage across it drops to zero. Note the time that the gate voltage spikes to 1 is the exact time that the TRIAC fires and allows the source voltage waveform to pass until the current drops below the holding current IH which occurs in this ideal case at I=0. Also notice the waveform that fires at approximately 10ms is slightly distorted – this asymmetrical firing of the TRIAC's occurs for a brief period until the converter stabilizes.

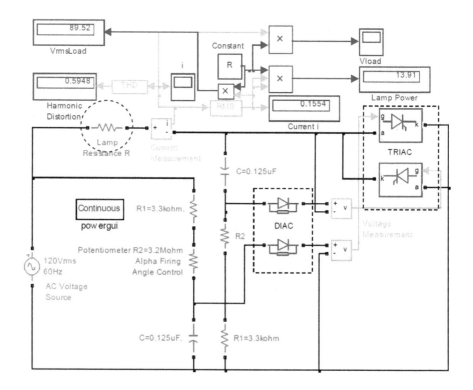

Figure 18. Light Dimmer Circuit

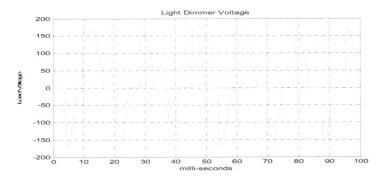

Figure 19. SimPower Light Dimmer Output Voltage Waveform - α=87°

The light dimmer circuit was also constructed using physical components and tested for validity. A 60 Watt light bulb was light controlled using the Littlefuse Q2015L5 TRIAC and the STMicroelectronics DB3 DIAC. The Fluke-41 Power Harmonics Analyzer was the primary waveform capturing device (Fig. 20).

Graphical comparison of simulated and experimental results shows very good agreement. Observe the symmetrical firing angle on both halves of the waveform as presented and discussed earlier – this provides confirmation of a successful design concerning firing angle symmetry. Simulated and experimental data were taken for firing angles ranging from 28° to 155° and recorded as presented in Table 6.

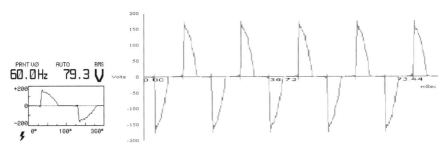

Figure 20. Experimental Light Dimmer Output Voltage Waveform - α=87°

Firing Angle α(deg)	Simulated in Simulink			Experimental		
	Vrms	Power (W)	THD(%)	Vrms	Power (W)	THD(%)
28	116.3	23.48	4.4	114.6	26	8.6
62	109.8	20.93	28.83	103.6	21	34.1
87	89.65	13.95	57.49	79.4	14	64.6
127	58.89	6.021	93.51	49.0	6	102.3
132	53.52	4.973	100.8	45.8	5	107.5
155	24.5	1.043	105.81	19.2	1	169.7

Table 6. Light Dimmer Characteristics – Experimental vs. Simulated Results

There is good agreement between the simulated and experimental data given in Table 6. The values diverge particularly toward the upper firing angles. Divergence and inconsistencies are expected due to variations in the load resistance due to thermal effects. THD is expected to be lower for low firing angles as less harmonic components are present in undisturbed waveforms closely resembling the smooth curve of the input sine wave. The more the voltage waveform is modified by the TRIAC firing at higher angles the more high frequency components are produced, and therefore the more total harmonic distortion.

4.2. DC-DC converter

A designer concerned with the behavior of DC-DC converters introduced in earlier sections may wish to consider the voltage gain of the buck, boost, and buck-boost converters as a starting point. The Matlab workspace can be used to plot V_{load}/V_{source} as introduced in section 2.2 for each converter to graphically represent the curves for consideration.

Recognizing that duty ratio ranges between 0 and 1 for all PWM converters, a Matlab workspace script program is used to create the plot shown in Fig. 21 to show output voltage of each type of DC-DC converter introduced in section 2 as a function of duty ratio. Note the asymptotic behavior of the boost and buck-boost at higher duty ratios.

4.3. Buck DC-DC converter

The buck converter was introduced in section 2.2.1 including equations 1 through 5 which describe buck converter behavior. To further develop tools in power electronics design in Matlab, consider the following design example.

It is desired to design a buck converter for a particular automotive application. The supply voltage in a typical automobile while running is 13.8 volts. The device to be powered is purely resistive at 100 ohms and requires a constant 5 volt supply. A maximum of 5% current and voltage ripple is desired. The design has physical size constraints, so a switching frequency of 100 kHz or above is decided upon to keep inductor size at a minimum. Analytically, minimum inductor size is given by Eq. (25) (Shaffer, 2007),

$$L_{CCM} = \frac{(V_S - V_O)R}{2fV_S} = \frac{(13.8 - 5)100}{2(100e3)(13.8)} = 318.8\,\mu H \tag{25}$$

To account for current ripple, the scaling factor lambda is developed,

$$\lambda = \frac{2V_O}{R(\Delta I)} = \frac{2(5)}{100(0.05)} = 2 \tag{26}$$

Inductor size accounting for current ripple follows with,

$$L = \lambda\left(L_{CCM}\right) = 2\left(318.8\right) = 637.6\,\mu H \tag{27}$$

Capacitor size determines output voltage ripple according to the relationship,

$$C = \frac{\left(1 - \dfrac{V_O}{V_S}\right)}{8Lrf^2} = \frac{\left(1 - \dfrac{5}{13.8}\right)}{8\left(637.6\mu\right)0.05\left(100e3\right)^2} = 250nF \tag{28}$$

```
%% Vload/Vsource as a function of duty
ratio
close; clear; %initialize workspace
d=0:0.01:0.9; %duty ratio ranges from 0 to
1

%buck
for x=1:length(d)
 Vbk(x)=d(x); %compute output voltage
end

%boost
for x=1:length(d) %intermediate variable
may be reused
 Vbst(x)=1/(1-d(x)); %compute output
voltage
end

%buck-boost
for x=1:length(d)
 Vbb(x)=d(x)/(1-d(x)); %compute output
voltage
end

%plot results
plot(d,Vbk); hold on; plot(d,Vbst,'r');
plot(d,Vbb,'g'); %hold allows plotting on
same graph
grid; xlabel('duty ratio');
ylabel('Vo/Vs'); %presentation
enhancements
legend('Buck','Boost', 'Buck-Boost',
'Location', 'NorthWest' )
```

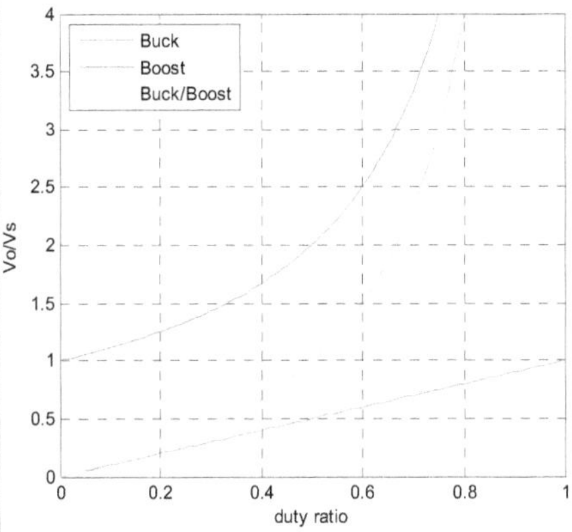

Figure 21. DC-DC Converter V_{load}/V_{source}

The analytic development of parameters may be used for simulation, but Matlab/Simulink offers another option. A Matlab program can be created to calculate and store system parameters, and used to support a Simulink simulation. First, the following script program is written to calculate system parameters (Fig. 22).

```
%Buck Evaluation Parameters
Vin=13.8; %Volt - Input Voltage, use highest value if source varies
Vout=5; %Volt - desired output voltage
fs=100e3; %1/Second - define switching frequency
vripple=0.05; %max acceptable voltage ripple
iripple=0.05; %max acceptable current ripple
R=100; %ohm - load resistance, purely resistive assumed (j0)
P=1/fs; %Second - switching period
d=Vout/Vin; %unitless ratio - duty ratio calculation
Lccm=(((Vin-Vout)*R)/(2*fs*Vin)); %Henry - minimum L value for CCM
Lambda=(2/iripple)*(Vout/R); %inductor scaling factor - intermediate
calculation
L=Lccm %Henry - inductor size at absolute minimum for CCM
%L=Lccm*Lambda %Henry - inductor size accounting for current ripple
C=(1-(Vout/Vin))/(8*L*vripple*fs^2) %Farad - capacitor calculation
```

Figure 22. Buck Converter Simulink Simulation

Merely by executing this program the values of C and L will be written to the Matlab workspace, and are also saved into temporary memory for use in a Simulink simulation. Such a simulation is constructed as shown in Fig. 23 for the buck converter.

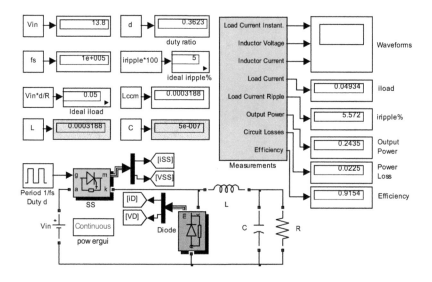

Figure 23. Buck Converter Simulink Simulation

Note the large red arrow in the script program which shows a command that is commented out. If we wished to evaluate this circuit with proper design considerations for current ripple, this line can be commented back in to the program. However, for the purpose of examining the behavior of the converter at the CCM/DCM borderline, the value of Lccm is used for the following evaluation. The capacitor size automatically changes accordingly when the program is reevaluated, highlighting the great advantage that computer-based systems have over analytic calculations: the ability to modify parameters at will without having to perform additional calculations. The circuit is set to run over the duration of 0 to 100*P, with all simulation settings default except Max step size set to P/20 to increase resolution. Examine and consider the actual simulation values shown in the Simulink simulation diagram of Fig. 23, and waveforms shown in Fig. 24. Note the values of L and C and other values shown in the upper left of the Simulink diagram as calculated from the workspace program.

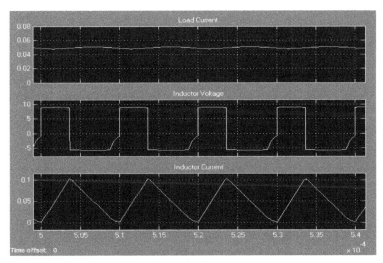

Figure 24. Buck Converter Voltage and Current Waveforms

Observe the buck converter's inductor current characteristics operating on the borderline of CCM and DCM behavior by nearly falling to zero. A related behavior is observed in the inductor voltage waveform as the energy contained in the inductor field exponentially decays nearly to zero before the source-switch closes and raises the voltage level. Also note the instantaneous voltage polarity change on the inductor – this capability is what makes power electronic converters possible (keep in mind that when the polarity across the inductor is negative, current is still flowing in the same direction through the load). The slight variation in load current is observed exhibiting ripple behavior. The circuit's efficiency is also evaluated at 92% with the loss model block developed in section 4.0.

4.4. Buck-boost DC-DC converter

Continuing with practical designs, consider an application for a portable electronic device that requires power such as a laptop or cellular phone. These devices require precisely controlled voltage levels for supply to sensitive electronics. Batteries, however, do not exhibit stable output voltage characteristics as illustrated in Fig. 25 for two typical battery types.

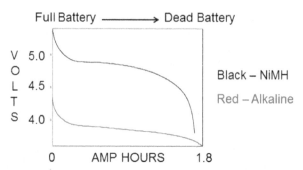

Figure 25. Typical Battery Output Voltage Discharge Characteristics

As the battery undergoes its normal discharge cycle, its supplied voltage varies significantly as Fig. 25 shows. A solution is required in order to provide a relatively constant input voltage to electronic devices fed from a source whose voltage varies. The buck-boost converter is very effective for this application as it can provide a well regulated load voltage, as discussed in Section 2.3.

Assume a designer wishes incorporate a converter for its voltage stability characteristics into a portable electronic device. Portable electronics require continuous current in order to retain information in volatile memory registers, therefore CCM mode is required. The designer will be concerned with minimizing the power losses of the converter in order to provide the maximum battery life possible. Simulink provides an effective option to determine optimal configuration of parameters to maximize efficiency. The synchronous converter as introduced earlier can be modeled in Simulink as shown in Fig. 26. The asynchronous converter is modeled by changing the active load switch to a diode, and changing the power & efficiency calculation block accordingly (see Fig. 15).

Parameters for simulation are defined in a workspace program according to data sheets for the IRFP450 MOSFET and SB245E Diode, as these are common devices. A median battery supply voltage of 5 volts is chosen as well as a 5 volt output from the converter as this is a common required voltage for electronic devices. Simulated buck-boost inductor behavior as described earlier is plotted in Fig. 27.

The synchronous and asynchronous buck-boost converters can be evaluated at various load currents in order to yield the overall efficiency of each in order to optimize power transfer. After some trial runs are executed to explore the range of load current that should be simulated, a minimum and maximum load current test range of 1mA to 1A are chosen. The converters are evaluated accordingly; efficiency data is recorded, and subsequently plotted in the Matlab workspace as shown in Fig. 28.

The curves shown in Fig. 28 can be used to select the appropriate buck-boost converter topology and design load current for various applications. If inductor size is not a consideration, the designer will elect to use a synchronous converter at a switching frequency of 10kHz as this configuration yields maximum efficiency for all loads examined (keep in mind that larger inductors allow lower switching frequencies). If perhaps size is a consideration and a minimum switching frequency of 50kHz must be used, the designer will choose a 50kHz asynchronous converter for loads ranging from 10mA to ~50mA, and a synchronous converter for loads above 50mA. Other considerations may regulate various switching frequencies, topologies, and load current such as harmonic considerations, available control circuitry for the load switch, etc. – Fig. 28 can be used for these various applications to choose the most efficient converter configuration.

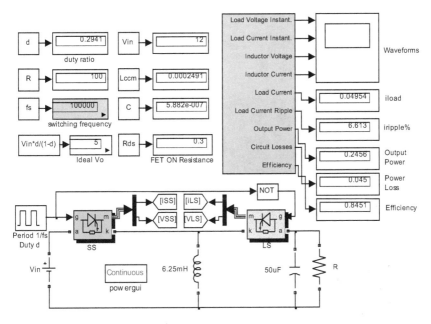

Figure 26. Buck-Boost Converter Simulation Diagram

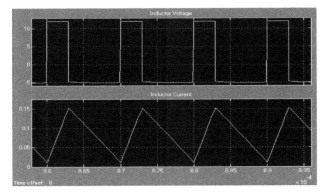

Figure 27. Buck-Boost Inductor Voltage and Current Waveforms

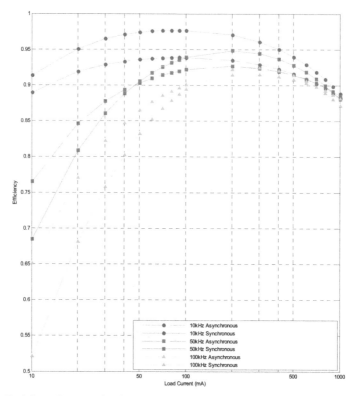

Figure 28. Buck-Boost Converter Synchronous and Asynchronous Efficiency

5. Conclusion

This chapter gave a general overview of AC and DC converters with special emphases on DC-DC converters and their applications. The different topologies were discussed and the importance of designing for efficiency and energy saving was emphasized. Design and analysis steps were illustrated using Matlab and Simulink as an engineering tool. The effectiveness of the SimPower toolbox was demonstrated via typical examples which lead the way for further investigation. The tools available for simulation were exploited to facilitate additional related studies.

Author details

Sven Fagerstrom
Pacific Gas and Electric (PG&E), Fresno, CA, USA

Nagy Bengiamin
California State University Fresno, Fresno, CA, USA

Acknowledgement

This work was supported partially by DPS Telecom, Inc. through a gift to enhance research and development projects in Electrical and Computer Engineering at California State University Fresno. DPS Telecom is located in Fresno, CA, USA.

6. References

Arbetter, B., Erickson, R., & Maksimović, D., (1995), *DC-DC Converter Design for Battery-Operated Systems*. University of Colorado at Boulder

Assi, A.H., (Ed.), (2011), *Engineering Research and Education using Matlab*. Capter *by* Carvalho, A., & Quterio, M.T., *Matlab in Model-based Design for Power Electronics Systems*, Intech, ISBN 978-953-307-656-0

Chen, Y., Lee, F.C., Amoroso, L., & Wu, H.P., (2000), *A Resonant MOSFET Gate Driver With Efficient Energy Recovery*, International Power Electronics and Motion Control (IPEMC) Conference

Djekic, O., & Brkovic, M., (1997), *Synchronous Rectifiers vs. Schottky Diodes in a Buck Topology for Low Voltage Applications*, Power Electronics Specialists Conference, Vol. 2, pp. 1974-1980.

Fagerstrom, S.E. & Bengiamin, N.N., (2011), *Buck/Boost Converter Modeling and Simulation*, IASTED Modeling and Simulation Conference (MS 2011), July 4-6, 2011, Calgary, Canada, paper # 735-059

Forsyth, A.J. &Mollov, S.V., (1998), *Modeling and Control of DC-DC Converters*, IEEE Power Engineering Journal, ISSN 0950-3366

Gildersleeve, M., Zadeh, H.P.F, & Mora, G.A.R, (2002), *A Comprehensive Power Analysis and a Highly Efficient, Mode-Hopping DC-DC Converter*, IEEE Asia-Pacific Conference on ASIC, pp. 153-156

Johansson, B., (2004),*DC-DC Converters – Dynamic Model Design and Experimental Verification*, Lund University, Sweden, ISBN 91-88934-34-9

Klein, J., (2006), *Synchronous buck MOSFET loss calculations with Excel Model*, Fairchild Semiconductor, www.fairchildsemi.com

Paul, B., (2001), *Industrial Electronics and Control, Prentice-Hall of India*, ISBN 81-203-1811-0

Rashid, M.H., (2004), *Power Electronics Handbook (third edition)*, Pearson Prentice Hall, ISBN 0-13-101140-5

Saggini, S., Trevisan, D., Mattavelli, P., Ghioni, M., (2007), *Synchronous-Asynchronous Digital Voltage-Mode Control for DC-DC Converters*, IEEE Transactions on Power Electronics, ISBN 0885-8993

Shaffer, R., (2007), *Fundamentals of Power Electronics with MATLAB*, Charles River Media, ISBN 1-58450-852-3

Skvarenina, T.L., (Ed.), (2002), *The Power Electronics Handbook*, CRC, ISBN-0-8493-7336-0

Stratakos, J., (1998), *High-Efficiency Low-Voltage DC-DC Conversion for Portable Applications*, University of California, Berkeley, Ph.D. Thesis

Wang, T.G., Zhou, X., & Lee, F.C., (1997), *A Low Voltage High Efficiency and High Power Density DC/DC Converter*, 28th Annual IEEE Power Electronics Specialists Conference, Vol. 1, pp. 240-245.

Xiong, Y., Sun, S., Jia, H., Shea, P., & Shen, Z.J., (2009), *New Physical Insights on Power MOSFET Switching Losses*, IEEE Transactions on Power Electronics, Vol. 24, No. 2

Zhou, S., (2003). *Fully Integrated Power-Saving Solutions for DC-DC Converters Targeted for the Mobile, Battery-Powered Applications*, Georgia Tech Analog Consortium Industry Research Review

Zhou, S. & Rincon-Mora, G.A., (2006),*A high Efficiency, Soft Switching DC-DC Converter with Adaptive Current-Ripple Control for Portable Applications*, IEEE Transactions on Circuits and Systems, Vol.53, No. 4

Dynamic and Quasi-Static Simulation of a Novel Compliant MEMS Force Amplifier by Matlab/Simulink

Ergin Kosa, Levent Trabzon, Umit Sonmez and Huseyin Kizil

Additional information is available at the end of the chapter

1. Introduction

MEMS are micro electromechanical systems having component sizes varying from 1 micrometer to 1 millimeter and provide specific engineering operations. MEMS are used as a micro sensor, micro actuator, micro accelerometer etc. and also have tendency to function rapidly due to having low inertia moment and affected less by disturbances coming from environment due to their small size (Hsu, 2002).

Compliant mechanisms having an ability to transmit motion and energy via their flexible hinges and/or flexible components instead of joints and rigid components, perform large deflections (Sreekumar et al, 2008). The large deflections of compliant mechanisms instead of rigid-body mechanisms depend on applied force that causes a much more complexity to nonlinear analysis (Ashok, 2000). Moreover, the geometry of several flexure hinges are modeled as torsion springs in its pseudo-rigid-body mechanisms (Howell, 2001). Flexible segments of compliant mechanism store and transfer energy when it is functioning (Howell, 2001; Tantanawat & S. Kota, 2007). Flexible links having small cross sections instead of traditional joints provide acting of mechanism due to its very low moment of inertia (Howell, 2001; Lobontiu et al, 2001).

Compliant four-link mechanism is designed as seen in Fig. 1 achieving force or displacement application according to the output spring constant and also, studied on size optimization to achieve maximum mechanical or geometric benefit at specific spring constants (Parkinson et al, 2001). Large displacement amplifier integrated with comb drive achieves 100 times amplifying of comb drive displacement by means of its design is modeled (Li et al, 2005).

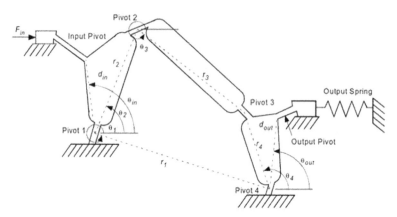

Figure 1. Schematic view of force or displacement amplifier' mechanism

Compliant MEMS have been used as a force amplifier in micro actuators and micro-mechanisms (Parkinson et al, 2001).

They are preferred since there is no need for assembly, no energy loss due to absence of friction, thus requiring no need for lubrication all of which providing high precision (Kosa et al, 2010). Besides, compliant micro mechanisms could be activated by mechanically (Han et al, 2007; Krishnan & Ananthasuresh, 2008), electro statically (Français et al, 2005; Millet et al, 2004), thermally (Lai et al, 2004; Terre & Shkel, 2004) or electrical (Gomm et al, 2002; Huang & Lan, 2006) induced forces.

Moreover, compliant MEMS having two or three clear stable states as named bi-stable or tri-stable behavior respectively were used in micro valve, micro switch, micro clasps applications (Chen et al, 2009; Jensen et al, 2001; Jensen & Howell, 2003; Nathan & Howell, 2003; Wilcox & Howell, 2005). For instance, Jensen designed several mechanisms such as double slider crank, slider-rocker mechanisms and explained the theory of bi-stable behavior (Jensen et al, 2004).

Recent studies on compliant mechanisms are focused on novel designs (Kosa et al, 2010), new developed methodologies and optimization in topology (Chour & Jyhjei, 2006; Krishnan & Ananthasuresh, 2008; Pedersen & Seshia, 2004), size and shape (Krishnan & Ananthasuresh, 2008) or the use of finite element methods (Jensen et al, 2001). Compliant micro mechanisms enable mechanical or geometric benefit meaning that the ratio of output force to input force and the ratio of output displacement to input displacement, respectively, and both mechanical and geometric advantage (MA and GA, respectively) are formulized as follows;

$$MA = F_{out}/F_{in} \qquad (1)$$

$$GA = d_{out}/d_{in} \qquad (2)$$

The energy is conserved during the motion transfer of compliant micro mechanism indicating that the increase in the output force causes decrease in the output displacement and vice versa. So, both mechanical and geometric benefits are significant to provide input to the micro actuators in MEMS applications (Kosa et al, 2010).

Optimization of compliant mechanisms such as topology and size optimization is a challenging issue. In topology optimization, it is critical to design a suitable functional configuration of the mechanism to provide desired output motion under applied forces while in size optimization, it is important to achieve desired force or displacement amplification so as to operate under maximum loads (Kota et al, 2001).

In this study, novel compliant MEMS force amplifier is designed and simulated by modeling its rigid body mechanism by Matlab/Simulink to determine the dynamic and quasi-static behavior. Kinematic approach is investigated and kinematic equations are derived and velocity and acceleration analysis of the micro mechanism are modeled. Dynamic response of MEMS amplifier is validated at a constant angular velocity and it is concluded that force amplification reaches to infinity at zero-crank angle. It is achieved that force amplification ratio reaches 5093, as the first stage crank angle, Θ_2 passes from $0°$ in quasi-static simulation.

2. Mechanism design

Compliant MEMS force amplifier's configuration is schematically shown in Fig. 2. Micro amplifier is composed of two slider-crank mechanisms. The two stage slider-crank amplifier provides force amplifying by means of its novel design. Its aim is to perform high output force at point B under low input forces. Two stages provide much more amplification compare to one stage. For both stages, rigid beams are linked by single thin flexible beams having a width of 3 µm. These flexible beams make the micro mechanism motion possible under operating forces. The micro mechanism stores energy and transfers force by elastic deformation of flexible beams linking rigid beams as both stage-slider cranks get close zero degree crank angle. Afterwards, input force is removed and micro amplifier springs back to its original position by means of flexible links having large deflections.

The beams in first stage have a length of 100 µm and width of 25 µm as the beams in second stage have a length of 800 µm and width of 25 µm, as all beams have rectangular cross sectional area. The depths of all beams are chosen as 25µm limited by SOI-MUMPs (Silicon on Insulator Multi User MEMS Process) manufacturing technology (Cohen et al, 2009).

2.1. Grashof theorem

In rigid body model of the MEMS amplifier, four-bar configuration is attained after vector loop equations are derived. Grashof theorem becomes significant to demonstrate the act of micro mechanism. Grashof theorem takes three cases into consideration and states that when both of beams are rocked it is called a double-rocker when both of beams are able to revolve, then it is called double-crank, when the short beam is able to rotate as the long one is rocked, then it is called a crank-rocker mechanism. To determine the moving limit of the micro mechanism, the relation between the lengths of beams turns out to be an important issue. Therefore, selecting the length of a beam plays a crucial role for the micro mechanism.

Due the fact that, x1, x2 are assumed as length of the shortest beam and length of the longest beam, respectively, as x3, x4 are the mean lengths of the beams. If x1+x2<= x3+x4, at least one of the beams can rotate and If x1+x2= x3+x4, the mechanism is activated and crank has limited rotation this feature enables beams to pass horizontal positions closely to each other achieving a high force amplifying.

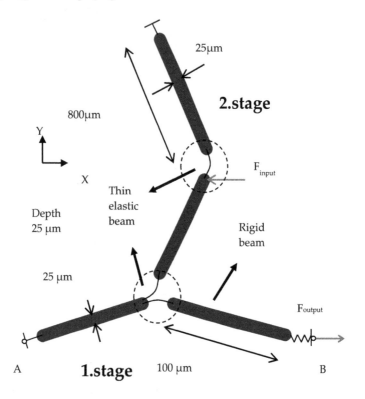

Figure 2. Novel compliant MEMS Force Amplifier

3. Analysis of quasi-static behavior

3.1. Force and moment equation derivation

Rigid body model of the compliant micro mechanism is considered. Free body diagram of each beam is sketched and a typical beam model is schematically shown in Fig. 3. Forces acting on each beam is broken down into x and y components as follows;

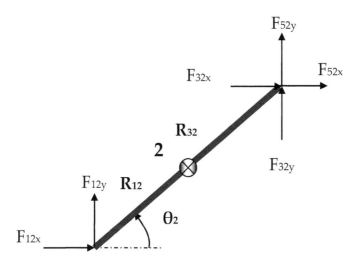

Figure 3. Free body diagram of beam 2

The static force and moment equations of beam 2 is typically shown and derived as; Equation derivation of forces acting on beam 2 along x axis;

$$\sum F_x = 0 \tag{3}$$

$$F_{12x} + F_{32x} + F_{52x} = 0 \tag{4}$$

Equation derivation of forces acting on beam 2 along y axis;

$$\sum F_y = 0 \tag{5}$$

$$F_{12y} + F_{32y} + F_{52y} = 0 \tag{6}$$

Equation derivation of moments acting on beam 2 along z axis;

$$\sum M_z = 0 \tag{7}$$

$$R_{12x} * F_{12y} - R_{12y} * F_{12x} + R_{32x} * F_{32y} - R_{32y} * F_{32x} + R_{52x} * F_{52y} - R_{52y} * F_{52x} = 0 \tag{8}$$

Free body diagram of beam 3 is shown in Fig. 4 and equation derivation of forces acting on beam 3 along x axis;

$$\sum F_x = 0 \tag{9}$$

$$F_{23x} + F_{43x} = 0 \tag{10}$$

Equation derivation of forces acting on beam 3 along y axis;

$$\sum F_y = 0 \tag{11}$$

$$F_{23y} + F_{43y} = 0 \tag{12}$$

Equation derivation of moments acting on beam 3 along z axis;

$$\sum M_z = 0 \tag{13}$$

$$R_{23x} * F_{23y} - R_{23y} * F_{23x} + R_{43x} * F_{43y} - R_{43y} * F_{43x} = 0 \tag{14}$$

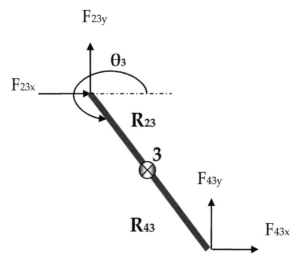

Figure 4. Free body diagram of beam 3

Free body diagram of beam 5 is shown in Fig. 5 and equation derivation of forces acting on beam 5 along x axis;

$$\sum F_x = 0 \tag{15}$$

$$F_{65x} + F_{25x} = 0 \tag{16}$$

Equation derivation of forces acting on beam 5 along y axis;

$$\sum F_y = 0 \tag{17}$$

$$F_{65y} + F_{25y} = 0 \tag{18}$$

Equation derivation of moments acting on beam 5 along z axis;

$$\sum M_z = 0 \tag{19}$$

$$R_{65x} * F_{65y} - R_{65y} * F_{65x} + R_{25x} * F_{25y} - R_{25y} * F_{25x} = 0 \tag{20}$$

Free body diagram of beam 6 is shown in Fig. 6 and equation derivation of forces acting on beam 6 along x axis;

$$\sum F_x = 0 \tag{21}$$

$$F_{g6x} + F_{56x} = 0 \tag{22}$$

Equation derivation of forces acting on beam 6 along y axis;

$$\sum F_y = 0 \tag{23}$$

$$F_{g6y} + F_{56y} = 0 \tag{24}$$

Equation derivation of moments acting on beam 6 along z axis;

$$\sum M_z = 0 \tag{25}$$

$$R_{g6x} * F_{g6y} - R_{g6y} * F_{g6x} + R_{56x} * F_{56y} - R_{56y} * F_{56x} = 0 \tag{26}$$

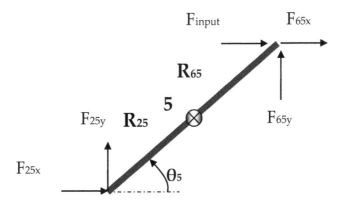

Figure 5. Free body diagram of beam 5

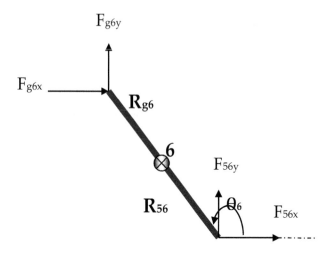

Figure 6. Free body diagram of beam 6

Free body diagram of slider is shown in Fig. 7 and equation derivation of forces acting on slider along x- and y- axes;

$$\sum F_x = 0 \tag{27}$$

$$F_{output} + F_{34x} = 0 \tag{28}$$

$$\sum F_y = 0 \tag{29}$$

$$F_{s4y} + F_{34y} = 0 \tag{30}$$

Thus, 14 force and moment equations are derived. Equations of relation between internal forces of beams;

$$F_{32x} = F_{23x} \tag{31}$$

$$F_{32y} = F_{23y} \tag{32}$$

$$F_{43x} = F_{34x} \tag{33}$$

$$F_{43y} = F_{34y} \tag{34}$$

$$F_{52x} = F_{25x} \tag{35}$$

$$F_{52y} = F_{25y} \tag{36}$$

$$F_{65x} = F_{56x} \tag{37}$$

$$F_{65y} = F_{56y} \tag{38}$$

8 equations are derived from the relations between internal forces of beams.

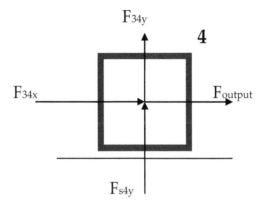

Figure 7. Free body diagram of slider

3.2. Equations and initial conditions

The vector loop equations are derived and broken down into x and y components as force and moment equations. It is seen that linear matrix method could not be used to solve the position problem. To analyze the position behavior of the micro mechanism, nonlinear and transcendental equations should be solved by Matlab and in quasi-static run, initial conditions of Θ_2 and (Θ_6-90°) are chosen as 10° and 20°, respectively.

3.3. Position analysis

The micro mechanism is a single degree of freedom mechanism and position analysis provides to inform the positions of other links and points as one of the links moves or rotates.

To find out position problem of the micro mechanism, nonlinear and transcendental vector loop equations that are derived and solved.

The vector loops are schematically shown in Fig. 8. There are two vector loop equations such as;

First vector loop equation:

$$R_2 + R_3 = R_1 \tag{39}$$

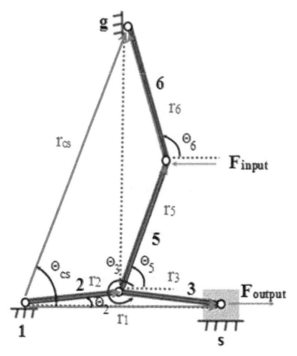

Figure 8. Vector loops for the force amplifier

Deriving equations according to coordinates of x and y:

$$r_2 * \cos\theta_2 + r_3 * \cos\theta_3 = r_1 \tag{40}$$

$$-r_2 * \sin\theta_2 - r_3 * \sin\theta_3 = 0 \tag{41}$$

Second vector loop equation:

$$R_2 + R_5 + R_6 = R_{cs} \tag{42}$$

Vector loop equations along x--axis

$$r_2 * \cos\theta_2 + r_5 * \cos\theta_5 + r_6 * \cos\theta_6 = r_{cs} * \cos\theta_{cs} \tag{43}$$

Vector loop equations along y--axis

$$r_2 * \sin\theta_2 + r_5 * \sin\theta_5 + r_6 * \sin\theta_6 = r_{cs} * \sin\theta_{cs} \tag{44}$$

By quasi-static analysis, it is claimed that (360°-Θ₃) and Θ₂ decreases linearly and are equal to each other during both quasi-static and dynamic simulations run by Matlab/Simulink. As seen in Fig. 9, it is calculated that as Θ₅ goes from 70° to 74.0248°, Θ₆ reduces from 110° to

105.9756°. Thus, as Θ_2 rotates 20°, both Θ_5 and Θ_2 rotates approximately 4.02° and slightly different from each other. The relation both between Θ_5 and Θ_2, Θ_6 and Θ_2 are linear.

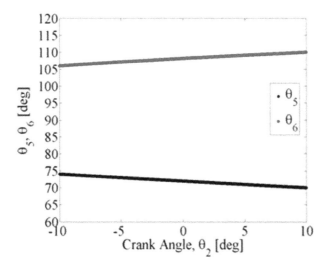

Figure 9. Plot of Θ_5 and Θ_6 according to first stage crank angle, Θ_2

Displacement ratio is defined as U_{output}/U_{input}. As the micro mechanism operates under an input force along – x direction, the first stage crank angle starts decreasing and pass from 0° and again starts increasing in an opposite direction and the ratio of output displacement to input displacement decreases as shown in Fig. 10. Beams 5 and 6 moves along –x and –y directions and the length of beams 5 and 6 are 8 times of beams 2 and 3. So, the input displacement increases rapidly than output displacement at close to zero degree crank angles. At negative crank angle values defining opposite directions, the slider gets close to initial position on contrast, beams 5 and 6 continue to get close to their vertical positions meaning that input displacement goes on to increase whereas output displacement begin to decrease. Therefore, after zero-crank angle, the displacement ratio continues to decrease according to Θ_2.

As the micro mechanism displays, both the second stage crank angle, $(\Theta_6-90°)$ and the first stage crank angle, Θ_2 get close to zero degree, the force amplification defined as F_{output}/F_{input} starts increasing and when Θ_2 is 0° and $(\Theta_6-90°)$ is at about small values, the micro mechanism provides high output force and force amplifying sharply increases as seen in Fig. 11 under $1.7*10^{-7}$ in [N]. Also, there are two peaks in force amplification by quasi-static run. As, the first crank angle is close to zero but at still positive value, the force amplifying reaches 5093 and after that step first crank angle gets negative value but it is still close to zero, the force amplification ratio is 4830 at negative direction due to the fact that the slider motion begin to move in opposite direction and also, output force is in opposite direction. It is claimed that the toggle position of the micro mechanism is a very crucial issue meaning that if the initial conditions such as crank angles are adjusted properly to enable both crank angle pass $0°$ at the same time, the ratio of the output to the input force applied to the mechanism goes to infinity at zero degree crank angles.

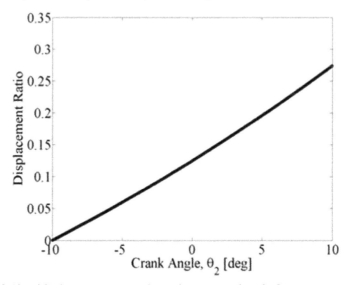

Figure 10. Plot of displacement ratio according to first stage crank angle, Θ_2

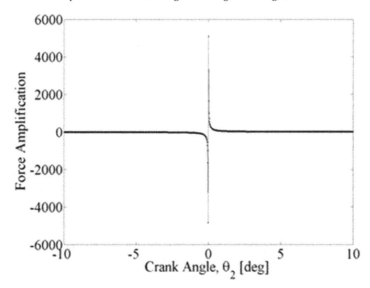

Figure 11. Plot of force amplifying according to first stage crank angle, Θ_2

4. Dynamic behavior of a novel MEMS amplifier

4.1. Inertial and geometric parameters:

It is assumed that micro mechanism is made up of silicon having a density of 2.33 g/cm³. For short length of beams, lengths are 100 micron, widths and heights are 25 micron. The mass of short beams is;

$$M_s = 2.33 * 100 * 25 * 25 * 10^{-15} = 145625 * 10^{-18} \text{ [kg]} \qquad (45)$$

For long length of beams, lengths are 800 micron, widths and heights are 25 micron. The mass of short beams is;

$$M_l = 2.33 * 800 * 25 * 25 * 10^{-15} = 1165000 * 10^{-18} \text{ [kg]} \qquad (46)$$

The mass of the slider is accepted as $145625 * 10^{-18}$ in kilograms.

The mass moments of inertia of the beams are calculated as follows;

For short beams;

$$I_s = M_s * (L^2 + a^2)/12 = 145625 * 10^{-18} * (100^2 + 25^2)/12 = 128938802.1 * 10^{-18} \text{ [kg*μm}^2\text{]} \qquad (47)$$

For long beams;

$$I_l = M_s * (L^2 + a^2)/12 = 1165000 * 10^{-18} * (800^2 + 25^2)/12 = 6.219401042 * 10^{-8} \text{[kg*μm}^2\text{]} \qquad (48)$$

4.2. Kinematic behavior

4.2.1. Velocity analysis

Kinematic simulation is used to calculate and to plot the velocities and acceleration of the beam of the MEMS amplifier.

To understand kinematic behavior of the mechanism, first of all, derivatives of vector loop equations derived in position analysis are taken with respect to time and the velocity equations are arranged as follows;

$$-r_2 * \sin\theta_2 * w_2 - r_3 * \sin\theta_3 * w_3 = \dot{r}_1 \qquad (49)$$

$$r_2 * \cos\theta_2 * w_2 + r_3 * \cos\theta_3 * w_3 = 0 \qquad (50)$$

$$-r_2 * \sin\theta_2 * w_2 - r_5 * \sin\theta_5 * w_5 - r_6 * \sin\theta_6 * w_6 = 0 \qquad (51)$$

$$r_2 * \cos\theta_2 * w_2 + r_5 * \cos\theta_5 * w_5 + r_6 * \cos\theta_6 * w_6 = 0 \qquad (52)$$

The beam 6 are rotated at a constant speed, 0.01 rad/s, in clockwise direction and the initial conditions of w_2, w_3, w_5, $\dot{r}_1$ are -0.059378175917485 [rad/s], 0.059378175917485 [rad/s], 0.011371580426033 [rad/s], 2.062182408251533 [μm/s], respectively.

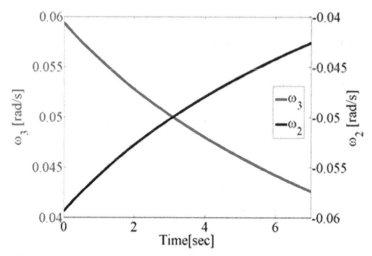

Figure 12. Plot of angular velocity of beam 2 and beam 3 versus time for simulation of force amplifier

The angular velocities of beams 2 and 3 in 1 stage are equal to each other in magnitude. As w_3 rotate counter clockwise direction, w_2 rotate clockwise direction and the absolute values of the changes in w_3 and w_2 equal to each other according to time as shown in Fig. 12.

Slider slows down until the first stage crank angle, Θ_2 pass from 0°. When first stage beams are fully open, as having horizontal position, slider velocity is equal to zero. Then the slider moves to along -x direction and angular velocity of beam 5 decreases according to time as in Fig. 13.

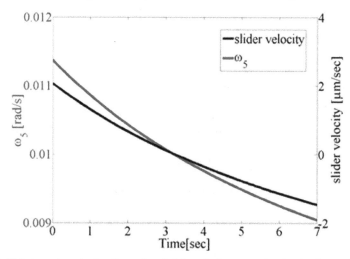

Figure 13. Plot of angular velocity of beam 5 and slider velocity versus time for simulation of force amplifier

4.2.2. Acceleration analysis

To analyze the acceleration of the beams, second derivatives of the terms must be handled. The second derivatives of the vector loop equations for the micro mechanism are as follows;

$$-r_2 * \cos\theta_2 * w_2^2 - r_2 * \sin\theta_2 * \alpha_2 - r_3 * \cos\theta_3 * w_3^2 - r_3 * \sin\theta_3 * \alpha_3 - \ddot{r}_1 = 0 \tag{53}$$

$$-r_2 * \sin\theta_2 * w_2^2 + r_2 * \cos\theta_2 * \alpha_2 - r_3 * \sin\theta_3 * w_3^2 + r_3 * \cos\theta_3 * \alpha_3 = 0 \tag{54}$$

$$\begin{aligned}
-r_2 * \cos\theta_2 * w_2^2 - r_2 * \sin\theta_2 * \alpha_2 - r_5 * \cos\theta_5 * w_5^2 \\
-r_5 * \sin\theta_5 * \alpha_5 - r_6 * \cos\theta_6 * w_6^2 - r_6 * \sin\theta_6 * \alpha_6 = 0
\end{aligned} \tag{55}$$

$$\begin{aligned}
-r_2 * \sin\theta_2 * w_2^2 + r_2 * \cos\theta_2 * \alpha_2 - r_5 * \sin\theta_5 * w_5^2 \\
+r_5 * \cos\theta_5 * \alpha_5 - r_6 * \sin\theta_6 * w_6^2 - r_6 * \cos\theta_6 * \alpha_6 = 0
\end{aligned} \tag{56}$$

In acceleration simulation by Simulink, the velocities such as w_2, w_3, w_5, r_1, w_6 are considered as known. The beam 6 rotates at a constant speed meaning that acceleration of beam 6 is zero.

Acceleration of beam 2 and beam 3 are shown in fig. 14. Both acceleration of beams decrease as the micro mechanism operates under constant w_6, angular velocity. The magnitude of acceleration of beam 2 and beam 3 are equal to each other during simulation. Also, as seen in Fig. 15, acceleration of beam 5 and slider decrease as function of time.

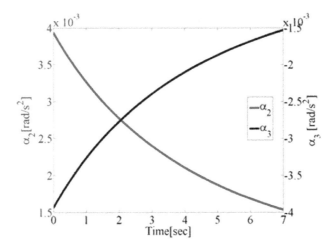

Figure 14. Acceleration of beam 2 and beam 3 under constant angular acceleration, α_2

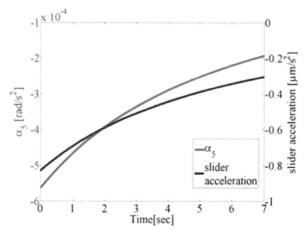

Figure 15. Acceleration of beam 5 and slider under constant angular acceleration, α_2

4.3. Acceleration vector equations according to center of mass

The linear acceleration of the center of mass equations are not present in vector loop equations that are previously derived. So, there must be equations relating to the acceleration of the center of mass of beams. Equation derivation is as follows and schematic representation of the center of mass acceleration in first and second loops is shown in Fig. 16 and Fig. 17, respectively.

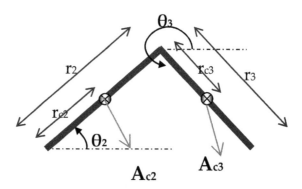

Figure 16. The center of mass acceleration in first loop

The center of mass acceleration of beam 2 along x and y direction;

$$A_{c2} = \ddot{R}_{c2} \qquad\qquad (57)$$

$$A_{c2x} = -r_{c2} * \sin\theta_2 * \alpha_2 - r_{c2} * \cos\theta_2 * w_2^2 \tag{58}$$

$$A_{c2y} = r_{c2} * \cos\theta_2 * \alpha_2 - r_{c2} * \sin\theta_2 * w_2^2 \tag{59}$$

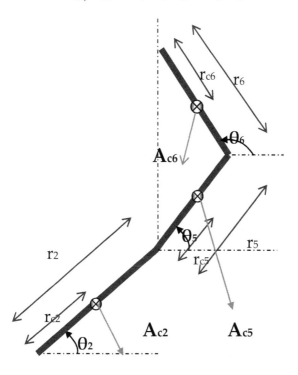

Figure 17. The center of mass acceleration in second loop

The center of mass acceleration of beam 3 along x and y direction;

$$A_{c3} = \ddot{R}_2 + \ddot{R}_{c3} \tag{60}$$

$$A_{c3x} = -r_2 * \sin\theta_2 * \alpha_2 - r_{c2} * \cos\theta_2 * w_2^2 - r_{c3} * \sin\theta_3 * \alpha_3 - r_{c3} * \cos\theta_3 * w_3^2 \tag{61}$$

$$A_{c3y} = r_2 * \cos\theta_2 * \alpha_2 - r_{c2} * \sin\theta_2 * w_2^2 + r_{c3} * \cos\theta_3 * \alpha_3 - r_{c3} * \sin\theta_3 * w_3^2 \tag{62}$$

The center of mass acceleration of beam 6 along x and y direction;

$$A_{c6} = \ddot{R}_{c6} \tag{63}$$

$$A_{c6y} = r_{c6} * \sin\theta_6 * \alpha_6 + r_{c6} * \cos\theta_6 * w_6^2 \tag{64}$$

$$A_{c6x} = -r_{c6} * \cos\theta_6 * \alpha_6 + r_{c6} * \sin\theta_6 * w_6^2 \tag{65}$$

The center of mass acceleration of beam 5 along x and y direction;

$$A_{c5} = \ddot{R}_2 + \ddot{R}_{c5} \tag{66}$$

$$A_{c5y} = r_6 * \sin\theta_6 * \alpha_6 + r_6 * \cos\theta_6 * w_6^2 + r_{c5} * \sin\theta_5 * \alpha_5 + r_{c5} * \cos\theta_5 * w_5^2 \tag{67}$$

$$A_{c5x} = -r_6 * \cos\theta_6 * \alpha_6 + r_6 * \sin\theta_2 * w_2^2 - r_{c5} * \cos\theta_5 * \alpha_5 - r_{c5} * \sin\theta_5 * w_5^2 \tag{68}$$

4.4. Force and dynamic analysis of the micro mechanism

The micro mechanism operates under constant angular velocity, 0.01 [rad/s], the slider crank starts increasing and reaches to its maximum value, 200 micron, meaning that the first stage slider crank is fully opened at 3.20 sec. then the first crank angle pass from 0° and slider begins to get close to its initial position and R_1 decreases as shown Fig. 18. According to both crank angles, Θ_2 and $(90-\Theta_6)$, the output force increases or decreases. In the first section of the F_{output} vs. time curve, first, both crank angles decrease, and two slider cranks start to open and at small crank angles, F_{output} sharply increase and at 3.20 sec Θ_2 is equal to 0.0013°

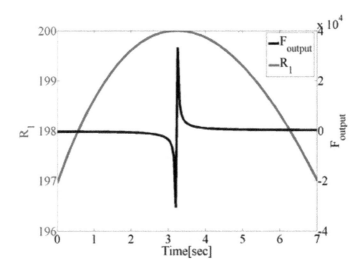

Figure 18. Displacement of slider and output force versus time

and at 3.25sec. Θ_2 is equal to -0.0012° and at Θ_2 these values, F_{output} goes to its peak values such as -3.07*10⁴ µN at 3.20 sec. and 3.32*10⁴ µN at 3.25 sec. Θ_2 decreases until 3.20 sec. and then it increases, whereas 90°-Θ_6 decreases and gets close to small values during the simulation. The magnitude of first peak of F_{output} at 3.25 sec. is higher than the magnitude of second peak of F_{output} at 3.20 sec. due to the fact that (90°-Θ_6) at 3.25 sec. is smaller than the value of (90°-Θ_6) at 3.20 sec., meaning that small crank angle value of (90°-Θ_6) contributes to get much more output force.

5. Conclusion

The MEMS force amplifier designed in this study is shown to provide high output to input ratio.

By quasi-static analysis, 5090 force amplifying is achieved as the first crank angle, Θ_2, rotates 10° and passes from its horizontal position and (90°-Θ_6) rotates 1.85° and continues to decrease.

The maximum amplifying ratio changes based on the initial position of the micro mechanism. So, the toggle of the micro mechanism has a crucial role to get high force output and high force amplification. If the mechanism's initial position is adjusted properly as both crank angles pass 0° at the same time, the force output and consequently force amplification go to infinity.

If pseudo rigid body of the compliant MEMS force amplifier having elastic hinges is modeled as a further study, it would provide us to get much more close response to the micro mechanism's real behavior. This novel MEMS amplifier design achieves high force amplifying due to its geometric design.

By dynamic analysis, high output force is achieved as the micro mechanism operates under 0.01 [rad/s] constant angular velocity of beam 6 at 3.20 sec and at about fully open position of first crank angle.

By Simulink, the simulation displays dynamic behavior of the micro compliant mechanism and it is claimed that second stage crank angle rotates 4.01°, whereas first stage crank angle, Θ_2, rotates 19.92°.

5.1. Nomenclauture

R_1, r_1	vector of beam 1
R_2, r_2	vector of beam 2
R_3, r_3	vector of beam 3
R_5, r_5	vector of beam 5
R_6, r_6	vector of beam 6
R_{cs}, r_{cs}	vector of beam cs
F_{12x}	force of beam ground acting on link 2 along x direction
F_{12y}	force of beam ground acting on link 2 along y direction

F_{23x}	force of beam 2 acting on link 3 along x direction
F_{23y}	force of beam 2 acting on link 3 along y direction
F_{32x}	force of beam 3 acting on link 2 along x direction
F_{32y}	force of beam 3 acting on link 2 along y direction
F_{43x}	force of beam 4 acting on link 3 along x direction
F_{43y}	force of beam 4 acting on link 3 along y direction
F_{34x}	force of beam 3 acting on link 4 along x direction
F_{34y}	force of beam 3 acting on link 4 along y direction
F_{52x}	force of beam 5 acting on link 2 along x direction
F_{52y}	force of beam 5 acting on link 2 along y direction
F_{25x}	force of beam 2 acting on link 5 along x direction
F_{25y}	force of beam 2 acting on link 5 along y direction
F_{65x}	force of beam 6 acting on link 5 along x direction
F_{65y}	force of beam 6 acting on link 5 along y direction
F_{56x}	force of beam 5 acting on link 6 along x direction
F_{56y}	force of beam 5 acting on link 6 along y direction
F_{g6x}	force of ground acting on link 6 along x direction
F_{g6y}	force of ground acting on link 6 along y direction
A_{c2x}	center of mass acceleration of beam 2 along x direction
A_{c2y}	center of mass acceleration of beam 2 along y direction
A_{c3x}	center of mass acceleration of beam 3 along x direction
A_{c3y}	center of mass acceleration of beam 3 along y direction
A_{c5x}	center of mass acceleration of beam 5 along x direction
A_{c5y}	center of mass acceleration of beam 5 along y direction
A_{c6x}	center of mass acceleration of beam 6 along x direction
A_{c6y}	center of mass acceleration of beam 6 along y direction
α_2	angular acceleration of beam 2
α_3	angular acceleration of beam 3
α_5	angular acceleration of beam 5
α_6	angular acceleration of beam 6
F_{in}	input force
F_{out}	output force
M_z	moment acting on a beam along z axis
w_2	angular velocity of beam 2
w_3	angular velocity of beam 3
w_5	angular velocity of beam 5
w_6	angular velocity of beam 6
$\dot{R}_1, \dot{r}_1$	velocity of slider
$\ddot{R}_1, \ddot{r}_1$	acceleration of slider
$\Theta 2$	first stage crank angle
$\Theta 3$	angle of beam 3 from +x axis in counter clockwise direction
$\Theta 5$	angle of beam 5 from +x axis in counter clockwise direction
$\Theta 6$	angle of beam 6 from +x axis in counter clockwise direction

Author details

Ergin Kosa* and Levent Trabzon
Mechanical Engineering, Istanbul Technical University, Istanbul, Turkey

Umit Sonmez
Mechanical Engineering, Sharjah University, Dubai, United Arab Emirates

Huseyin Kizil
Metallurgical and Materials Engineering, Istanbul Technical University, Istanbul, Turkey

6. References

Ashok, M.; Howell, L. L. & Norton, T. W. (2000). Limit Positions of Compliant Mechanisms Using the Pseudo-Rigid-Body Model Concept. Mechanism and Machine Theory, Vol. 35, pp. 99-115

Chen, G.; Wilcox, D. L. & Howell L. L. (2009). Fully Compliant Double Tensural Tristable Micromechanisms (DTTM), *Journal of Micromechanics and Microengineering*, Vol., 19, pp. 1-8

Cohen, A.; Hames, G.; Monk, D., Wilcenski, S. & Hardy B. (2009). Soimumps Design Handbook, MEMSCAP Revision 5.

Français, O.; Rousseau, L., Bourouina, T., Haussy, J. & Tissot, A. (2005). MEMS Memory Based on Bi-stable Mechanical Structures, Proceedings of DTIP of MEMS and MOEMS, ISBN 2-84813-0357-1, Montreux, Switzerland, June, 2005

Gomm, T.; Howell, L. L. & Selfridge, R. H. (2002). In-plane Linear Displacement Bistable Microrelay, *Journal of Micromechanics and Microengineering*, Vol. 12, pp. 257–264

Han, J. S.; Müller, C., Wallrabe, U. & Korvink, J. G. (2007). Design, Simulation, and Fabrication of a Quadstable Monolithic Mechanism with X- and Y-Directional Bistable Curved Beams. *Journal of Mechanical Design*, Vol. 129, pp. 1198-2003

Hsu, Tai Ran. (2002). *MEMS & Microsystems Design and Manufacture*, McGraw Hill (1st edition), ISBN 0-07-113051, USA

Huang, S. C. & Lan, G. J. (2006). Design and Fabrication of a Micro Compliant Amplifier with a Topology Optimal Compliant Mechanism Integrated with a Piezoelectric Microactuator. *Journal of Micromechanics and Microengineering*, Vol. 16, pp. 531–538. ISSN 0960-1317

Jensen, B. D.; Parkinson, Matthew B., Kurabayashi, Katsuo, Howell, Larry L. & Baker, Michael S. (2001). Design Optimization of a Fully-Compliant Bistable Micromechanism, Proceedings of 2001 ASME International Mechanical Engineering Congress and Exposition, New York, November, 2001

Jensen, B. D. & Howell, L. L. (2003). Identification of Compliant Pseudo-Rigid-Body Four-Link Mechanism Configurations Resulting in Bistable Behavior. *Journal of Mechanical Design*, Vol. 125, pp. 701-708

---

* Corresponding Author

Jensen, B. D. & Howell, L. L. (2004). Bistable Configurations of Compliant Mechanisms Modeled Using Four Links and Translational Joints. *Journal of Mechanical Design.* Vol. 126 , pp. 657-666

Kosa, E.; Sonmez, U., Kizil, H. & Trabzon L. (2010). The Design and Analysis of a Novel MEMS Force Amplifier. *Turkish Journal of Engineering & Environmental Sciences,* Vol. 34, pp. 253–259

Kota, S.; Joo J., Li Z., Rodgers, S. M. & Sniegowski J. (2001). Design of Compliant Mechanisms: Applications to MEMS. *Analog Integrated Circuits and Signal Processing,* Vol. 29, pp. 7-15

Krishnan , G. & Ananthasuresh G. K. (2008). Evaluation and Design of Displacement-Amplifying Compliant Mechanisms for Sensor Applications. *Journal of Mechanical Design,* Vol. 130, pp. 1-9

Lai, Y.; McDonald , J., Kujath, M. & Hubbard, T., (2004). Force, Deflection and Power Measurements of Toggled Microthermal Actuators. *Journal of Micromechanics and Microengineering,* Vol. 14, pp. 49–56

Larry, H. L. (2001). *Compliant Mechanisms,* John Wiley & Sons, ISBN 0-471-38478-X, USA.

Li, J.; Liu, Z. S., Lu, C., Zhang, Q. X. & Liu, A. Q. (2005). A Self Limited Large Displacement Ratio Micromechanical Amplifier. *Proceedings of The 13th International Conference on Solid-State Sensors, Actuators and Microsystems,* ISBN 0-7803-8952-2, Seoul, Korea, June, 2005

Lobontiu, N.; Paine, J. S. N., Garcia, E. & Goldfarb, M. (2001). Corner-Filleted Flexure Hinges. *Journal of Mechanical Design,* Vol. 123, pp. 346-352

Millet, O.; Bernardoni, P., Régnier, S., Bidaud, P., Tsitsiris, E., Collard, Dominique. & Buchaillot, Lionel. (2004). Electrostatic Actuated Micro Gripper using an Amplification Mechanism, *Sensors and Actuators A,* Vol. 114, pp. 371–378

Nathan, D. & Howell, Larry L. (2003). A Self-Retracting Fully Compliant Bistable Micromechanism. *Journal of Microelectromechanical Systems,* Vol. 12, pp. 273-280

Parkinson, M. B.; Jensen, B. D. & Kurabayashi K. (2001). Design of Compliant Force and Displacement Amplification Micro-Mechanisms. *Proceedings of DETC'01 ASME, Design Engineering Technical Conferences and Computers and Information in Engineering Conference,* Pittsburgh, Pennsylvania, September, 2001

Pedersen, C. B. W. & Seshia, A. A. (2004). On the Optimization of Compliant Force Amplifier Mechanisms for Surface Micromachined Resonant Accelerometers. *Journal of Micromechanics and Microengineering,* Vol. 14, pp. 1281–1293

Sreekumar, M.; Nagarajan, T. & Singaperumal, M. (2008). Experimental Investigations of the Large Deflection Capabilities of a Compliant Parallel Mechanism Actuated by Shape Memory Alloy Wires. *Smart materials and structures,* Vol. 17, pp. 1-12

Tantanawat , T. & Kota, S. (2007). Design of Compliant Mechanisms for Minimizing Input Power in Dynamic Applications. *Journal of Mechanical Design,* Vol. 129, pp. 1064-1075

Terre, J. C. & Shkel, A. (2004). Dynamic Analysis of a Snap-Action Micromechanism, *IEEE,* pp. 1245-1248

Wilcox, D. L. & Howell, L. L. (2005). Fully Compliant Tensural Bistable Micromechanisms (FTBM). *Journal of Microelectromechanical Systems,* Vol. 14, pp. 1-8

Chapter 7

Voltage Sag Waveform Using SagWave GUI

Kosol Oranpiroj, Worrajak Moangjai and Wichran Jantee

1. Introduction

A recent survey attributes that 92% of all disturbances in power system is caused by voltage sags. Three-phase voltage sag can be classified in seven types as shown in Fig.1 (Bollen MHJ, 2000). The electrical sensitive load often trips of shunts down when voltage sag occur. It's very important to know how these sensitive equipment works when the voltage sag occur. This is the reason to develop the voltage sag generator that can created varied type of voltage sag waveform. The purpose of voltage sag generator is use to test the immunity of equipment against the voltage sag.

The magnitude and angle of three phase voltage sag can calculate form equation 1 to equation 7(Bollen MHJ, 2000).

Type A

$$
\left.
\begin{aligned}
V_a &= V \\
V_b &= -\frac{1}{2}V - j\frac{1}{2}\sqrt{3}V \\
V_c &= -\frac{1}{2}V + j\frac{1}{2}\sqrt{3}V
\end{aligned}
\right\} \tag{1}
$$

Type B

$$
\left.
\begin{aligned}
V_a &= V \\
V_b &= -\frac{1}{2} - j\frac{1}{2}\sqrt{3} \\
V_c &= -\frac{1}{2} + j\frac{1}{2}\sqrt{3}
\end{aligned}
\right\} \tag{2}
$$

Type C

$$\left. \begin{array}{l} V_a = 1 \\ V_b = -\dfrac{1}{2} - j\dfrac{1}{2}\sqrt{3}V \\ V_c = -\dfrac{1}{2} + j\dfrac{1}{2}\sqrt{3}V \end{array} \right\} \tag{3}$$

Type D

$$\left. \begin{array}{l} V_a = V \\ V_b = -\dfrac{1}{2}V - j\dfrac{1}{2}\sqrt{3} \\ V_c = -\dfrac{1}{2}V + j\dfrac{1}{2}\sqrt{3} \end{array} \right\} \tag{4}$$

Type E

$$\left. \begin{array}{l} V_a = 1 \\ V_b = -\dfrac{1}{2}V - j\dfrac{1}{2}\sqrt{3}V \\ V_c = -\dfrac{1}{2}V + j\dfrac{1}{2}\sqrt{3}V \end{array} \right\} \tag{5}$$

Type F

$$\left. \begin{array}{l} V_a = V \\ V_b = -j\dfrac{\sqrt{3}}{3} - \dfrac{1}{2}V - j\dfrac{\sqrt{3}}{6}V \\ V_c = +j\dfrac{\sqrt{3}}{3} - \dfrac{1}{2}V + j\dfrac{\sqrt{3}}{6}V \end{array} \right\} \tag{6}$$

Type G

$$\left. \begin{array}{l} V_a = \dfrac{2}{3} + \dfrac{1}{3}V \\ V_b = -\dfrac{1}{3} - \dfrac{1}{6}V - j\dfrac{\sqrt{3}}{2}V \\ V_c = -\dfrac{1}{3} - \dfrac{1}{6}V + j\dfrac{\sqrt{3}}{2}V \end{array} \right\} \tag{7}$$

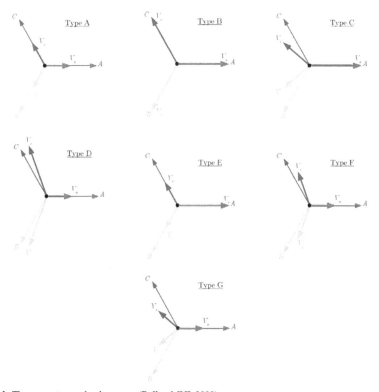

Figure 1. The seven type of voltage sag (Bollen MHJ, 2000).

2. Voltage sag generator

Previous works (Takahashi *et al.*, 2008; Rylander *et al.*, 2007; Bhavar *et al.*, 2008; Teke *et al.*, 2008; Ma and Karady, 2008), have developed voltage sag generator which can be simply classified into 4 types. These four types of voltage sag generator are transformer, switching-impedance, generator and amplifier. The transformer type uses a switch to adjust both pre-sag voltage and sag magnitudes. The switching-impedance type creates voltage sags by switching impedance into a power system by using a thyristor-controlled reactor (TCR). The generator type uses a synchronous generator to give controlled 3-phase voltage sags. The amplifier type uses a waveform generator to create controlled 3-phase voltage sags.

An autotransformer is used as the 1-phase voltage sag generator as demonstrated (Rylander *et al.*, 2007, Bhavar *et al.*, 2008); Rylander, *et al* .used MOSFET to turn-on/turn-off for changing between the primary source and the secondary source. Bhavsar, *et al.* used motorized variac with multi tapping transformer, the position of the variac is changed using a signal generated by the PIC. The main disadvantage of this method is that the non-conducting pairs connected to the unselected taps dissipate power due to the taps. It has a complex structure and requires control of signal processors. The TCR type creates a difference in voltage by firing the TCR at different angles. The disadvantages of TCR are the generation of low frequency harmonic current components and higher losses when working in the inductive region (Teke *et al.*, 2008). The generator type uses a synchronous generator that provides voltage sag by changing the exciting current of the generator. The control of sag generator's operation and monitoring of the system under test in performed by the Visual Basic programming (Collins and Morgan, 1996). The software of this paper had not displayed the waveform of voltage sag and disadvantages of this type are that it needs more space to install and is more expensive (Ma & Karady, 2008). The amplifier type can provide voltage sags with varying magnitude, duration, frequency and harmonics. After defining the desired waveform data is passed to power amplifier, at which outputs of adequate voltage levels of voltage sag are produced. This type is more convenient than others types, because it enables more precise control of all voltage sag characteristics and also allows testing of equipment in context of frequency variations and harmonic distortions. Therefore, a power amplifier type of voltage sag generator is selected for designing the voltage sag generator in this study. This chapter presents a 3-phase 4-wire voltage sag generator based on an *abc* algorithm((Oranpiroj *et al.*, 2009). Voltage sag generator has been created waveform by SagWave software. The actual voltage sag is created by the 3-phase 4-wire inverter which is controlled by low-cost dsPIC.

3. Graphic user interface (GUI) waveform generator

The graphic user interface (GUI) "SagWave" (Oranpiroj *et al.*, 2010, Oranpiroj *et al.*, 2011) is designed for easy input of the designed waveform. The user can create sag magnitude, sag duration, phase angle jump and point on wave for a designed sag waveform from the front panel of GUI. Users can verify the desired waveform in time domain or vector form as shown in windows. Then, parameters of desired sag waveform can be sent to dsPIC microcontroller directly from GUI to control voltage sag generator. From the requirement, the SagWage GUI had designed consisted of:

1. The window for showing the 3-phase voltage.
2. The window for showing vector of A, B and C phase.
3. Magnitude of Voltage (A, B and C phase), user had used value box or slider bar.
4. Phase angle jump of voltage sag on A, B or C phase.
5. Sag type for selected the voltage sag type (single-phase, two-phase and three-phase).
6. Display normal or repeat mode of voltage sag.
7. Point on wave in degree.
8. Sag duration time for period time of voltage sag.
9. Number of repeat of voltage sag.
10. The button "Plot" for generated the voltage sag waveform.
11. The button "Send" for send the data from SagWave to the dsPIC microcontroller.
12. The button "Refresh" for clear the value and graphic display.

The layout of GUI "SagWave" designed as shown in Fig.2. The SagWave development on MATLAB's Graphical User interface Development Environment (GUIDE)(Patrick Marchand & O. Thomas Holland., 2003).

3.1. The window for showing the 3-phase voltage

This is an "Axes" object in component palette ([icon]) on the left-side of window. The "Axes" can move and resize by drag it with the mouse. This "Axes" to shown the 3-phase voltage of voltage sag, then we assigned name to "Time_Plot" in Property inspector by double click on "Axes1" as shown in Fig. 3.

3.2. The window for showing vector of A, B and C phase

This "Axes2" to shown the vector of A, B and C of voltage sag, then we assigned name to "Com_pass" in Property inspector by double click on "Axes2" as shown in Fig. 4.

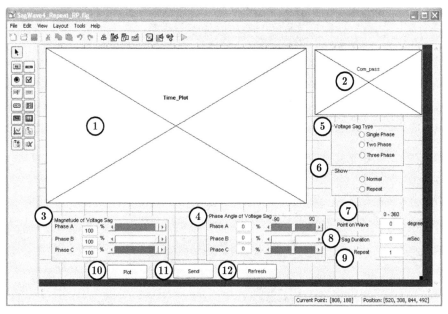

Figure 2. GUI "SagWave" designed.

3.3. Magnitude of Voltage (A, B and C phase), user had used value box or slider bar

This group used the Edit Text and Slider object. The Edit Text and Slider object set the default value as 100%. In the property inspector of three Edit Text changed the String to "100", Max to "1.0" and Min to "0.0", as shown in Fig. 5. The String in Edit Text property to changed to the number value in m-file. In the property inspector of three Slider changed the Value to "[100.0]", Max to "100.0" and Min to "0.0", as shown in Fig. 6.

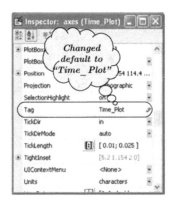

Figure 3. The property inspector of Axes1 assigned name to "Time_Plot".

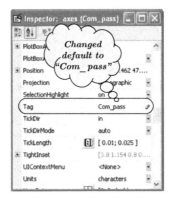

Figure 4. The property inspector of Axes2 assigned name to "Com_pass".

Figure 5. The property inspector of Edit Text (Magnitude) set Max and Min. (Magnitude) set Max and Min.

Figure 6. The property inspector of Slider.

3.4. Phase angle jump of voltage sag on A, B or C phase

This group used the Edit Text (⬛) and Slider (⬛) object, that the same as Magnitude group. In the property inspector of three Edit Text changed the String to "0", Max to "1.0" and Min to "0.0", as shown in Fig. 7. The String in Edit Text property to changed to the number value in m-file. In the property inspector of three Slider changed the Value to "[0,0]", Max to "90.0" and Min to "-90.0", as shown in Fig. 8.

3.5. Sag type for selected the voltage sag type (single-phase, two-phase and three-phase)

This group are "Radio Button" objects in component palette (⬛) on the left-side of window. The Radio Button of this group used to select the voltage sag type, Single-phase, Two-phase and Three-phase type. The property inspector was shown in Fig. 9.

Figure 7. The property inspector of Edit Text of the Magnitude group.

Figure 8. The property inspector of Slider of the Magnitude group.

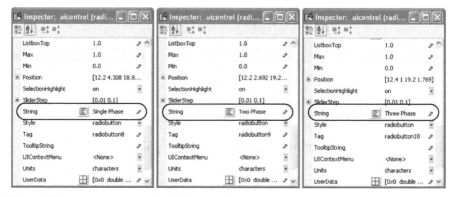

Figure 9. The property inspector of Radio Button of voltage sag type group.

3.6. Display normal or repeat mode of voltage sag

These groups are "Radio Button" objects same as the voltage type group. The Radio Button of this group used to select the graph to shown normal and repeat mode of voltage sag. The property inspector was shown in Fig. 10.

3.7. Point on wave in degree

This object is the Edit Text for input degree of voltage on wave. The property inspector was shown in Fig.11.

3.8. Sag duration time for period time of voltage sag

This object is the Edit Text for input time duration of voltage sag. The property inspector was shown in Fig.11.

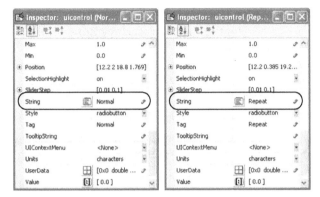

Figure 10. The property inspector of Radio Button of show group set to Normal and Repeat.

3.9. Number of repeat of voltage sag

This object is the Edit Text for input the repeated number of voltage sag. The property inspector was shown in Fig.11.

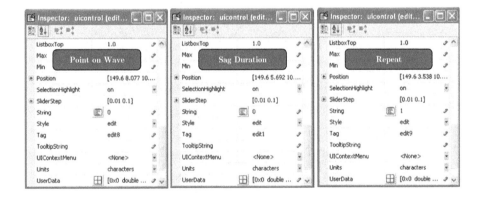

Figure 11. The property inspector of Point on Wave, Sag Duration and Repeat.

3.10. The button "Plot" for generated the voltage sag waveform

This object is "Button" objects in component palette (0K) on the left-side of window. The "Plot" button is the main object of the GUI "SagWave", this button used to calculate and showed the graph of voltage sag. The property inspector was shown in Fig.12.

3.11. The button "Send" for send the data from SagWave to the dsPIC microcontroller

The "Send" button used to send the wave form data of voltage sag to dsPIC microcontroller. The property inspector was shown in Fig.12.

3.12. The button "Refresh" for clear the value and graphic display

The "Refresh" button used to clear the graphic, all of the value in program to provide the new value. The property inspector was shown in Fig.12.

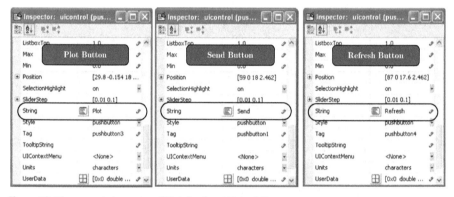

Figure 12. The property inspector of Plot, Send and Refresh Button.

Finally users are ready to let GUIDE create the Fig-file and M-file. They are two options to create; one, simply select menu File → Save As.., or users can run GUI by select menu Tools

→ Run or click ![ ] on tool bar. GUIDE will save user's GUI to file with the name as gave by user with extension *.fig and *.m of the same name.

4. SagWave programming

The concept of SagWave programming shown in Fig. 13. Form the 3th topic, GUIDE will create an M-File with callback function prototypes. The callback function was response to an event by MATLAB code. There must be a callback to implement the function of each graphical component on the GUI. Now we must be programming the callback to implement the function of each component on the SagWave.

4.1. Magnitude of Voltage Sag

These groups to input the magnitude of the voltage sag. There are two ways to input the magnitude;

1.   Edit Text (Phase A, Phase B, Phase C Magnitude)

The Edit Text is an element that user to enter a text string(0 to 100). The program of this element is shown in Fig.14, in this program shown how to converse string to numeric.

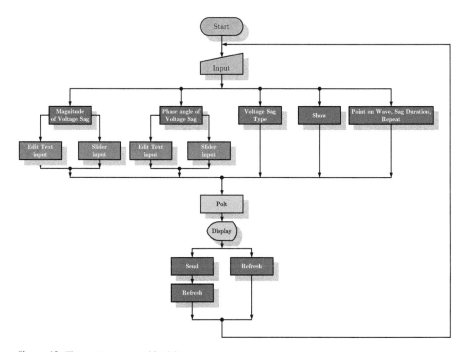

Figure 13. The main concept of SagWave programming.

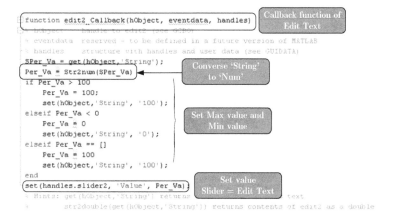

Figure 14. Program on Edit Text(Magnitude) callback function for input Magnitude.

2.   Slider (Phase A, Phase B, Phase C Magnitude)

The Slider is the element that user to select values from continuous range between a specified minimum and maximum value by moving a bar with mouse. The program of this element is shown in Fig.15.

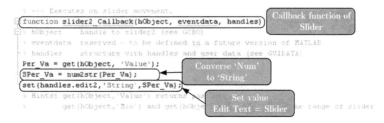

Figure 15. Program on Slider(Magnitude) callback function for input Magnitude.

4.2. Phase angle of Voltage Sag

These groups to input the phase angel of voltage sag. There are two ways to input the magnitude;

1.   Edit Text (Phase A, Phase B, Phase C Phase angle)

The Edit Text is an element that user to enter a text string (-90 to +90). The program of this element is shown in Fig.16, in this program shown how to converse string to numeric.

2.   Slider (Phase A, Phase B, Phase C Phase angle)

The program of this element is shown in Fig.17.

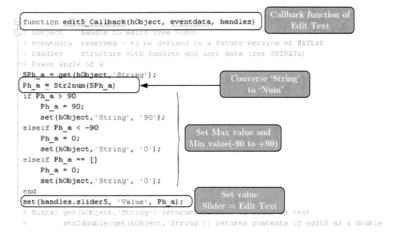

Figure 16. Program on Edit Text(Phase angle) callback function for input phase angle.

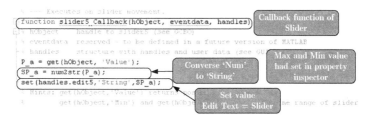

Figure 17. Fig. 17. Program on Slider(Phase angle) callback function for input phase angle.

4.3. Voltage Sag Type

These groups to select the voltage sag type, the program of this element shown in Fig. 18.

```
% --- Executes on button press in radiobutton8.
function radiobutton8_Callback(hObject, eventdata, handles)
% hObject    handle to radiobutton8 (see GCBO)
% eventdata  reserved - to be defined in a future version of MATLAB
% handles    structure with handles and user data (see GUIDATA)
set(ShowPlot1,'Value',1);
set(ShowPlot2,'Value',0);
set(ShowPlot3,'Value',0);
% Hint: get(hObject,'Value')
        set(ShowPlot1,'Value',0);
        set(ShowPlot2,'Value',1);
       set(ShowPlot3,'Value',0);  set(ShowPlot1,'Value',0);
                                   set(ShowPlot2,'Value',0);
                                   set(ShowPlot3,'Value',1);
```

Selected Single Phase

Selected Two Phase

Selected Three Phase

Figure 18. Program on Radio Button callback function for select voltage sag type.

4.4. Show

These groups to select the program to show single or repeat of voltage sag, program of this element shown in Fig. 19.

```
% --- Executes on button press in Normal.
function Normal_Callback(hObject, eventdata, handles)
% hObject    handle to Normal (see GCBO)
% eventdata  reserved - to be defined in a future version of MATLAB
% handles    structure with handles and user data (see GUIDATA)
set(handles.Repeat,'Value',0)
Sh_Nor = set(handels.Normal,'Value',1)
Sh_Rep = set(handels.Repeat,'Value',0)      set(handles.Normal,'Value',0)
                                            Sh_Rep = 1
                                            Sh_Nor = 0
```

Selected Normal

Selected Repeat

Figure 19. Program on Radio Button callback function for show Normal and Repeat.

4.5. Point on Wave, Sag Duration and Repeat

These groups to enter the value of Point on Wave, Sag duration and Repeat of voltage sag, the program of this element shown in Fig. 20.

4.6. Send Button

The Send Button is the button for user to send the data from SagWave to dsPIC microcontroller. The Duty.dat was generated by SagWave. The user clicked the "Send" button to send the Data.dat to dsPIC microcontroller by a RS-232 port. The program of this element shown in Fig. 21.

```
function edit8_Callback(hObject, eventdata, handles)
% hObject      handle to edit8 (see GCBO)
% eventdata    reserved - to be defined in a future version of MATLAB
% handles      structure with handles and user data (see GUIDATA)

% Hints: get(hObject,'String') returns contents of edit8 as text
%        str2double(get(hObject,'String')) returns contents of edit8 as a double

Point = str2num(get(handles.edit8,'String'));
    if Point > 360
        Point = 360
        set(hObject,'String','360');
    elseif Point <0
        Point = 0
        set(hObject,'String','0')
    elseif Point ==[]
        Point = 0
        set(hObject,'String','0')
    end
```

```
% handles     structure with handles and user data
Sagdura = str2num(get(handles.edit1,'String'));
% Hints: get(hObject,'String') returns contents
```

```
% handles     structure with handles and user data
Repeat = str2num(get(handles.edit9,'String'));
% Hints: get(hObject,'String') returns contents of
```

Figure 20. Program on Edit Text(Point on Wave, Sag Duration and Repeat) callback function.

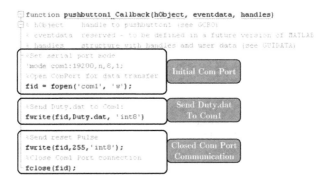

```
function pushbutton1_Callback(hObject, eventdata, handles)
% hObject      handle to pushbutton1 (see GCBO)
% eventdata    reserved - to be defined in a future version of MATLAB
% handles      structure with handles and user data (see GUIDATA)

%Set serial port mode
'mode com1:19200,n,8,1;
%Open ComPort for data transfer
fid = fopen('com1', 'w');

%Send Duty.dat to Com1:
fwrite(fid,Duty.dat, 'int8')

%Send reset Pulse
fwrite(fid,255,'int8');
%Close Com1 Port connection
fclose(fid);
```

Figure 21. Program on "Send" Button callback function for open communication port and send file.

4.7. Refresh Button

The Refresh Button is the button for user to clear the parameter and graph in SagWave for the next simulation. The program of this element shown in Fig. 22.

```
% --- Executes on button press in pushbutton4.
function pushbutton4_Callback(hObject, eventdata, handles)
% hObject      handle to pushbutton4 (see GCBO)
% eventdata    reserved - to be defined in a future version of MATLAB
% handles      structure with handles and user data (see GUIDATA)
cla(handles.Time_Plot)            Clear graph on
cla(handles.Com_pass)        Time_Plot and Com_pass

%cla(figure1)            Clear figure
%k = figure('HandleVisibility','off');
close(figure(1))
set(handles.edit1,'String',  '0')        Set Edit Text
set(handles.edit2,'String', '100')        to default value
set(handles.edit3,'String', '100')
set(handles.edit4,'String', '100')
set(handles.edit5,'String',  '0')
set(handles.edit6,'String',  '0')
set(handles.edit7,'String',  '0')
set(handles.edit8,'String',  '0')
set(handles.edit9,'String',  '1')
zero1 = num2str(0);
set(handles.slider2,'Value',100)
set(handles.slider3,'Value',100)        Set Slider
set(handles.slider4,'Value',100)        to default value
set(handles.slider5,'Value',0)
set(handles.slider6,'Value',0)
set(handles.slider7,'Value',0)
```

Figure 22. Program on "Refresh" Button callback function to clear all parameter.

4.8. Plot Button

The Plot Button is a main element of the SagWave, when user clicked this button the callback program calculated and plot graph of voltage sag. The program of this element shown in Fig. 23 to Fig. 25.

```
% --- Executes on button press in pushbutton3.
function pushbutton3_Callback(hObject, eventdata, handles)
% hObject      handle to pushbutton3 (see GCBO)
% eventdata    reserved - to be defined in a future version of MATLAB
% handles      structure with handles and user data (see GUIDATA)
Point = str2num(get(handles.edit8,'String'));

PP_on_Wave = (Point)*(2D*1e-3/38D);
dural = str2num(get(handles.edit1,'String'));    %sag duration
nn = (dural*3D)+3;
d1 = mod(dural,2D);                              % d1 is mod of dural
d2 = dural - d1;                                % inter and even sine wave
dural = dural*1e-3;
dura2 = (d2*1e-3)+ PP_on_Wave;
dura = (dura2*2)+dural;                          Initial variable
P_a = get(handles.slider2, 'Value');
P_b = get(handles.slider3, 'Value');
P_c = get(handles.slider4, 'Value');
Ph_a = get(handles.slider5, 'Value');
Ph_a1 = ((Ph_a*pi)/18D);
Ph_b = get(handles.slider6, 'Value');
Ph_b1 = ((Ph_b*pi)/18D);
Ph_c = get(handles.slider7, 'Value');
Ph_c1 = ((Ph_c*pi)/18D);
x = 0:1e-3:dura;
```

Figure 23. Initial variable sections of Plot button.

5. Simulation result

From equation 1 to equation 7 in Topic 1, if we need 60%(V = 0.6) voltage sag there can be calculate and result in Table. 1. The operation of this program with the user designing the voltage sag wave form SagWave software. Then the user clicks the "Send" button to send the parameters to dsPIC microcontroller. The actual voltage sag is created by a 3-phase 4-leg 4-wire inverter based on an *abc* algorithm.

```
plot(handles.Time_Plot,x4,Va4,'r','LineWidth',2)
grid on
hold on                                                    Plot voltage sag
plot(handles.Time_Plot,x4,Vb4,'b','LineWidth',2)               graph
plot(handles.Time_Plot,x4,Vc4,'g','LineWidth',2)
axis(handles.Time_Plot,[0 dura -1.2 1.2]);

      axes(handles.Com_pass)

      VecA = (P_a/100)*exp(i*Ph_a1);
      VecB = (P_b/100)*exp(i*(-(2*pi/3)+Ph_b1));
      VecC = (P_c/100)*exp(i*((2*pi/3)+Ph_c1));

compass(handles.Com_pass,VecA,'r')
hold on;                                                   Plot voltage sag
compass(handles.Com_pass,VecB,'k')                             Phasor
set(findobj('type','line'),'linewidth',3)
compass(handles.Com_pass,VecC,'b')
set(findobj('type','line'),'linewidth',3)

compass(handles.Com_pass,1,'r')
text(1.3,0,'Va')
compass(handles.Com_pass,(1*exp(i*(-(2*pi/3)))),'k')
text(-0.75,-1.1,'Vb')
compass(handles.Com_pass,(1*exp(i*(2*pi/3))),'b')
text(-0.75,1.1,'Vc')
```

Figure 24. The program of graph and vector of phase voltage plotting section.

For example, the designed waveforms have parameters as found in "Bollen, (2000)". The parameters in Table 1. are used to generate seven types of voltage sag. Users can verify waveforms through graphic display windows as shown in Fig. 24.

Voltage	Phase Voltage									
Sag	A		B				C			
Type	Magnitude	Phase	Magnitude	Phase	Lag	Lead	Magnitude	Phase	Lag	Lead
A	V	0°	0.6	−120°	-	-	0.6	120°	-	-
B	V	0°	1	−120°	-	-	1	120°	-	-
C	1	0°	0.72	−133.9°	−13.39°	-	0.72	133.9°	-	13.39°
D	0.6	0°	0.92	−109.1°	-	10.9°	0.92	109.1°	−10.9°	-
E	1	0°	0.6	−120°	-	-	0.6	120°	-	-
F	V	0°	0.808	−111.79°	-	8.21°	0.808	111.79°	−8.21°	-
G	0.867	0°	0.6	−129.83°	−9.83°	-	0.6	129.83°	-	9.83°

Table 1. Parameter for seven type of voltage sag.

SagWave software can create point on wave single-phase(phase A) voltage sag, the parameters are shown in Table 2. The display of waveforms was is in Fig. 25. The parameters of single-phase(phase A) repeated voltage sag is shown in Table 3, and the simulation waveform in Fig.26.

```
if Sh_Nor == 1 & Sh_Rep == 0               % Normal Show
     dura = (dura2*2)+dura1;
     axes(handles.Time_Plot);
     %set(findobj('type','line'),'linewidth',0.5)

     plot(handles.Time_Plot,x4,Va4,'r','LineWidth',2)
     grid on                                          Normal Display
     hold on
     plot(handles.Time_Plot,x4,Vb4,'b','LineWidth',2)
     plot(handles.Time_Plot,x4,Vc4,'g','LineWidth',2)
     axis(handles.Time_Plot,[0 dura -1.2 1.2]);
     %title(200,1000,'Phase Voltage Va, Vb, Vc');

elseif Sh_Rep == 1 & Sh_Nor == 0           % if 1 show sag wave RF and duty cycl

Repeat = str2num(get(handles.edit9,'String'));
```

```
case 3
    dura = 4*dura2 + 3*dura1 - (3*d1*1e-3);
    x3 = (dura2+dura1):0.01e-3:(dura2+dura1)+(dura2-d1*1e-3);
    Va2 = sin(pi*2*50*x3);
    x5 = (dura2+dura1)+(dura2-d1*1e-3):0.01e-3:(dura2+dura1)+(dura2-d1*1e-3)+dura1;
    x6 = ((dura2+dura1)+(dura2-d1*1e-3)+dura1): 0.01e-3 :((dura2+dura1)+(dura2-(d1*1e-3))+ dura1 + (dura2-(d1*1e-3)));
    y3 = 1*x3;
    y3(:)=1;
    y5 = 1*x5;
    Va5 = sin((pi*2*50*x5)+Ph_a1);
    y5(:) = P_a/100;
    y6 = 1*x6;
    y6(:)= 1;
    Va6 = sin(pi*2*50*x6);
    x7 = (3*dura2)+(2*dura1)-((d1*1e-3)*2): 0.01e-3 : (3*dura2)+(3*dura1)-((d1*1e-3)*2);
    x8 = (3*dura2)+(3*dura1)-((d1*1e-3)*2): 0.01e-3 : (4*dura2) + (3*dura1) - ((d1*1e-3)*3);
    Va7 = sin((pi*2*50*x7)+Ph_a1);
    Va8 = sin(pi*2*50*x8);              Repeat Display
    y7 = 1*x7;                          Repeat = 3
    y7(:) = P_a/100;
    y8 = 1*x8;
    y8(:)= 1;
    ya1 = [y1 ya y3 y5 y6 y7 y8];
    x4 = [x1 x2 x3 x5 x6 x7 x8];
    Va3 = [Va Va1 Va2 Va5 Va6 Va7 Va8];
    Va4 = Va3.*ya1;
    axes(handles.Time_Plot);
    plot(handles.Time_Plot,x4,Va4,'r','LineWidth',0.5)
    grid on
    axis(handles.Time_Plot,[0 dura -1.2 1.2]);
    figure(1)
    plot(x4,Va4)
    axis([0 dura -1.2 1.2]);
    grid on
```

Figure 25. The program of Normal and Repeat as Repeat = 3.

Case	Manitude(%)	Duration(ms)	Point on Wave (degree)
1	5	60	45
2	25	60	45
3	25	60	270

Table 2. Parameter of point on wave voltage sag.

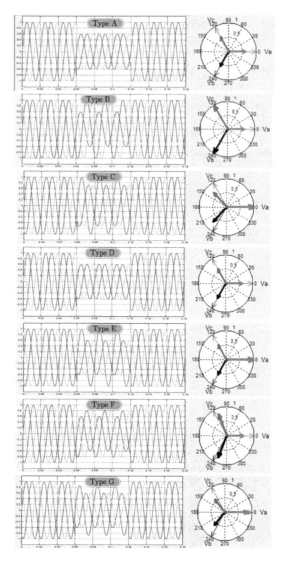

Figure 26. The seven types of voltage sag created using SagWave software.

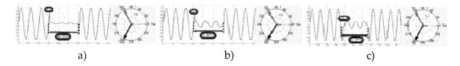

a)   b)   c)

Figure 27. a) The point on wave at $45°$; b) The point on wave at $45°$; c) The point on wave at $270°$

Case	Manitude(%)	Duration(ms)	Number of repeated
1	60	60	4
2	60	60	6

Table 3. Parameter of repeated voltage sag.

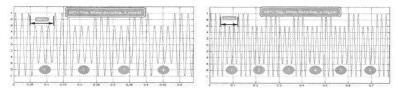

Figure 28. The simulation of single-phase voltage sag repeated.

6. Experimental of 3-phase 4-wire voltage sag generator

From section 3 the SagWave software generates the parameter file and sends it to the dsPIC microcontroller. The dsPIC uses this file to control the 3-phase 4-leg 4-wire inverter in order to create the actual waveform. Experimental results for voltage sag types A, B and E are shown in Fig. 27-29, respectively.

The experimental results in Fig. 27 are according with simulation results in Fig.24 (Type A). Fig.27 shows the 3-phase voltage and 3-phase current of voltage sag Type A. During voltage sag, the voltage on phase A (V_a), phase B (V_b) and phase C (V_c) are reduced to 60%. The current on phase A (I_a), phase B (I_b) and phase C (I_c) also are reduced to 60%. Before voltage sag occurs, the neutral current (I_n) has zero currents due to the balanced load condition. However during voltage sag transition, the unbalance load currents causes non-zero in the neutral current (I_n).

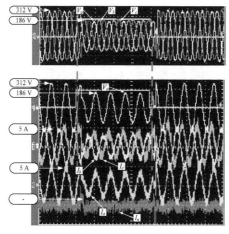

Figure 29. Voltage sag Type A.

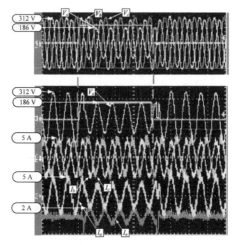

Figure 30. Voltage sag Type B.

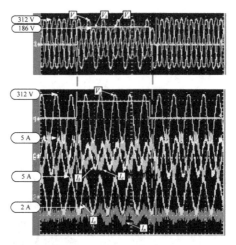

Figure 31. Voltage sag Type E.

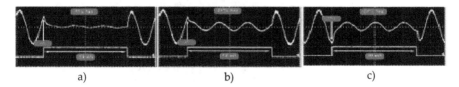

Figure 32. Experimental result: a) point on wave at 45° b) point on wave at 45° c) point on wave at 270°

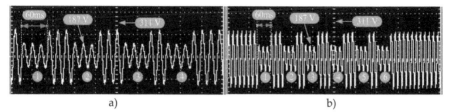

Figure 33. Experimental results: a) 4 repeated voltage sag b) 6 repeated voltage sag

The experimental results in Fig. 28 are according with simulation results in Fig.24(Type B). Fig.28 shows the 3-phase voltage and 3-phase current of voltage sag Type B. During voltage sag, the voltage on phase A (V_a) is reduced to 60%. The current on phase A (I_a) also is reduced to 60%. Before voltage sag occurs, the neutral current (I_n) has zero currents due to the balanced load condition. However during voltage sag, the unbalance load causes an increase in the neutral current (I_n) that the return current in fourth leg of inverter.

The experimental results in Fig. 29 are according with simulation results in Fig.24 (Type E). Fig. 29 shows the 3-phase voltage and 3-phase current of voltage sag Type E. During voltage sag, the voltage on phase B (V_b) and phase C (V_c) are reduced to 60%. The current on phase A(I_a) is constant, while current on phase B (I_b) and current on phase C (I_c) are reduced to 60%. Before voltage sag occurs, the neutral current (In) has zero currents due to the balanced load condition. However during voltage sag, the unbalance load causes an increase in the neutral current (I_n) that the return current in fourth leg of inverter.

The experimental results of point on wave are shown in Fig. 30. The sag generator can generate waveform at any point of wave of sine wave as desired.

The experimental results of repeated voltage sags are shown in Fig. 31. The sag generator can generate repeated voltage sag waveform as many as desired.

7. Conclusions

This chapter has proposed the use of GUI SagWave software to provide a visual interactive capability generating data for the dsPIC controller. SagWave software can show the waveform and the phasor of the three-phase voltage. The simulation and experimental results have shown a simple control algorithm for generating the sag signal for testing. The experimental results have shown the main advantages of this prototype: point on wave, sag duration, magnitude of voltage sag and varied type of voltage sag. A future study will design software for the dsPIC microcontroller to generate all seven types of voltage sag and to test the dynamic and nonlinear loads.

Author details

Kosol Oranpiroj, Worrajak Moangjai and Wichran Jantee
Rajamangala University of Technology Lanna Chiangmai, Thailand

8. References

Bollen MHJ (2000). Understanding Power quality problems voltage sags and interruption. New York, IEEE Press. 193 – 196.

Bhavsar S, Shah VA, Gupta V. "Voltage dips and short interruption immunity test generator as per IEC 61000-4-11". *in Proc. of 15th National Power Systems Conference. Bombay, India,* 2008.

Collins ER, Morgan RL. "A Three-Phase Sag Generator for Testing Industrial Equipment". *IEEE Transaction on Power Delivery.* 11(1): 526 – 532, 1996.

Ma Y, Karady GG . "A single-phase voltage sag generator for testing electrical equipments". *in Proc. of Transmission and Distribution Conference and Exposition, Chicago IL,* pp 1 – 5, 2008.

Oranpiroj K, Premrudeepreechacharn S, Ngoudech M, Muangjai W, Yingkayun K, Boonsai T. "The 3-phase 4-wire voltage sag generator based on three dimensions space vector modulation in abc coordinates". *In Proc. of International Symposium on Industrial Electronics ISIE2009,* 275 – 280, 2009.

Oranpiroj K, Premrudeepreechacharn S, Ngoudech M, Muangjai W, Yingkayun K, Boonsai T. "The 3-phase 4-wire voltage sag generator based on abc algorithm". *in Proc. of Electrical Engineering/Electronics, Computer, Telecommunications and Information Technology ECTI-CON 2009,* 82 – 85, 2009.

Oranpiroj K, Premrudeepreechacharn S, Higuchi K. "SagWave for the 3-phase 4-wire voltage sag generator prototype". *in Proc. of IEEE International conference on Control Applications CCA 2010,* 2209 – 2212, 2010.

Oranpiroj K, Premrudeepreechacharn S,Muangjai W, C.V. Nayar., "Development of the 3-phase 4-wire voltage sag generator". *Scientific Research and Eassys,* 6(23): 4960 – 4974, 2011.

Patrick Marchand, O.Thomas Holland, *Graphics and GUIs with MATLAB.* (CHAPMAD & HALL/CRC, LTD, 2003)

Rylande M, Grady WM, Arapostathis A. "Enhancement and application of a voltage sag station to test transient load response". *in Proc. of IEEE Electric Ship Technology Symposium, Arlington VA.* pp. 428 – 433, 2007.

Takahashi R, Cortez JA, da Silva VF, Rezek AJJ. "A prototype implementation of a voltage sag generator". *VIII Conferencia Internacional de Aplicacoes Industriais, Poços de Caldas, Brazil,* 2008

Teke A, Meral ME, and Tümay M. "Evaluation of available power quality disturbance generators for testing of power quality mitigation devices". *Int. J. of Sciences and Techniques of Automatic Control and Computer Engineering, (special issue),* pp. 624 – 635, 2008

Improved DTC Algorithms for Reducing Torque and Flux Ripples of PMSM Based on Fuzzy Logic and PWM Techniques

Khalid Chikh, Mohamed Khafallah and Abdallah Saâd

Additional information is available at the end of the chapter

1. Introduction

Permanent Magnet Synchronous Motors (PMSM's) are widely used in high-performance drives such as industrial robots, automotive hybrid drive trains and machine tools thanks to their advantages as: high efficiency, high power density, high torque/inertia ratio, and free maintenance. In the recent years, the magnetic and thermal capabilities of the Permanent Magnet (PM) have been considerably increased by employing the high-coercive permanent magnet material.

Direct Torque Control (DTC) method has been first proposed and applied for induction machines in the mid-1980s, by Takahachi and Noguchi, for low and medium power applications. This concept can also be applied to synchronous drives. Indeed, PMSM DTC has appeared in the late 1990s. However, for some applications, the DTC has become unusable although it significantly improves the dynamic performance (fast torque and flux responses) of the drive and is less dependent on the motor parameters variations compared to the classical vector control due to torque and flux ripples. Indeed, hysteresis controllers used in the conventional structure of the DTC generates a variable switching frequency, causing electromagnetic torque oscillations. Also this frequency varies with speed, load torque and hysteresis bands selected. In addition, a high sampling frequency is needed for digital implementation of hysteresis comparators and a current and torque distortion is caused by sectors changes.

In the last decade, several contributions have been proposed to overcome these problems by using the three level or the multilevel inverter: more voltage space vectors are available to control the flux and torque. However, more power switches are needed to achieve a lower ripple and almost fixed switching frequency, which increases the system cost and complexity. In order to improve the DTC performance and overcome the above cited problems, another solution combines basic DTC and fuzzy logic control advantages in one control strategy, named Fuzzy Direct Torque Control (FDTC). In this technique, the hysteresis comparator and the switching table used in basic DTC are replaced by a fuzzy logic switcher, which decides directly on the switches states of the Voltage Source Inverter (VSI). In addition, it's known that fuzzy control works as well for complex non-linear multi-dimensional system, system with parameter variation problem and/or cases where the sensor signals are not precise. The fuzzy control is basically nonlinear and adaptive in nature, giving robust performance under parameter variation and load disturbance effect. For all these reasons, a Fuzzy Logic Controller can be used instead of the speed PI controller in FDTC in order to achieve a complete fuzzy control for the PMSM. Also, much interest has been focused on the use of modified DTC structures to improve basic DTC performances by replacing the hysteresis controllers and the switching table by a PI regulator, predictive controller and Space Vector Modulation (SVM). Indeed, under DTC-SVM strategy, both torque and flux linkage ripples are greatly reduced when compared with those of the basic DTC, because the application of SVM guarantees lower harmonics current by eliminating the distortion caused by sector changes in case of DTC switching table and by fixing the switching frequency.

Moreover, the design of the speed controller used in basic DTC or in modified DTC strategies, greatly affects the performance of the drive. The PI controllers have a simple structure and can offer satisfactory performances over a wide range of operations. However, due to the uncertainties, the variations in the plant parameters and the nonlinear operating conditions, the fixed gains of the PI controller may become unable to provide the required control performance. In order, to realize a good dynamic behaviour of the PMSM, a perfect speed tracking with no overshoot and a good rejection of impact loads disturbance, the speed PI controller can be replaced by a PI-Fuzzy speed controller.

This chapter is organized as follows: PMSM modelling and simulation results of the basic DTC by using Matlab/Simulink environment with a simple speed PI corrector, will be presented and discussed in Section 2 and 3, respectively. Whereas in Section 4 a complete Fuzzy Direct Torque Control (FDTC), which uses a fuzzy switching table and a PI-Fuzzy speed controller, for PMSM is proposed to reduce the torque and flux ripples. In addition, the simulation results show the effectiveness of this strategy when compared with the basic DTC and a classical speed PI controller. Section 5 and 6 are devoted to presenting a fixed switching-frequency DTC with two approaches: Sinusoidal Pulse With Modulation (SPWM) and Space Vector Modulation (SVM). The objective, of these two strategies, is reducing the flux and torque ripples and fixing the switching-frequency. Of course, the simulation results of these two approaches will be discussed and compared with those of basic DTC and FDTC, in section 7. Section 8 is devoted to study DTC performances under PMSM parameters variation, also a solutions have been proposed to overcome this issue. Eventually, conclusion and simulation results interpretations are included in Section 9.

2. Modelling of the VSI and the PMSM

2.1. Voltage Source Inverter (VSI) for adjustable speed or torque drive

In large number of industries the PMSM's are required to be operated at different speeds or torques. In order to obtain variable speed or torque, these motors are fed from inverters with variable voltage and variable frequency supply. Figure 1 shows the VSI structure used to produce well the voltage waveforms at the terminal of the motor. The voltage control of this inverter is obtained by using switching table in case of basic DTC or by pulse width modulation (PWM) in case of modified DTC techniques.

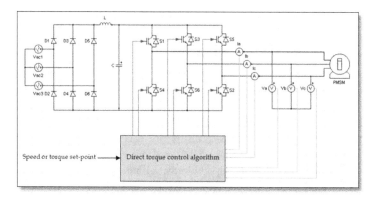

Figure 1. Three phase voltage source bridge inverter structure

The model of the VSI is given by:

$$\begin{bmatrix} V_a \\ V_b \\ V_c \end{bmatrix} = \frac{U_{dc}}{3} \begin{bmatrix} 2 & -1 & -1 \\ -1 & 2 & -1 \\ -1 & -1 & 2 \end{bmatrix} \begin{bmatrix} C_{s1} \\ C_{s3} \\ C_{s5} \end{bmatrix} \tag{1}$$

Where U_{dc} is the DC bus voltage and C_{s1}, C_{s3}, C_{s5} are the transistor states.

2.2. Modeling of the PMSM

The stator voltages equation for a PMSM in the rotor oriented coordinates d-q can be expressed as:

$$\begin{bmatrix} U_{sd} \\ U_{sq} \end{bmatrix} = \begin{bmatrix} R_s + s.L_d & -P.\omega_m.L_q \\ P.\omega_m.L_d & R_s + s.L_q \end{bmatrix} \begin{bmatrix} I_{sd} \\ I_{sq} \end{bmatrix} + \begin{bmatrix} 0 \\ P.\omega_m.\Phi_{PM} \end{bmatrix} \tag{2}$$

Where I_{sd} and I_{sq} are the d - q axis stator currents, R_s is the stator resistance, Ψ_{PM} is the flux linkage of the rotor magnets linking the stator, L_d and L_q are the d - q axis stator inductances, P is the number of pole pairs and ω_m is the mechanical speed.

And the electromagnetic torque equation in the rotor oriented coordinates d-q can be expressed as (3):

$$\Gamma_{em} = \frac{3}{2}P(\Phi_{sd}I_{sq} - \Phi_{sq}I_{sd}) = \frac{3}{2}P[\Phi_{PM}I_{sq} + (L_d - L_q)I_{sd}I_{sq}] \tag{3}$$

Where Φ_{sd} and Φ_{sq} are d - q components of the stator flux linkage, which are expressed as:

$$\begin{bmatrix} \Phi_{sd} \\ \Phi_{sq} \end{bmatrix} = \begin{bmatrix} L_d & 0 \\ 0 & L_q \end{bmatrix} \begin{bmatrix} I_{sd} \\ I_{sq} \end{bmatrix} + \begin{bmatrix} \Phi_{PM} \\ 0 \end{bmatrix} \tag{4}$$

Finally, when the dry friction torque is neglected; the motion equation is expressed as:

$$J\frac{d\omega_m}{dt} = \Gamma_{em} - \Gamma_{r-}f_r\omega_m \tag{5}$$

Where J moment of inertia, Γ_r motor load and f_r damping constant.

3. Basic direct torque control for PMSM

DTC is a vector control method used to control the torque and therefore the speed of the motor bycontrolling the switching sequence of the inverter transistors. Figure 2 shows the DTC for a PMSM block diagram. It can be seen that once one has the estimated and reference instantaneous values of electromagnetic torque and stator flux, we proceed to calculate the error between them; these errors are used as inputs for the hysteresis controllers, which aim to maintain the torque and flux errors within upper and lower limits allowed, so that when evaluating within these limits an output level is obtained to know the status of the variable. The output levels achieved in this stage of the control are input signals to the block that is responsible for finding the right vector to get rid of the speed error. This procedure is made for each sampling instant to drive the PMSM to the desired speed value.

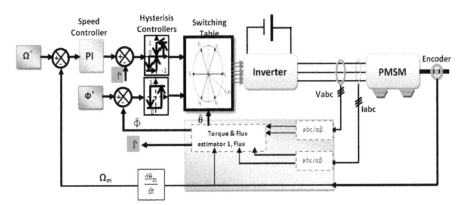

Figure 2. DTC scheme for PMSM with Classical Torque and Flux Estimator (CTFE)

In the DTC, the motor torque control is achieved with two hysteresis controllers, one for stator flux magnitude error and the other for the torque magnitude error. The selection of one switching vector per sampling time depends on the sign of these two controllers without inspections of the magnitude of the errors produced in the transient and dynamic situations per sampling time and level of the applied stator voltage.

3.1. Stator flux control

The stator voltage vector equation, in a stator reference frame, is given by:

$$\overline{V_s} = R_s . \overline{I_s} + \frac{d\overline{\Phi}_s}{dt} \tag{6}$$

Where R_s is the stator resistance and $\overline{V_s} = V_{s\alpha} + jV_{s\beta}$.

So

$$\overline{\Phi}_s = \overline{\Phi}_o + \int_0^t (\overline{V_s} - R_s . \overline{I_s}) \, dt \tag{7}$$

For high speeds, the term $R_s . \overline{I_s}$ can be neglected, so the equation 7 is given by:

$$\overline{\Phi}_s \approx \overline{\Phi}_o + \int_0^t \overline{V_s} \, dt \tag{8}$$

$\overline{\Phi}_o$ is the initial stator flux at the instant t_0.

Because during one sampling period T_e the selected stator voltage vector is always constant, the last question becomes:

$$\overline{\Phi}_s(k + 1) \approx \overline{\Phi}_s(k) + \overline{V_s} . T_e \tag{9}$$

$$\Delta\overline{\Phi}_s = \overline{V_s} . T_e = \overline{\Phi}_s(k + 1) - \overline{\Phi}_s(k) \tag{10}$$

With: T_e is the sampling period.
         $\overline{\Phi}_s$ (k) is the stator flux vector at the actual sampling period.
         $\overline{\Phi}_s$ (k + 1) is the stator flux vector at the next sampling period.
         $\Delta\overline{\Phi}_s$ is the variation of stator flux vector.

From equation 10, it is seen that the variation of the stator flux is directly proportional to the stator voltage; consequently the control is carried out by varying the stator flux vector by selecting a suitable voltage vector with the Voltage Source Inverter (VSI).

Figure 3 shows that the stator flux vector is varied in the same direction as the applied stator voltage vector. Therefore, applied a collinear stator voltage vector as the stator flux vector and in the same direction as it is a sufficiently condition to increase it, and vice versa. Indeed, to control the stator flux vector $\overline{\Phi}_s(k)$ an estimator of its module $\hat{\Phi}_s$ and its argument $\hat{\theta}_s$ is needed; the stator flux can be estimated from the measure of stator currents and voltages and their transformation in the $\alpha\beta$ subspace, by integrating of difference between the input voltage and the voltage drop across the stator resistance as given by:

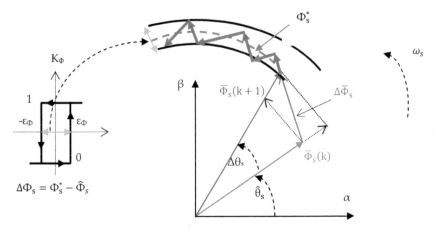

Figure 3. Stator flux vector evolution in the $\alpha\beta$ subspace

$$\Phi_{s\alpha} = \Phi_{PM} + \int_0^t (V_{s\alpha} - R_s . I_{s\alpha})\, dt \tag{11}$$

$$\Phi_{s\beta} = \int_0^t (V_{s\beta} - R_s . I_{s\beta})\, dt \tag{12}$$

Note that Φ_{PM} is the permanent magnet flux. From equations 11 and 12, the stator flux module and its argument are given by:

$$\hat{\Phi}_s = \sqrt{\Phi_{s\alpha}^2 + \Phi_{s\beta}^2} \tag{13}$$

$$\hat{\theta}_s = \tan^{-1}\left(\frac{\Phi_{s\beta}}{\Phi_{s\alpha}}\right) \tag{14}$$

A two level hysteresis controller, as indicated in figure 3, is used to control the stator flux, which compares the reference stator flux Φ_s^* with the estimated stator flux $\hat{\Phi}_s$. The flux hysteresis comparator output is denoted by Boolean variable K_Φ which indicates directly if the amplitude of flux must be increased $K_\Phi = 1$ or decreased $K_\Phi = 0$: if $K_\Phi = 1$, it means that the actual value of the flux linkage is below the reference value and outside the hysteresis limit; so the stator flux must be increased, while if $K_\Phi = 0$, it means that the actual value of the flux linkages is above the reference value and outside the hysteresis limit; so the stator flux must be decreased.

The two level VSI, as shown in figure 1, is used to select proper voltage vectors from the output of flux and torque hysteresis controller (will be presented in the next part). The inverter has eight permissible switching states (V_0, V_1 ... V_7), out of which six are active (V_1, V_2... V_6) and two zero or inactive states (V_0 and V_7). The voltage vector plane is divided into six sectors so that each voltage vector divides each region in two equal parts as shown in Figure 4. In each sector four of the six non-zero voltage vectors along with zero vectors may be used.

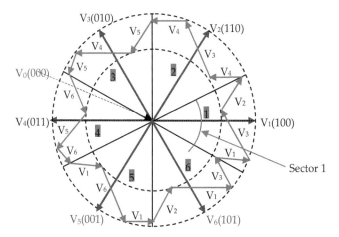

Figure 4. Control of stator flux by selection of the suitable voltage vector $V_{i(i=0,...,7)}$

3.2. Torque control

The electromagnetic torque equation is defined as follows:

$$\Gamma = k.(\overline{\Phi}_s.\overline{\Phi}_r) = \|\overline{\Phi}_s\|.\|\overline{\Phi}_r\|.\sin\delta \qquad (15)$$

Where δ is the angle between the rotor and the stator flux vectors and the constant k is expressed as (when $L_d = L_q$):

$$k = \frac{3P}{2L_q}$$

The equation 15 indicates that the electromagnetic torque depends to the rotor and stator amplitude, and the angle δ. So, if the stator flux vector is perfectly controlled, by mean of the stator voltage vector $\overline{V}_s$, in module and in position; consequently, the electromagnetic torque can be controlled by the same stator voltage vector.

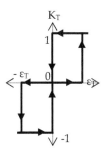

Figure 5. Three level hysteresis controller

Note that the electromagnetic torque can be controlled by mean of a two level comparator as the same as stator flux (see figure 3) or by using a three level comparator as shown in figure 5. In this work, a three level comparator has been used in order to minimize the switches commutation numbers and to have the two senses of the motor rotation. The output of this controller is represented by a Boolean variable K_T which indicates directly if the amplitude of the torque must be increased, maintained constant or decreased, respectively, when K_T is equal 1, 0 or -1. The goal of this controller is to maintain the torque variation $\Delta\Gamma$ in the bandwidth $[-\varepsilon_T, \varepsilon_T]$ chosen by the programmer of DTC algorithm. Indeed, this controller adjusts the torque variation generated by a comparator of electromagnetic torque reference (Γ^*) and the estimated torque ($\hat{\Gamma}$).

$$\Delta\Gamma = \Gamma^* - \hat{\Gamma} \tag{16}$$

3.3. Switching table for controlling flux and torque

According to the signal generated by the hysteresis controller of stator flux and electromagnetic torque presented in figure 3 and 5, respectively; just one voltage vector can be selected to adjust the torque and flux. The choice of this vector depends on the outputs of the torque and flux controller and the position of the stator flux vector, as shown in table 1.

K_Φ	K_T	θ_1	θ_2	θ_3	θ_4	θ_5	θ_6
	1	V_2	V_3	V_4	V_5	V_6	V_1
1	0	V_7	V_0	V_7	V_0	V_7	V_0
	-1	V_6	V_1	V_2	V_3	V_4	V_5
	1	V_3	V_4	V_5	V_6	V_1	V_2
0	0	V_0	V_7	V_0	V_7	V_0	V_7
	-1	V_5	V_6	V_1	V_2	V_3	V_4

Table 1. Takahashi and Noguchi switching table

3.4. Torque and flux estimator

In this chapter, two estimators of torque and stator flux will be presented.

3.4.1. Classical Torque and Flux Estimator (CTFE)

The figure 2 shows that the torque and stator flux can be estimated by measuring the mechanical position, stator voltages and currents. Indeed, the stator flux is estimated by using equations 11, 12 and 13. Whereas, the torque is estimated by using equation 17:

$$\hat{\Gamma} = \frac{3}{2}P\left[\Phi_{s\alpha}I_{s\beta} - \Phi_{s\beta}I_{s\alpha}\right] \tag{17}$$

Note that the stator voltages used in this estimator can be measured directly by mean of two or three sensors, or indirectly by combining the measured DC bus voltage and the transistor states (C_{s1}, C_{s3}, C_{s5}) of the VSI.

$$\begin{bmatrix} V_{s\alpha} \\ V_{s\beta} \end{bmatrix} = U_{dc}\sqrt{\frac{2}{3}}\begin{bmatrix} 1 & -\frac{1}{2} & -\frac{1}{2} \\ 0 & 1 & 1 \end{bmatrix}\begin{bmatrix} C_{s1} \\ C_{s3} \\ C_{s5} \end{bmatrix} \tag{18}$$

C_{s1}, C_{s3} and C_{s5} are the switching commands of each VSI leg and they are complementary. For the first leg (transistors S_1 and S_4), C_{s1} is 1 if the upper switch (S_1) is commanded to be closed and 0 if the lower one (S_4) in commanded to be closed first.

The drawbacks of this estimation technique are: In addition to stator current sensors, at least one voltage sensor is necessary. In addition, the estimated torque and stator flux dependent to the stator resistance.

3.4.2. Robust Torque and Flux Estimator (RTFE)

In order to estimate stator flux and electromagnetic torque with this estimator, just current components and rotor position are measured without measuring stator voltages directly or by using transistor states and DC bus voltage sensor. The bloc diagram of this estimation technique is shown in figure 6.

The advantages of this NTFE are: Any stator voltage sensor is necessary to estimate stator flux or electromagnetic torque and the estimated stator flux and electromagnetic torque are independent to the stator resistance variations, which can improve the performances of the drive and reduce the cost of this equipment.

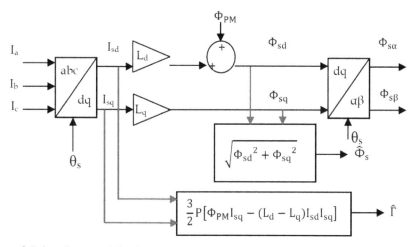

Figure 6. Robust Torque and Flux Estimator structure

3.5. Speed PI controller synthesis

The speed closed loop with the PI controller is presented by the bloc diagram in Figure 7. To eliminate the zero effect due to corrector, the compensation method is used to the corrector synthesis. In this case the regulator parameters are given by the relationships:

$$k_p = \frac{J}{K_T.\tau_w} \text{ and } k_i = \frac{J}{K_T.\tau_w} \text{ where } \tau_w = 0.1 \text{ second}$$

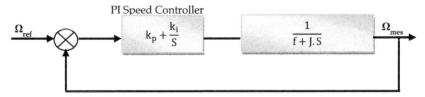

Figure 7. Closed loop PI speed controller

3.6. Simulation results

The PMSM parameters used in this simulation are shown in table II. These parameters will be used in all the simulations of this chapter.

Rated output power (Watt)	Rated phase voltage (Volt)	Magnetic flux linkage (Wb)
500	190	0.052
Rated torque (Nm)	Rated speed (r/min)	Maximum speed (r/min)
0.8	1000	6000
d-axis inductance (mH)	q-axis inductance (mH)	Inertia (Kg.m²)
3.3	3.3	0.003573
Poles	Stator resistance (Ω)	friction coefficient (Nm.s/rd)
3	1.59	0.00047

Table 2. PMSM parameters

The models of the PMSM, VSI and basic DTC algorithm are developed in Matlab/Simulink in order to examine the complete behaviour of the basic DTC. The sampling period has been chosen equal to 50 μs (20 KHz) for basic DTC. Various tests have been carried out in order to investigate the drive performance and to characterize the steady-state and transient behavior.

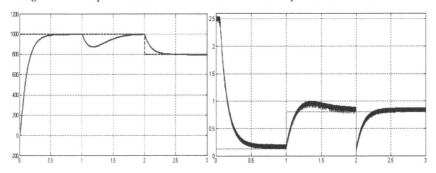

Figure 8. Mechanical speed (on the left) and electromagnetic torque (on the right) tracking performance under load variations in case of basic DTC

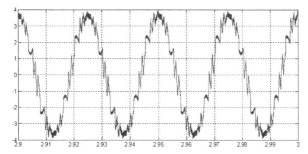

Figure 9. Stator current waveform at 800 rpm with nominal load under basic DTC

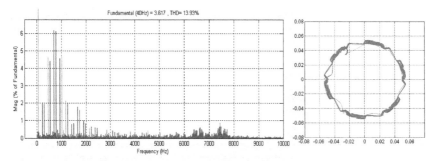

Figure 10. Stator current spectrum at 800 rpm with nominal load (on the left) and Stator flux in (α,β)
axes under load variations (on the right) in case of basic DTC

4. Fuzzy direct torque control for PMSM

4.1. FDTC strategy

Figure 11 shows the complete FDTC structure which combines FDTC and PI-Fuzzy speed
controller. Indeed, the switching table used in basic DTC and the hysterisis controllers are
replaced by a fuzzy switching table, whose inputs are electromagnetic torque and stator flux
errors denoted respectively $\Delta\Gamma$ and $\Delta\Phi_s$, and the argument θ_s of the stator flux (should
remain between $\pm\pi$).Whereas its outputs are the states of the VSI switches. In other hand,
the classical speed PI corrector is replaced by a PI-Fuzzy speed controller in order to
improve the dynamic performance of the DTC.

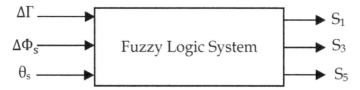

Figure 11. Fuzzy logic switching table used in FDTC

Figure 12 shows the design of this fuzzy logic system in Matlab/Simulink and also the configuration of its inputs and outputs as membership functions.

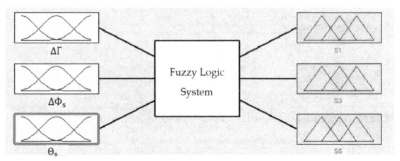

Figure 12. Matlab/Simulink design of the fuzzy logic switching table used in FDTC

4.2. Inputs fuzzification and outputs defuzzification

In order to examine the fuzzy logic contribution to DTC, the choice of the membership functions number for the fuzzification of flux and torque errors has been repected in this part, i.e two membership functions for $\Delta\Phi_s$, because a two level hysteresis controller was utilized to control the stator flux in basic DTC. Whereas three membership functions for the fuzzification of $\Delta\Gamma$ because a three level hysteris controller was used to adjust the torque.

4.2.1. Stator flux error fuzzification

Two trapezoidal membership functions are selected to fuzzify the stator flux error, so the following two fuzzy sets are used, N signify Negative and P for Positive. The parameters of these two functions are indicated in figure 13.

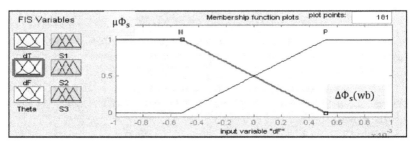

Figure 13. Membership functions for stator flux error

4.2.2. Electromagnetic torque error fuzzification

Three trapezoidal membership functions are selected to fuzzify the torque error as shown in figure 14, so the following three fuzzy sets are used, N signify Negative, EZ for Zero and P for Positive.

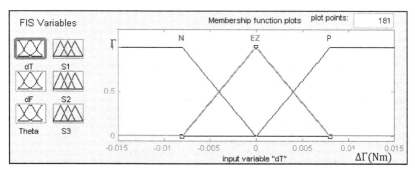

Figure 14. Membership functions for electromagnetic torque error

4.2.3. Stator flux angle fuzzification

The flux angle has a universe of discours equal 2π radians, as shown in figure 15. It is divided into six zones or sectors in order to be equivalent to that of the basic DTC. "thetai" means sector i, i.e "theta1" means sector 1 (θ_1) and so on.

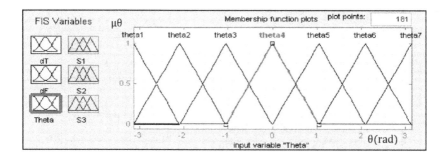

Figure 15. Membership functions for stator flux position

4.2.4. State switches defuzzification

The sole output control variable of fuzzy logic system is the inverter switching states S_1, S_3 and S_5 or the selected voltage vector. Figure 16, illustrates the suggested output fuzzy set as singletons. Indeed, the choice of the stator volt dge vector is based on the rules indicated in table 3. Each control rule can be described using the state variables $\Delta\Phi$, $\Delta\Gamma$ and θ_s and the control variables. The ith rule Ri can be written as:

$$Ri : \text{if } \Delta\Phi, \text{ is } A_i, \Delta\Gamma \text{ is } B_i \text{ and } \theta_s \text{ is } C_i \text{ then } S_1 \text{ is } a, S_3 \text{ is b and } S_5 \text{ is c}$$

Where a, b and c are a boolean variable. A_i, B_i and C_i denote the fuzzy set of the variables $\Delta\Phi$, $\Delta\Gamma$ and θ_s, respectively.whereas Ri is the control rule number i.

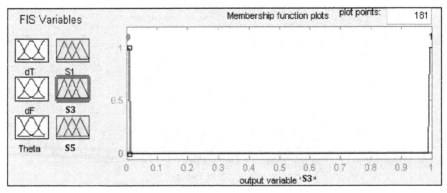

Figure 16. Membership functions for state switches as singletons

4.3. Fuzzy logic switcher rules

The most important part of designing the fuzzy controller (fuzzy logic system) is to design the rule base, because it gouverns the behiviour of fuzzy controller and stores the expert knowledge on how to control the plant. The fuzzy associative memory of Mamdani rule base model to develop DTFC is as shown in Table 3.

θ_1, θ_7			θ_2			θ_3		
$\Delta\Gamma\backslash\Delta\Phi$	P	N	$\Delta\Gamma\backslash\Delta\Phi$	P	N	$\Delta\Gamma\backslash\Delta\Phi$	P	N
P	V_5	V_6	P	V_6	V_1	P	V_1	V_2
Z	V_0	V_7	Z	V_7	V_0	Z	V_0	V_7
θ_4			θ_5			θ_6		
$\Delta\Gamma\backslash\Delta\Phi$	P	N	$\Delta\Gamma\backslash\Delta\Phi$	P	N	$\Delta\Gamma\backslash\Delta\Phi$	P	N
P	V_2	V_3	P	V_3	V_4	P	V_4	V_5
Z	V_7	V_0	Z	V_0	V_7	Z	V_7	V_0

Table 3. Fuzzy logic switcher rules

4.4. PI-Fuzzy speed controller synthesis

The speed closed loop with the PI-Fuzzy controller structure is shown in Figure 17. The inputs of this FLC are the normalized values of the speed error denoted "e" and its rate of change denoted "de" that should remain between ±1. Wherefore, two scaling factors (K_{ne} and $K_{\Delta ne}$) are used to normalize the actual speed error and its rate of change. The output of the controller is the normalized change of the motor torque command which generates the actual value of the motor torque demand when it's multiplied by a third scaling factor (K_{nc}).

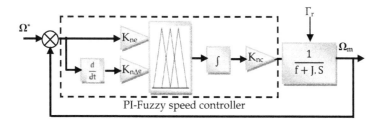

Figure 17. Closed loop PI-Fuzzy speed controller

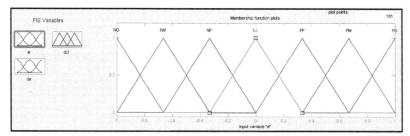

Figure 18. Membership functions for speed error

The membership functions used, in this chapter, for the inputs and the output are the same, as shown in figure 18. Where, the following fuzzy sets used in these membership functions: NG is negative big, NM is negative medium, NP is negative small, EZ is equal zero, PP is positive small, PM is positive medium and PG is positive big.

From the speed behavior analysis, the table 4 has been developed to obtain a good performance in the speed closed loop. Whereas, from the membership functions of inputs and the output, and the rules presented in this table, the FLC elaborates the electromagnetic torque reference to be developed by the PMSM.

$e \backslash \Delta e$	NG	NM	NP	EZ	PP	PM	PG
PG	EZ	PP	PM	PG	PG	PG	PG
PM	NP	EZ	PP	PM	PG	PG	PG
PP	NM	NP	EZ	PP	PM	PG	PG
EZ	NG	NM	NP	EZ	PP	PM	PG
NP	NG	NG	NM	NP	EZ	PP	PM
NM	NG	NG	NG	NM	NP	EZ	PP
NG	NG	NG	NG	NG	NM	NP	EZ

Table 4. PI-Fuzzy speed controller rules

4.5. Simulation results

The sampling period has been chosen equal to 100 μs (10 KHz) for FDTC; in order to compare this strategy with basic DTC; despite the fact that the sampling time used to simulate DTC is less than that used in case of FDTC.

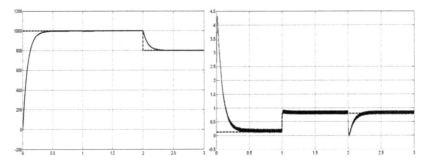

Figure 19. Mechanical speed (on the left) and electromagnetic torque (on the right) tracking performance under load variations in case of FDTC

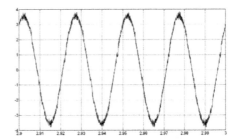

Figure 20. Stator current waveform at 800 rpm with nominal load under FDTC

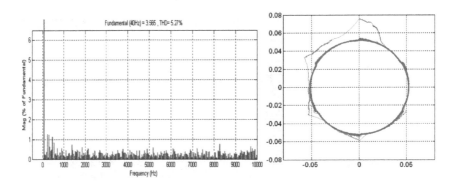

Figure 21. Stator current spectrum at 800 rpm with nominal load (on the left) and Stator flux in (α, β) axes under load variations (on the right) in case of FDTC

5. Direct Torque Control with Space Vector Modulation for PMSM

Figure 22 shows the DTC with SVM scheme for PMSM drive, this technique is a solution to overcome the drawbacks of the basic DTC by using the same torque and flux estimators and the same speed PI controller. In this modified DTC, torque and flux hysteresis controllers and the switching table used in basic DTC are replaced by a PI torque controller and a predictive calculator of vector voltage reference to be applied to stator coils of the PMSM.

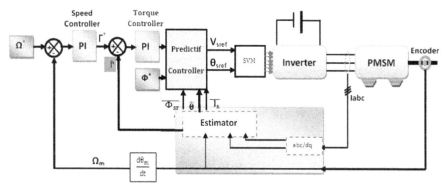

Figure 22. DTC-SVM scheme for PMSM drive

In the proposed scheme of DTC-SVM with speed loop control, shown in this figure, after correction of the mechanical speed through a PI controller, the torque PI controller delivers V_{sq} voltage to the predictive controller and also receives, more the reference amplitude of stator flux $\Phi^* = \Phi_{PM}$, information from the estimator namely, the position of the actual stator flux, estimated flux vector and measured current vector, where:

$$\overline{\Phi}_s = \Phi_{s\alpha} + j\Phi_{s\beta} \text{ and } \overline{I_s} = i_{s\alpha} + ji_{s\beta}$$

After calculation, the predictive controller determinates the polar coordinates of stator voltage command vector $\overline{V_{sref}} = [V_{sref}, \theta_{sref}]$ for space vector modulator, which finally generates the pulses S_1, S_3 and S_5 to control the VSI.

5.1. Torque and flux control by means of SVM

The electromagnetic torque of the PMSM can be expressed as:

$$\Gamma_{em} = \frac{3}{2} P \frac{\Phi_{sr}}{L_d L_q} \left[\Phi_{PM} L_q \sin \delta + \frac{1}{2} \Phi_{sr} (L_d - L_q) \sin \delta \right] \tag{19}$$

Where δ is the angle between the stator and rotor flux linkage (or the torque angle).

Above equation consist of two terms, the first is the excitation torque, which is produced by permanent magnet flux and the second term is the reluctance torque.

In the case where $L_d = L_q = L$, the expression of electromagnetic torque becomes:

$$\Gamma_{em} = \frac{3}{2} P \frac{\Phi_{sr}}{L} \Phi_{PM} \sin \delta \qquad (20)$$

Under the condition of constant stator flux amplitude Φ_{sr}, by diffentiating equation 20 with respect to time, the rate of increasing of torque at t=0 can be obtained in equation 21.

$$\frac{d\Gamma}{dt} = \left(\frac{3}{2} P \frac{\Phi_{sr}}{L} \Phi_{PM} \cos \delta \right) \frac{d\delta}{dt} \qquad (21)$$

From equations 20 and 21, it can be seen that for constant stator flux amplitude Φ_{sr} and flux produced by Permanent Magnets (PM) Φ_{PM}, the electromagnetic torque can be changed by control of the torque angle; quick dynamic reponse can be achieved by changing this angle as quickly as possible, this is the basis of DTC for PMSM (Tang et al., 2003). This is the angle between the stator and rotor flux linkage, when the stator resistance is neglected. The torque angle δ, in turn, can be changed by changing position of stator flux vector in respect to PM vector using the actual voltage vector supplied by PWM inverter.

When the PMSM drive, we distinguish between two cases:

- Steady state: the angle δ is constant and its value is the load torque of the machine, while the stator flux and rotor rotate at the same speed is the synchronous speed.
- The transient state, the angle δ is variable then the stator and rotor flux rotate at different speeds (see figure 23).

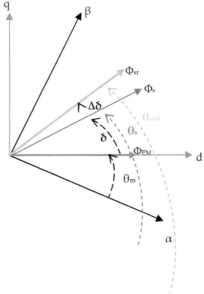

Figure 23. Vector diagram of illustrating torque and flux control conditions

The change of the angle δ is done by varying the position of the stator flux vector relative to the rotor flux vector with the vector V$_{sref}$ provided by the predictive controller to the power of the SVM. The figure 23 above shows the evolution of the stator flux vector at the beginning and the end of a period vector modulation. At the beginning, stator flux vector is at the position δ with an amplitude Φ_s, it's at this moment that the predictive controller calculated the variation Δδ of the stator flux angle, it's also at this same moment that the space vector modulator receives the new position and amplitude of the voltage vector that must be achieved at the end of the modulation period. Of course, this vector will allow the stator flux to transit to the location as defined by the predictive controller to adjust the torque fluctuations, and this by calculating the time of application of the adjacent vectors V_1, V_2 and V_0 as well as their sequence that depends on the symmetry of the modulation vector.

The internal structure of the predictive torque and flux controller is shown in figure 24. So the average change Δδ of the angle δ is expressed as:

$$\Delta\delta = T_s \frac{d}{dt}\left[Arcsin(\frac{\Phi_{sr}}{L_q\,I_{sq}})\right] \tag{22}$$

where: T_s is the sampling time.

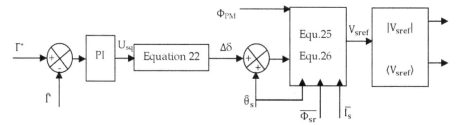

Figure 24. Internal structure of predictive controller used in DTC-SVM

From equation 22, the relation between error of torque and increment of load angle Δδ is non linear. In odrder to generate the load angel increment required to minimize the instantaneous error between reference and actual estimated torque; a PI controller has been applied as indicated in figure 24. The step change Δδ that corresponds to the torque error is added to the current position $\hat\theta_s$ of the stator flux vector to determine the new position of this vector at the next simple time.

The module and argument of the reference stator voltage vector is calculated by the following equations, based on stator resistance R_s, Δδ signal and actual stator flux argument:

$$|V_{sref}| = \sqrt{V_{s\alpha-ref}^2 + V_{s\beta-ref}^2} \tag{23}$$

$$\langle V_{sref}\rangle = \arctan(\frac{V_{s\beta-ref}}{V_{s\alpha-ref}})\ \# \tag{24}$$

Where:

$$V_{s\alpha-ref} = \frac{\Phi_{sr}\cos(\hat\theta_s+\Delta\delta)-\Phi_s\cos\hat\theta_s}{T_s} + R_s\cdot I_{s\alpha} \tag{25}$$

$$V_{s\beta-ref} = \frac{\Phi_{sr}\sin(\theta_s+\Delta\delta)-\Phi_s\sin\theta_s}{T_s} + R_s \cdot I_{s\beta} \qquad (26)$$

The figure 25 shows the application sequence of the two adjacent vectors and zero vector in the first sector of the vector V_{sref}. Indeed, after the vector modulation algorithm computation times T_1, T_2 and T_0 successively apply the voltage vectors V_1, V_2 and V_0, we choose the symmetry in the schematic figure 25 of dividing each modulation period T_s into two sequences and transistor control of the upper arms of the VSI, in the second half of the period are an image of themselves in relation to the vertical axis passing through the point $T_s/2$.

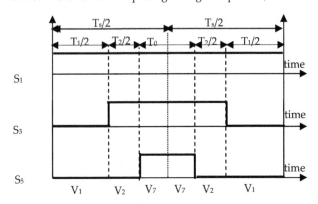

Figure 25. Time sequences and applications of adjacent vectors in the first sector

So to have a fast transit of stator flux vector, very low flux ripple and fast torque response, the space vector modulator generates a voltage vector V_{sref} governed by the following law:

$$V_{sref} = \frac{1}{T_s}\left[\left(\frac{T_1}{2}V_1 + \frac{T_2}{2}V_2 + \frac{T_0}{2}V_0\right) + \left(\frac{T_0}{2}V_0 + \frac{T_2}{2}V_2 + \frac{T_1}{2}V_1\right)\right] \qquad (27)$$

So at each modulation period and in this case, the sequence of adjacent vectors in the first sector is applied $(V_1\text{-}V_2\text{-}V_7\text{-}V_7\text{-}V_2\text{-}V_1)$ respectively during the time $\left(\frac{T_1}{2},\frac{T_2}{2},\frac{T_0}{2},\frac{T_0}{2},\frac{T_2}{2},\frac{T_1}{2}\right)$ to rebuild the better the rotating vector.

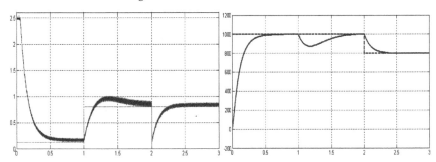

Figure 26. Stator current spectrum at 800 rpm with nominal load (on the left) and Stator flux in (α,β) axes under load variations (on the right) in case of DTC-SVM

5.2. Simulation results

The sampling period has been chosen equal to 100 μs (10 KHz) for DTC-SVM; in order to compare this strategy with basic DTC; despite the fact that the sampling time used to simulate DTC is less than that used in case of DTC-SVM. Whereas, the sampling frequencies used to simulate FDTC and DTC-SVM are equal; so as to compare these two techniques in the same conditions.

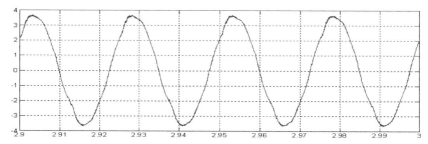

Figure 27. Stator current waveform at 800 rpm with nominal load under DTC-SVM

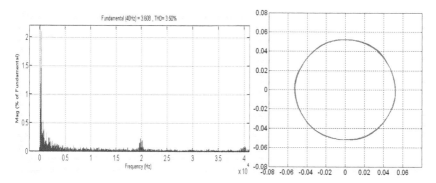

Figure 28. Stator current spectrum at 800 rpm with nominal load (on the left) and Stator flux in (α,β) axes under load variations (on the right) in case of DTC-SVM

6. Direct Torque Control with Sinusoidal Pulse with Modulation for PMSM

DTC-SPWM for PMSM is based on the same algorithm used in DTC-SVM already presented in figure 22, but instead of using SVM pulses generator, a simple and fast SPWM pulses generator is investigated to control the VSI. Indeed, after transformation of $V_{s\alpha-ref}$ and $V_{s\beta-ref}$ produced by the predictive controller (from the stator flux reference frame $(\alpha-\beta)$ to the (a-b-c) frame). These three signals, used as reference signals, will be compared with a triangular signal (figure 29); then the inverter is controlled by the SPWM.

In this proposed technique, the same flux and torque estimators and the predictive torque and flux controller as for the DTC-SVM are still used. Instead of the SVM generator, a SPWM technique is used to determine reference stator flux linkage vector. It is seen that the proposed scheme retains almost all the advantages of the DTC-SVM, such as no current control loop, constant switching frequency, low torque and flux ripple, etc. But, the main advantage of the DTC-SPWM is the simple algorithm of PWM (SPWM) used to control the VSI. Of course, the SVM algorithm needs more calculation time than SPWM and the same advantages of DTC-SVM will be obtained by using DTC-SPWM. Whatever is the load torque and speed variation, SPWM guarantees a constant switching frequency, which greatly improves the flux and torque ripples.

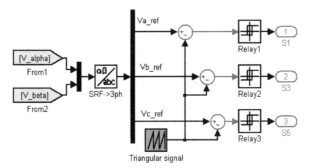

Figure 29. Sinusoidal PWM pulses generator scheme

6.1. Simulation results

The sampling period has been chosen equal to 100 μs (10 KHz) for DTC-SVM; in order to compare this strategy with basic DTC; despite the fact that the sampling time used to simulate DTC is less than that used in case of DTC-SVM. Whereas, the sampling frequencies used to simulate FDTC and DTC-SVM are equal; so as to compare these two techniques in the same conditions.

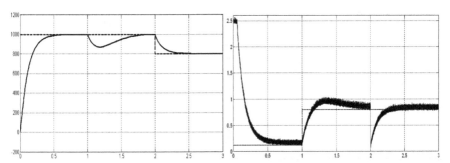

Figure 30. Stator current spectrum at 800 rpm with nominal load (on the left) and Stator flux in (α,β) axes under load variations (on the right) in case of DTC-SPWM

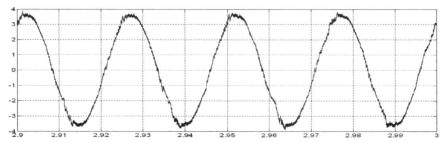

Figure 31. Stator current waveform at 800 rpm with nominal load under DTC-SPWM

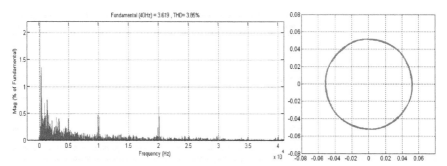

Figure 32. Stator current spectrum at 800 rpm with nominal load (on the left) and Stator flux in (α, β) axes under load variations (on the right) in case of DTC-SPWM

7. Comparison of DTC strategies

To verify and to compare the four DTC strategies proposed in this chapter, digital simulations have been carried out, by using the environment Matlab/Simulink, for the same PMSM parameters and conditions, except the sampling frequency utilized to simulate basic DTC which was taken equal to 20 KHz while for the FDTC, DTC-SVM and DTC-SPWM was taken equal to 10 KHz. Taking into consideration those conditions, the strategies' performances have been compared for both regimes dynamic and steady state.

Dynamic state: Figures 8, 26 and 30 shows that DTC, DTC-SVM and DTC-SPWM present the same speed and torque response time. Whereas, it's seen in figure 19 that torque and speed response time was greatly improved; at start time and at load toque or speed set-point variation. Indeed, speed FLC used in FDTC improves the dynamic state performances when compared to speed PI controller used in the other strategies.

Steady state: Figure 10 (on the left) show the spectral analysis of current presented in figure 10, it's seen that the Total Harmonic Distortion (THD) of the current waveform under basic DTC is 13.93 %. Whereas, figure 21 show that FDTC allows to decrease the THD value to 5.27 % with a variable switching frequency as indicated in the current spectral analysis. In addition, torque and stator flux ripple are reduced in case of FDTC in comparison with basic DTC, and also the current quality was improved. Figure 28 (on the left) shows that the current THD under DTC-SVM is 3.5 %, which is smother than that of basic DTC and FDTC. Also, it's seen that torque and flux ripples are greatly reduced under DTC-SVM when compared to DTC and FDTC (compare figures 26 and 28 with figures 8, 10, 19 and 21). Figure 32 shows that the THD of the current waveform under DTC-SPWM is 3.85%, which is almost the same as DTC-SVM, also DTC-SVM guarantees a constant switching frequency; as shown in figure 32 which allow to reduce torque and flux ripple as the same as DTC-SVM. Furthermore, the calculation time of the DTC-SPWM is much inferior to the DTC-SVM, this is because SPWM algorithm is very simple than SVM. Note that the SVM symmetry used in this work eliminates the harmonics which are around the uneven switching frequency (Chikh et al., 2011a). The same performances for DTC-SVM and DTC-SPWM can be obtained if an asymmetric SVM has been used instead of symmetrical SVM.

8. Effect of PMSM parameters variations and their compensation

This part is devoted to compare two speed controllers performances used in DTC under PMSM parameters variations. Also, a comparison between classical and novel torque and flux estimators has been developed in order to show their performances under PMSM parameters variations.

8.1. PI and FLC performances

Figure 33 shows the rotation speed and motor torque evolution for PMSM DTC strategy by using PI speed controller (green color) and speed FLC (red color). Indeed, the FLC has exhibited high performance in tracking the speed reference, as compared with speed PI controller. This figure confirms that the motor torque response with fuzzy controller is faster than PI controller during the start up regime and during a step change in load torque. The speed dynamic state imposes the motor torque response time because these two variables are regulated in cascade: the inner loop controls the motor electromagnetic torque and the outer loop regulates the motor rotation speed.

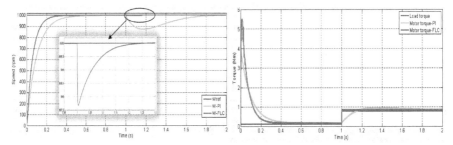

Figure 33. Rotation speed (on the left) and motor torque (on the right) performances under DTC for PMSM drive by using speed PI controller (green color) or speed FLC (red color)

8.2. Classical and novel estimators under stator resistance variation

The simulation results presented in this part shows the robustness of the classical and the novel flux and torque estimators, described at the beginning of this chapter, under stator resistance variation. Figure 34 shows the stator resistance variation applied to examine DTC for PMSM drive by using classical or novel estimator. In this case, the value of stator resistance was changed from the nominal value 1.59 Ω to the double of this value 3.18 Ω. Where, the reference stator flux and load torque are kept constant at 0.052 Wb and 0.8 Nm, respectively.

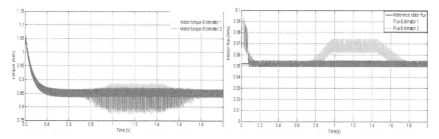

Figure 34. Stator resistance variation

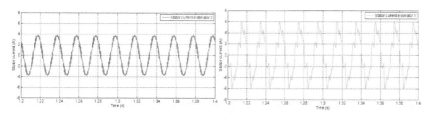

Figure 35. Motor torque (on the left) and stator flux (on the right) evolution by using classical estimator (green color) or by using novel estimator (red color)

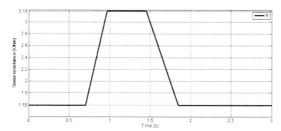

Figure 36. Stator current waveform in case of classical estimator (on the left) and novel estimator (on the right)

It's seen in figure 35 that the estimated stator flux was affected, when the stator resistance was changed at t=0.75 s; when the stator flux was estimated by using classical estimator.

This figure shows that, in spite of stator resistance variation, the stator flux was maintained constant when it is estimated by the novel estimator, because this estimator does not depends to the stator resistance variation. This stator flux deviation is normal and forecasted because the estimated flux value by using classical estimator depends on the stator resistance. When the PMSM stator resistance varies; while this classical estimator still uses the nominal stator resistance to estimate the actual stator flux; the estimated stator flux differ significantly from the real stator flux.

As shown in figure 35, the torque and flux ripples are increased when stator resistance varies in case of classical estimator, because the stator flux deviation causes the DTC algorithm to select a wrong switching state, which can result in unstable operation of the PMSM. Indeed, figure 36 shows that the stator current waveform in case of the novel estimator presents a good THD than the current in case of classical estimator, this is due to the wrong selection of the switching state.

8.3. Classical and Robust estimators under PMSM parameters variation

The simulation results below presents the DTC for PMSM performances in case of speed PI controller and Robust estimator, and speed FLC and this estimator under motor parameters variation, which are stator resistance, friction coefficient and motor inertia. Figure 37 (on the left) shows the variations, of these three parameters, applied to examine DTC robustness: the stator resistance was changed from the nominal value 1.59 Ω to the double of this value 3.18 Ω, the friction coefficient was changed from the nominal value f=0.00047 Nm.s/rd to f1=100*f and the motor inertia was changed from the nominal value J=0.003573 Kg.m^2 to J1=100*J.

It's seen in figure 37 (on the right) that the speed FLC allows to achieve a faster response and reject the perturbations (motor parameters variations), whereas the speed PI controller takes much time, in comparison with FLC, to reject these perturbations. Also, a faster motor torque response has been achieved with speed FLC compared to speed PI controller; as shown in figure 38 (on the left). Indeed, combining speed FLC and the novel estimator allow DTC for PMSM to reject stator resistance variation thanks to this estimator and reject motor inertia and friction coefficient thanks to speed FLC, which is shown in figure 38 (on the right).

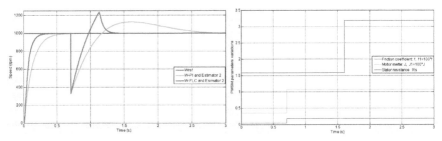

Figure 37. PMSM parameters variation (on the left) and rotation speed evolution (on the right) in case of DTC for PMSM drive using speed PI controller and novel estimator (green color), and speed FLC and novel estimator (red color)

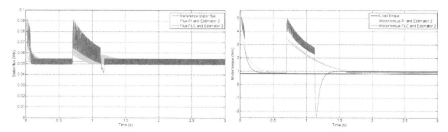

Figure 38. Motor torque (on the left) and stator flux (on the right) in case of DTC for PMSM drive using speed PI controller and novel estimator (green color), and speed FLC and novel estimator (red color)

9. Conclusion

Another solution has been presented to overcome the problems associated to DTC for PMSM in case of motor parameters variation and/or nonlinear operating conditions, which utilize speed FLC and an independent stator resistance estimator. Of course, FDTC allows rejecting the perturbations and minimizing torque and flux ripple. For all these reasons, a fixed switching frequency (DTC-SVM or DTC-SPWM) presented in this chapter can be combined with speed FLC and this independent stator resistance estimator to develop a robust DTC for PMSM.

Author details

Khalid Chikh, Mohamed Khafallah and Abdallah Saâd
Hassan II University, National Higher School of Electricity and Mechanics (ENSEM),
Department of Electrical Engineering, Energy and Electrical Systems Research Group, Morocco

10. References

Chikh, K.; Saad, A.; Khafallah, M. & Yousfi, D. (2011a). PMSM Vector Control Performance Improvement by Using Pulse with Modulation and Anti-windup PI Controller, *Proceedings of IEEE 2011 2nd International Conference on Multimedia Computing and Systems*, pp. 1-7, ISBN 978-1-61284-730-6, Ouarzazate, MOROCCO, April 07-09, 2011

Chikh, K.; Khafallah, M.; Saad, A. & Yousfi, D. (2011b). Drive with Low Torque and Flux Ripple for PMSM by Using Direct Torque Control with Space Vector Modulation, *Proceedings of WASET 2011 International Conference on Computer, Electrical, and System Sciences, and Engineering*, pp. 1130-1137, ISSN 2010-3778, Paris, FRANCE, June 24-26, 2011

Chikh, K.; Khafallah, M.; Saad, A. & Yousfi, D. (2011c). A Novel Drive Implementation for PMSM by Using Direct Torque Control with Space Vector Modulation. *Canadian Journal on Electrical and Electronics Engineering*, Vol.2, No.8, (September 2011), pp. 400-408, ISSN 1923-0540

Lokriti, AS.; Zidani, Y. & Doubabi, S. (2011). Fuzzy Logic Control Contribution to the Direct Torque and Flux Control of an Induction Machine, *Proceedings of IEEE 2011 2nd International Conference on Multimedia Computing and Systems*, pp. 1-6, ISBN 978-1-61284-730-6, Ouarzazate, MOROCCO, April 07-09, 2011

Ningzhou, L.; Xiaojuan, W. & Xiaoyun, F. (2010). An Improved DTC algorithm for Reducing Torque Ripples of PMSM Based on Cloud Model and SVM, *Proceedings of International Conference on Multimedia Information Networking and Security*, pp. 274-277, ISBN 978-1-4244-8626-7, Nanjing, Jiangsu, November 04-06, 2010

Pujar, HJ. & Kodad, SF. (2009). Digital Simulation of Direct Torque Fuzzy Control of PMSM Servo System. *International Journal of Recent Trends in Engineering*, Vol.2, No.2, (November 2009), pp. 89-93, ISSN 1797-9617

Tang, L.; Zhong, L.; Fazlur Rahman, M. & Hu, Y. (2003). A Novel Direct Torque Control for Interior Permanent-Magnet Synchronous Machine Drive with Low Ripple in Torque and Flux- A Speed-Sensorless Approach. *IEEE Transactions on Industry Applications*, Vol.39, No.6, (November 2003), pp. 1748-1756, ISSN 0093-9994

Tlemcani, A.; Bouchhida, O.; Benmansour, K.; Boudana, D. & Boucherit, M.S. (2009). Direct Torque Control Strategy (DTC) Based on Fuzzy Logic Controller for a Permanent Magnet Synchronous Machine Drive, *Journal of Electrical Engineering & Technology*, Vol.4, No.1, (December 2009), pp. 66-78, ISSN 1975-0102

Ziane, H.; Retif, J.M. & Rekioua, T. (2008). Fixed-Switching-Frequency DTC Control for PM Synchronous Maching with Minimum Torque Ripples, *Canadian Journal on Electrical and Computer Engineering*, Vol.33, No.3/4, (December 2008), pp. 183-189, ISSN 0840-8688

Haque, M.E. & Rahman, M.F. (2002). Influence of Stator Resistance Variation on Direct Torque Controlled Interior Permanent Magnet Synchronous Motor Drive Performance and Its Compensation, *IEEE-Industry Applications Conference-Thirty Sixth IAS annual meeting*, Vol.4, (Aout 2002), pp. 2563-2569, ISSN 0197-2618

Chapter 9

Digital Differential Protection of Power Transformer Using Matlab

Adel Aktaibi and M. Azizur Rahman

Additional information is available at the end of the chapter

1. Introduction

Power system development is reflected in the development of all the power system devices generators, transformers with different sizes, transmission lines and the protection equipment. Modern power transformer is one of the most vital devices of the electric power system and its protection is critical. For this reason, the protection of power transformers has taken an important consideration by the researchers. One of the most effective transformer protection methods is the differential protection algorithm. Typically, transformer protection is focused on discriminating the internal faults from the magnetizing inrush currents in the power transformers and overcoming the CTs related issues [1 -5].

2. Conventional differential protection scheme

This scheme is based on the principle that the input power to the power transformer under normal conditions is equal to the output power. Under normal conditions, no current will flow into the differential relay current coil. Whenever a fault occurs, within the protected zone, the current balance will no longer exist, and relay contacts will close and release a trip signal to cause the certain circuit breakers (CBs) to operate in order to disconnect the faulty equipment/part. The differential relay compares the primary and secondary side currents of the power transformer. Current transformers (CTs) are used to reduce the amount of currents in such a way their secondary side currents are equal. Fig. 1 shows the differential relay in its simplest form. The polarity of CTs is such as to make the current circulate normally without going through the relay, during normal load conditions and external faults.

Current transformers ratings are selected carefully to be matched with the power transformer current ratings to which they are connected so as the CTs secondary side currents are equal. However, the problem is that the CTs ratios available in the market have standard ratings. They are not available exactly as the desired ratings. Therefore, the primary ratings of the CTs are usually limited to those of the available standard ratio CTs. Commonly the primary side of the current transformer has only one turn (1) and the secondary side has many turns depending on the transformation ratio (N) of the CT, which is selected to match the ratings of the power transformer. Since the transformation ratio of transformers is the ratio between the number of turns in the primary side to the number of the turns in the secondary side. Therefore, the turn ratio of the primary current transformer is $\frac{1}{N_1}$ and the turn ratio of the secondary side current transformer is $\frac{1}{N_2}$. The secondary current of the CT located in the primary side of the power transformer is [2], [6-7];

$$I_1 = \frac{I_p}{N_1} \tag{1}$$

Where:

I_p : the primary side current of the power transformer,
I_1 : the secondary side current of CT_1.
N_1 : the number of turns in the secondary side of CT_1

In the same manner for the CT located at the secondary side of the power transformer, the CT secondary current is:

$$I_2 = \frac{I_s}{N_2} \tag{2}$$

Where:

I_s : secondary side current of the power transformer,
I_2 : secondary side current of CT_2.
N_2 : number of turns in the secondary side of CT_2

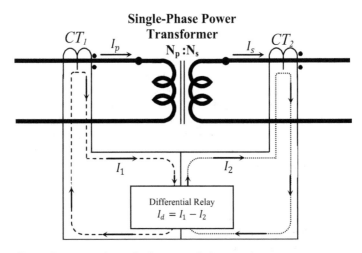

Figure 1. Differential protection for single phase two winding transformer

Since the differential current is: $I_d = I_1 - I_2$, then, from equation (1) and equation (2) the differential current flowing in the relay operating coil current I_d can be calculated as;

$$I_d = \frac{I_p}{N_1} - \frac{I_s}{N_2} \qquad (3)$$

If there is no internal fault occurring within the power transformer protected zone, the currents I_1 and I_2 are assumed equal in magnitude and opposite in direction. That means the differential current $I_d = 0$ as shown in figure 2. The primary and secondary side current of the power transformer are related to each other by equation (4);

$$\frac{I_p}{I_s} = \frac{N_s}{N_p} \qquad (4)$$

Where:

N_p and N_s: primary and secondary side turns of the power transformer, respectively

$\frac{N_p}{N_s}$: power transformer transformation ratio.

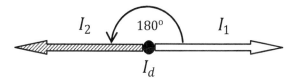

Figure 2. Output currents of the CTs are equal in magnitude and opposite in direction

If there is any fault in the power transformer protected zone, the currents I_1 and I_2 are no longer equal in magnitude and opposite in direction. That means the differential current $I_d = I_d \angle \theta$ has a significant value as shown in figure 3.

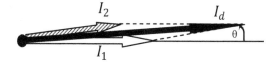

Figure 3. Output currents of the CTs are not equal in magnitude and not opposite in direction

The amount of current $I_d = I_d \angle \theta$ induces the relay operating coil to operate in order to send a trip signal to the circuit breakers to isolate the transformer.

From equation (4) the secondary current with respect to the primary current of the power transformer is [2], [6-7];

$$I_s = \frac{I_p \times N_p}{N_s} \qquad (5)$$

Therefore, by manipulating equations (3) and (5),

$$I_d = \frac{I_p}{N_1} - \frac{I_p \times (N_p/N_s)}{N_2}$$

$$I_d = \frac{I_p}{N_1}\left(1 - \frac{N_p/N_s}{N_2/N_1}\right) \tag{6}$$

$$\lambda = \left(1 - \frac{N_p/N_s}{N_2/N_1}\right)$$

From equation (6) it is obvious that the term λ must be equal to zero in order to make $I_d = 0$

$$\left(1 - \frac{N_p/N_s}{N_2/N_1}\right) = 0$$

$$\frac{N_2}{N_1} = \frac{N_p}{N_s} \tag{7}$$

Equation (7) gives the condition for the security of the differential relay, which means the reciprocal of the ratio of the secondary side turns of the CTs must equal to the turns ratio of the power transformer.

In power transformers, the input power is equal to the output power. However, the voltage and the current in both the primary and secondary sides are different depending on whether the transformer is step up or step down. For instance, if the transformer is step up that means; the input voltage of the power transformer is low and the current is high, meantime the voltage in the secondary side is high and the current is low. This action makes both the input and output power equal. Due to this nature the CTs in the primary and the secondary sides of the power transformer do not have same turn ratio. However, they are carefully selected, in terms of turn ratio and magnetizing characteristics, so that they have the same output current at normal conditions of operations. If identical CTs are not available, the closer ones are chosen and then the mismatch between them is compensated by using the interposing CTs. The interposing CTs can fix the mismatch in the CTs; however they add their own burden to the output of the main CTs.

The same argument is applied for three phase (3ϕ) transformers, except some extra issues may appear in polyphase transformers. Figure 4 shows the schematic diagram of the 3ϕ differential protection.

In some cases, of 3ϕ power transformer connections as shown in figure 5, a $30°$ phase shift between primary and secondary currents is taking place. This phase shift occurs in the Y-Δ or Δ-Y connected transformers due to the transformation of the current from Y-Δ or Δ-Y as illustrated in the figure 4. This phase shift can be corrected easily by connecting the CTs secondary circuits in opposite way to the way that the power transformer phases are connected. I.e. if the transformer windings are connected in Y-Δ the CTs secondary windings should be connected in Δ-Y and vice versa [20]. As shown in figure 4 the relation between the line-to-line voltage (V_{LL}) to the phase voltage (V_{ph}) can explain the phase shift between the Δ-Y transformer connection. The following equation gives the relationship between the line-to-line voltage (V_{LL}) to the phase voltage (V_{ph}) [2], [3], [6], [7]:

$$\frac{V_{ab}}{2} = V_{an} \cos$$

$$\frac{V_{ab}}{2} = V_{an} \frac{\sqrt{3}}{2} \qquad (8)$$

$$V_{ab} = \sqrt{3}\, V_{an}$$

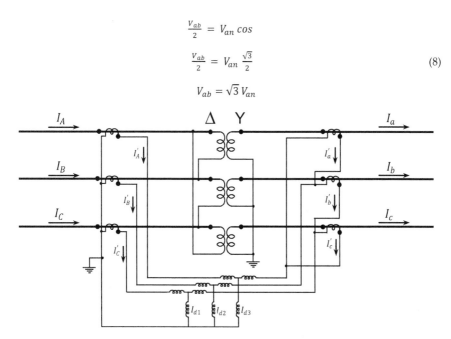

Figure 4. Connection of differential protection of 3-phase Δ-Y transformer

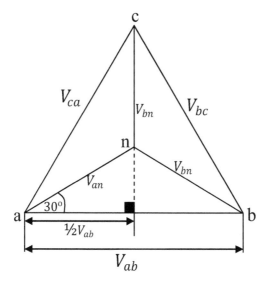

Figure 5. The relationship between line to line voltage and the phase to neutral voltage and the phase shift between them which reflects the phase shift in Y-Δ or Δ-Y connected transformers

3. Differential protection difficulties

Generally, three main difficulties handicap the conventional differential protection. They induce the differential relay to release a false trip signal without the existing of any fault. These complications must be overcome in order to make the differential relay working properly [2], [3]:

- Magnetizing inrush current during initial energization,
- CTs Mismatch and saturation,
- Transformation ratio changes due to Tap changer.

3.1. Magnetizing inrush current

This phenomenon, the transient magnetizing inrush or the exciting current, occurs in the primary side of the transformer whenever the transformer is switched on (energized) and the instantaneous value of the voltage is not at 90^0. At this time, the first peak of the flux wave is higher than the peak of the flux at the steady state condition. This current appears as an internal fault, and it is sensed as a differential current by the differential relay. The value of the first peak of the magnetizing current may be as high as several times the peak of the full load current. The magnitude and duration of the magnetizing inrush current is influenced by many factors, some of these factors are [2], [6], [7];

- The instantaneous value of the voltage waveform at the moment of closing CB,
- The value of the residual (remnant) magnetizing flux,
- The sign of the residual magnetizing flux,
- The type of the iron laminations used in the transformer core,
- The saturation flux density of the transformer core,
- The total impedance of the supply circuit,
- The physical size of the transformer,
- The maximum flux-carrying capability of the iron core laminations,
- The input supply voltage level,

The effect of the inrush current on the differential relay is false tripping the transformer without of any existing type of faults. From the principle of operation of the differential relay, the relay compares the currents coming from both sides of the power transformer as explained above. However, the inrush current is flowing only in the primary side of the power transformer. So that, the differential current will have a significant value due to the existence of current in only one side. Therefore, the relay has to be designed to recognize that this current is a normal phenomenon and to not trip due to this current.

3.2. False trip due to C.T characteristics

The performance of the differential relays depends on the accuracy of the CTs in reproducing their primary currents in their secondary side. In many cases, the primary ratings of the CTs, located in the high voltage and low voltage sides of the power transformer, does not exactly match the power transformer rated currents. Due to this discrepancy, a CTs mismatch takes place, which in turn creates a small false differential current, depending on the amount of this mismatch. Sometimes, this amount of the differential current is enough to operate the differential relay. Therefore, CTs ratio correction has to be done to overcome this CTs mismatch by using interposing CTs of multi taps [8].

Another problem that may face the perfect operation of the CTs is the saturation problem. When saturation happens to one or all CTs at different levels, false differential current appears in the differential relay. This differential current could cause mal-operation of the differential relay. The dc component of the primary side current could produce the worst case of CT saturation. In which, the secondary current contains dc offset and extra harmonics [9], [10].

3.3. False trip due to tap changer

On-Load Tap-Changer (OLTC) is installed on the power transformer to control automatically the transformer output voltage. This device is required wherever there are heavy fluctuations in the power system voltage. The transformation ratio of the CTs can be matched with only one point of the tap-changing range. Therefore, if the OLTC is changed, unbalance current flows in the differential relay operating coil. This action causes CTs mismatches. This current will be considered as a fault current which makes the relay to release a trip signal [11], [12].

4. Digital differential protection

Many digital algorithms have been used so far after the invention of the computer. These algorithms do the same job with different accuracy and speed. The acceptable speed according to IEEE standard for transformer protection is 100 msec. All modern algorithms are faster than this IEEE standard. Nowadays, there are some algorithms performs their function in less than 10 msec. In this chapter, a fast algorithm is introduced. Its speed is in the range of 1 to 15 msec. This algorithm is based on the Fast Fourier algorithm (FFT). This algorithm is not new, however, significant changes has been introduced to make it much faster.

The proposed digital differential relay is designed using a simulation technique in Matlab Simulink environment. The design is implemented to protect the power transformer against internal faults and prevent interruption due to inrush currents.

This algorithm is built on the principle of harmonic-current restraint, where the magnetizing-inrush current is characterized by large harmonic components content that are not noticeably present in fault currents. Due to the saturated condition of the transformer iron, the waveform of the inrush current is highly distorted. The amplitude of the harmonics, compared with the fundamental is somewhere between 30% to 60% and the third harmonic 10% to 30%. The other harmonics are progressively less [3] [6], [13]. Fast Fourier Transform (*FFT*) is used to implement this approach. In general, any periodic signal $f(t)$ can be decomposed to its sine and cosine components as follows:

$$f(t) = \frac{a_0}{2} + \sum_{k=1}^{\infty} C_k \cos(kwt) + S_k \sin(kwt)$$

Where: a_0 is the DC component of the f (t), and C_k, S_k are the cosine and sine coefficients of the frequencies present in $f(t)$, respectively. The discrete forms of the coefficients C_k, S_k are expressed in the following equations:

$$C_k = \frac{2}{N} \sum_{n=1}^{N-1} x(n) \cos\left(\frac{2kwt}{N}\right)$$

$$S_k = \frac{2}{N} \sum_{n=1}^{N-1} x(n) \sin\left(\frac{2kwt}{N}\right)$$

The Fourier harmonic coefficients can be expressed as [13]:

$$F_k = \sqrt{S_k^2 + C_k^2}$$

Where: F_k is the kth harmonic coefficient for k = 1, 2,...,N and $x(n)$ is the signal $f(t)$ in its discrete form. The FFT produces exactly the same results as the DFT; however, the FFT is much faster than DFT, where the speed of calculation is the main factor in this process [13-16].

Fig 6 illustrates the flow chart of the designed digital Fourier Transform based logic technique algorithm. In this algorithm the output currents of the *CTs* undergo over two analysis processes, amplitude comparison process and harmonic content calculation process. The amplitude comparison between the *RMS* values of the *CTs* output currents ($|I_{d1} - I_{d2}|$) is in the left hand side of the flowchart, and the harmonic calculation is in the right hand side of the flowchart.

The software is implemented according to the following steps [15-17]:

Step 1. Reading data from the *CTs*.
Step 2. Data calculation, which is given as follows;

For the amplitude calculation, if the absolute difference ($|I_{d1} - I_{d2}|$) between the *CTs* output currents is greater than zero the logic (1) takes place, which indicates the case of an inrush current or an internal fault. Otherwise, the logic (0) takes place, which indicates a detection of an external fault.

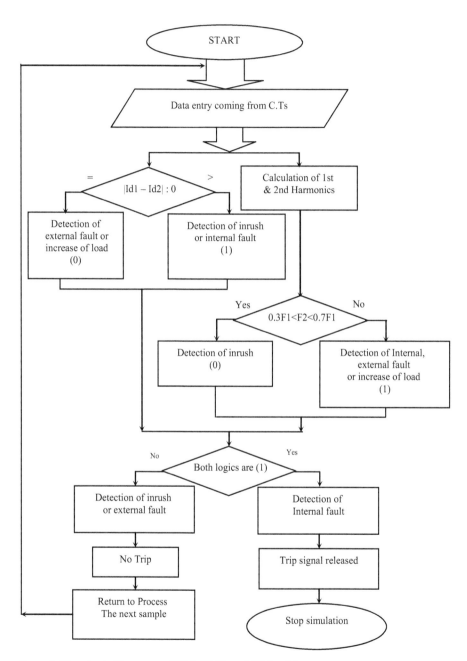

Figure 6. Flow chart of the proposed Digital Differential Relay Scheme

In the meantime, the harmonic calculation is performed. If the percentage value of the second harmonic amplitude is in the range of (0.3 to 0.6) of the fundamental component amplitude, then the logic (0) occurs, that means recognition of inrush current. Otherwise, the logic (1) takes place, which indicates a detection of an internal or external fault.

Step 3. Taking the final decision:

If the logic cases received from both cases (a & b) in step two are both (1), that indicates a detection of an internal fault. Then a trip signal is released to stop the simulation.

For the other logic options of (0,1) means an external fault, (1,0) means an inrush current, or (0,0) indicate an occurrence of an inrush current or an external fault, and the simulation goes back to step two to start the calculation again for the next sample.

5. Implementation of the digital differential protection using matlab

This implementation is done using Matlab/Simulink environment. Figure 7 shows the simulated power system built in Matlab/Simulink environment. In which a three phase, 250MVA, 60Hz, (735/315) kV, Y/Δ power transformer is used in this system. The contents of each designed block are illustrated in separate figs. 8 to 12.

There are some coefficients are kept hidden for the reader to find them. These coefficients can change the behavior of the design.

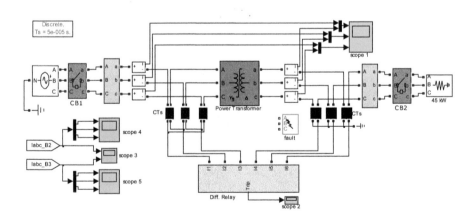

Figure 7. Matlab/Simulink Model of the proposed system

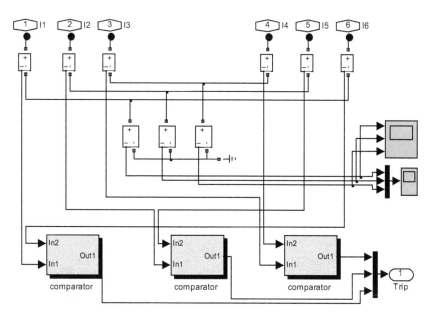

Figure 8. The differential relay block contents

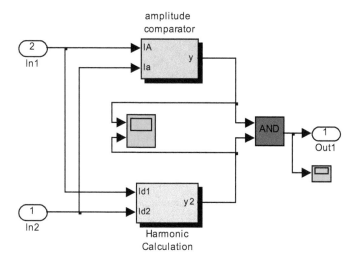

Figure 9. The comparator block contents

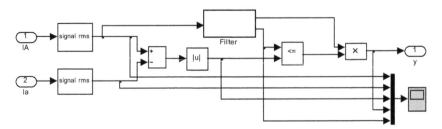

Figure 10. The amplitude comparator block contents

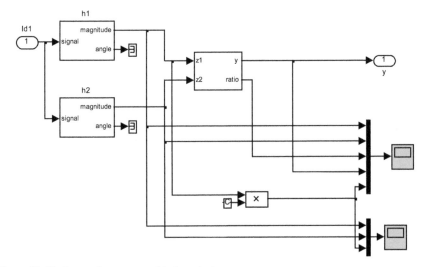

Figure 11. The harmonic comparator block contents

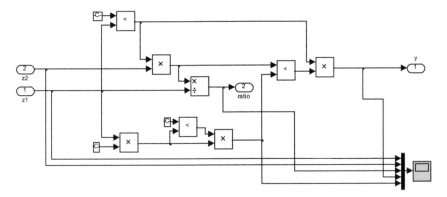

Figure 12. The ratio block contents

6. The results and discussions

The results will be given for different cases:

Case 1: magnetizing inrush current,
Case 2: magnetizing inrush with adding load,
Case 3: Three phase to ground fault at loaded transformer,
Case 4: Phase A to ground external fault at loaded transformer,

Other cases of different types of faults and inrush currents such as single line to ground fault, line-to-line fault, line to line to ground fault and three phase fault in both cases loaded and unloaded transformer are illustrated.

Case 1: Magnetizing inrush current:

In this section of simulation, when the primary side CB1 is closed at 0.1 sec, only the inrush current flows in the primary circuit of the power transformer and no current passes through the power transformer to the secondary side as shown in Fig. 13. The harmonic comparator shows in Fig. 14 that the value of the 2nd harmonic is higher than 0.3 of the fundamental component.

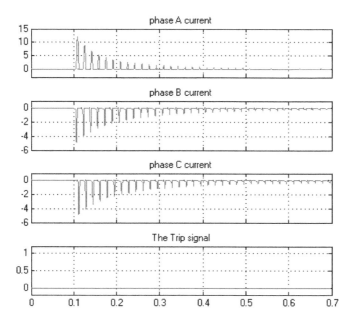

Figure 13. Inrush currents waveforms of the three phases at the primary side of the power transformer.

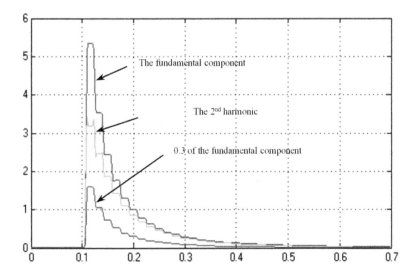

Figure 14. Harmonic comparator result: the 2nd harmonic and the fundamental component for the 1st case.

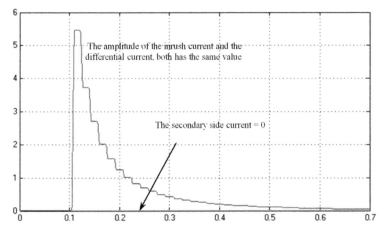

Figure 15. Amplitude comparator results for the 1st case.

In this case the harmonic calculation part released logic (0) but the amplitude comparator showed in Fig. 15 that the differential current is equal to the inrush current, where both curves are drown over each other, then the amplitude comparator release logic (1). For this logic coordination (0,1) no trip signal is released.

Case 2: Magnetizing inrush with adding load:

This test is carried out after the energization of the power transformer by switching ON the CB1 at 0.1sec and CB2 at 0.3 sec from the beginning of the simulation to see the effect of load excursion on the accuracy of the designed approach. Therefore, a 500W resistive load is added to the system at 0.3 sec. Consequently, the inrush current disappeared and load current started to flow in the primary and secondary circuits of the transformer according to the transformation ratio of the power transformer as shown in Fig. 16. However, the amplitude of the output currents of the primary and secondary CTs are equal due to the proper selection of the transformation ratio of the primary and secondary CTs, which can obviously noticed in Fig. 18. Where, before the time 0.3 sec the differential current was equal to the inrush current, but after the swathing ON of the load the differential current went to zero and the primary and secondary currants became equal.

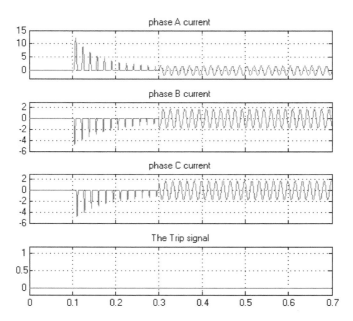

Figure 16. Normal load current starts flowing at 0.3sec.

As shown in Fig. 17, after the switching of CB2, the value of the 2nd harmonic become lower than 0.3 of the fundamental component. Accordingly, the harmonic calculation part released logic (1) but the amplitude comparator released logic (0). Consequently, for this logic coordination (1,0) no trip signal is released. Figure 18 shows the amplitude comparator results.

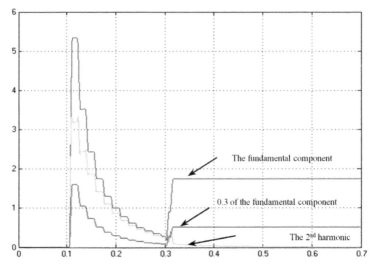

Figure 17. 2nd harmonic and the fundamental component for the 2nd case.

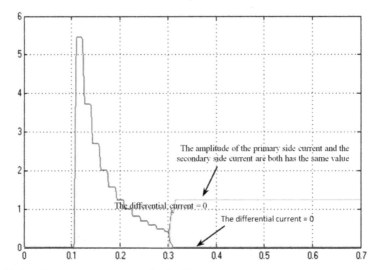

Figure 18. Amplitude comparator results for the 2nd case.

Case 3: Three phase to ground fault at loaded transformer:

In this section, a three phase to ground fault is created to test the security of the algorithm. After the switching of CB1 at 0.1sec, an internal fault is created at 0.5 sec at the secondary side of the power transformer by connecting the three phases A, B and C of the secondary side of the power transformer to the ground. In this case, a significant increase of the primary current takes place due to the fault occurrence inside the protected zone at 0.5 sec as shown in Fig. 19. The relay detected this increase using the harmonic and amplitude comparators and realized it as an internal fault. Consequently the transformer is isolated from the grid. Also it is obvious from Fig. 20 that the relay has released a trip signal after 0.57 msec after the occurrence of the fault, which can be considered as a very good speed to isolate the transformer.

As shown in Fig. 21, after the occurrence of the fault at time 0.5 sec, the value of the 2nd harmonic increased during the transient time and then decreased rapidly to a value lower than 0.3 of the fundamental component once the steady state is achieved. Accordingly, the harmonic calculation part released logic (1). Also from Fig. 22 which shows the result of the amplitude comparator the value of the differential current is no longer equal to zero. Accordingly the amplitude comparator released logic (1). Therefore, for this logic coordination (1,1) a trip signal is released in order to isolate the power transformer from the grid.

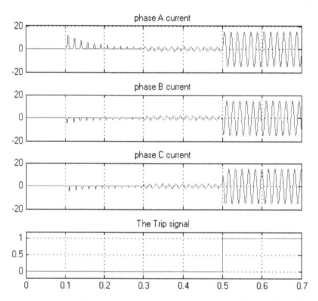

Figure 19. Increase of phase A, B & C currents due to the occurrence of the fault at 0.5 sec for loaded transformer

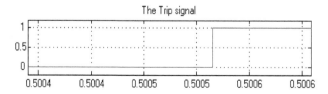

Figure 20. Zoomed trip signal, trip time is around 0.57 msec

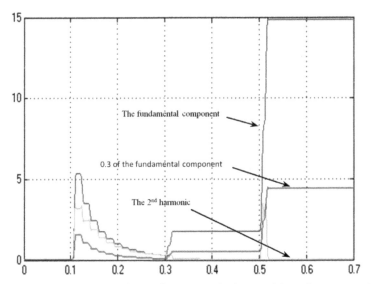

Figure 21. 2nd harmonic and the fundamental component for the case of three phase to ground fault at loaded transformer.

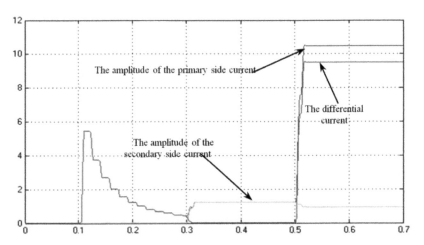

Figure 22. Amplitude comparator result for the 3rd case.

Case 4: Phase A to ground external fault at loaded transformer.

This case is similar to case 2, where the occurrence of the fault current outside the protected zone leaded to the increase of fault currents in both sides of the power transformer. Therefore the relay considered this case as a sever increase in load currents. Fig. 23 shows the increase in phase A currant and no trip signal is released

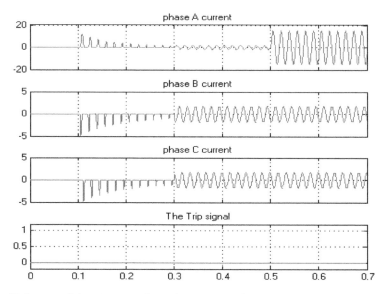

Figure 23. Increase of phase A current due to the occurrence of the fault at 0.5 sec for loaded transformer

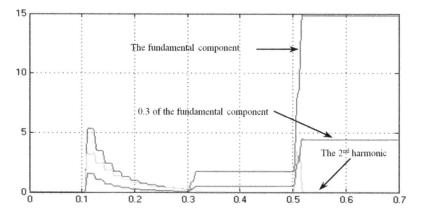

Figure 24. 2nd harmonic and the fundamental component for the Case for the 4th case.

As illustrated in Fig. 24, after the occurrence of the external fault at 0.5 sec, the value of the 2nd harmonic decreased to a value less than 0.3 of the fundamental component. Accordingly, the harmonic calculation part released logic (1) but the amplitude comparator released logic (0) because the differential current is almost zero as it can be seen from Fig. 25. Consequently, for this logic coordination (1,0) no trip signal is released.

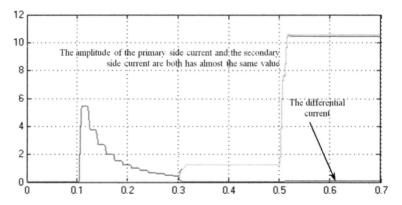

Figure 25. Amplitude comparator result for the 4th case.

Similarly, the relay is tested for all other cases of different types of faults such as single line to ground, line to line, line to line to ground and three phase faults in both cases loaded and unloaded transformer. In all cases the relay has successfully released a trip signal in each case. The results of some of these different types of faults are shown in Figs (26 - 30).

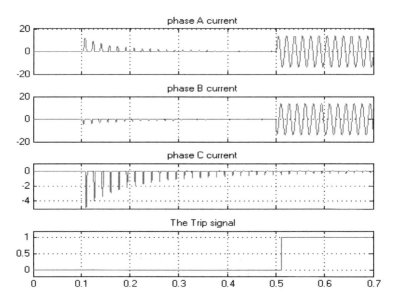

Figure 26. Increase of phase A & B currents due to the occurrence of the fault at 0.5 sec, for unloaded transformer

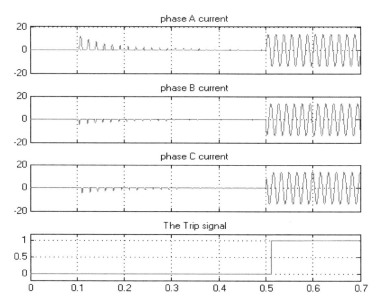

Figure 27. Increase of phase A , B & C currents due to the occurrence of the fault at 0.5 sec, for unloaded transformer

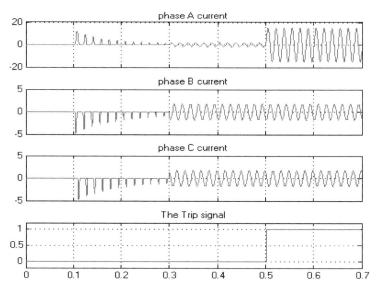

Figure 28. Increase of phase A current due to the occurrence of the fault at 0.5 sec for loaded transformer

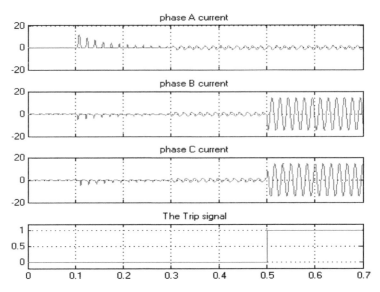

Figure 29. Increase of phase B & C currents due to the occurrence of the fault at 0.5 sec for loaded transformer

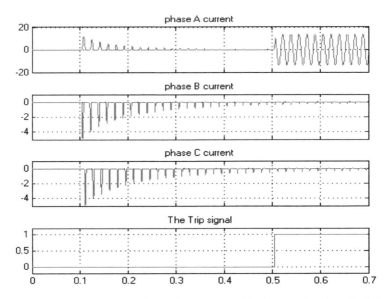

Figure 30. Increase of phase A current due to the occurrence of the fault at 0.5 sec, for unloaded transformer

7. Summary of all tested cases

case type	Relay response	Trip signal release time (m sec)	
		Loaded	unloaded
Phase A to ground	Trip	1.7	4.7
Phase B to ground	Trip	0.6	12
Phase C to ground	Trip	0.6	15
Phase A to phase B	Trip	0.8	12.2
Phase B to phase C	Trip	0.6	12.2
Phase A to phase C	Trip	1.3	14.6
Phase A to phase B to ground	Trip	0.6	12
Phase B to phase C to ground	Trip	0.6	12
Phase A to phase C to ground	trip	0.6	13.2
Three phase to ground	Trip	0.6	0.57
Three phase	Trip	0.6	12
Inrush current	Restrain	No trip signal	
Load current	Restrain	No trip signal	
External fault	Restrain	No trip signal	

Table 1. Summary of the performance of the designed differential relay at different types of disturbances that may occur to the power transformer

8. Conclusions

This chapter is talking about the implementation and simulation of a small power system with a differential protection for the power transformer. The implementation is shown in step by step. This simulation is tested for various cases and for all cases it gave satisfactory results. All the tests gave satisfactory results. There are some difficulties are faced in the implantation of this system such as the lack of some toolbox in the Sim-power-system. For example, there is no current transformer in the toolbox. In this case, there are two choices to solve this problem. The first one is to use a regular single phase and make some changes in its specification to fit the current transformer specifications. The second one is to use a current measurement, but this one will not simulate the problems of the CTs.

Author details

Adel Aktaibi and M. Azizur Rahman
Memorial University of Newfoundland, Canada

9. References

[1] M. A. Rahman and B. Jeyasurya, "A state-of-the-art review of transformer protection algorithms", IEEE Trans. Power Delivery, vol. 3, pp. 534–544, Apr. 1988.

[2] P. M. Anderson, "Power System Protection", Piscataway, NJ: IEEE Press, 1999.

[3] C. D. Hayward, "Harmonic-Current Restrained Relays for Transformer Differential Protection", AIEE trans., vol. 60, pp 276, 1941.

[4] M. S. Sachdev, T. S. Sidhu, H. C. Wood, "A Digital Relaying Algorithm for Detecting Transformer Winding Faults", IEEE Transactions on Power Deliver, vol. 4, No. 3. July 1989.

[5] K. Yabe, "Power Differential Method for Discrimination between Fault and Magnetizing Inrush Current in Transformers", IEEE Transactions on Power Delivery, Vol. 12, No. 3, July 1997.

[6] A. R. Van C. Warrington, "Protective Relays Their Theory and Practice", vol. 1, Chapman Hall Press, 3rd edition, 1985.

[7] J. Duncan Glover and Mulukutla Sarma, "power system analysis and design", PWS publishing company, 2nd ed., 1994.

[8] AREVA, "KBCH 120, 130, 140 Transformer Differential Protection Relays Service Manual", KBCH/EN M/G11, France, 2001.

[9] W. Rebizant, T. Hayder, L. Schiel, "Prediction of C.T Saturation Period for Differential Relay Adaptation Purposes", web site, 2004.

[10] A. G. Zocholl, G. Benmouyal and H. J. Altuve, "Performance Analysis of Traditional and Improved Transformer Differential Protective Relays", web site, 2000.

[11] Y. Marty, W. Smolinski, and S. Sivakumar, "Design of a digital protection scheme for power transformer using optimal state observers," IEE Proceedings Vol. 135,pt. C, No.3 May 1988.

[12] ABB relays, "Power transformer protection application guide", AG03-5005E, 1998.

[13] M. A. Rahman, Y.V.V.S. Murthy and Ivi Hermanto, "Digital Protective Relay for Power Transformers", U.S. Patent No. 5,172,329, December 1992.

[14] P.K. Dash and M.A. Rahman, "A New Algorithm for Digital Protection of Power Transformer", Canadian Electrical Association Transactions, Vol. 26, Part 4, 1987, pp. 1-8, (87-SP-169), 1987.

[15] A. Gangopadhay, M.A. Rahman, B. Jeyasurya, "Simulation of Magnetizing Inrush Currents in Single Phase Transformers", International Journal of Energy Systems, Vol. 7, No. 1, 1987, pp. 34-38.

[16] M.A. Rahman and A. Gangopadhay, "Digital Simulation of Magnetizing Inrushes Currents in Three-Phase Transformers", IEEE Transactions on Power Delivery, Vol. PWRD-1, No. 4, October 1986, pp. 235-242. (Over 100 citations)

[17] Adel Aktaibi and M. A. Rahman, "A Software Design Technique for Differential Protection of Power Transformers", International Electric Machines & Drives Conference (IEMDC 2011), IEEE, 15-18 May 2011, Page(s): 1456–1461.

Chapter 10

PH Control Using MATLAB

Mostefa Ghassoul

Additional information is available at the end of the chapter

1. Introduction

Wastewater neutralization plays an important part in a wastewater treatment process. It provides the optimum environment for microorganism activity between pH 6.5 and 7.5{1}, and the right water discharge to the public sewage as mandated by the Department of Environment of between pH 5 and 9 (Environmental Quality Act, 1974) {2}. Wastewater of pH below 4.5 and above 9 may greatly reduce the activity of the microorganisms which treat the water and may not support their life at all {3}.

For a number of years, Hydrogen chloride (HCL) acid was used in wastewater treatment facilities to control alkalinity. It's a product that works, but it also has many potential problems. HCL acid can be difficult to apply and control. Correcting the pH of alkaline wastewater is usually required either for discharge to sewer, in preparation to further biological, physical/chemical treatment or direct discharge to the environment. Strong acids such as hydrochloric acid have traditionally been used to neutralize alkaline waste streams prior to discharge {4}.

On the control side, It is well known that controlling pH is very difficult, and specially neutralization in industry, due to the high non linearity of the system. In fact the pH dynamics are not only time variant, but change with each pH value and becomes oscillatory around the 7 mark as well. Even by placing the pH probe in the proximity of a mixer or in a turbulent flow could result in a big change in the pH. It has been reported in literature that researchers have been trying for ages to control the pH with a tuned classical PID controller with many additional restrictions; but experience has shown that this is not satisfactory because of the changing of dynamics hence the transfer function where when the PID is tuned for a certain characteristics, it becomes completely un-tuned for the next. To overcome this problem, we (here at the chemical engineering department University of Bahrain) have engaged in finding a solution to the problem. One of the option possible is the use of fuzzy logic. For the last fifty years, since Zadeh {5} introduces his famous paper on fuzzy logic and control, fuzzy logic control has been widely implemented successfully in many industrial applications ranging from home appliances such as washing machines to heavy industries such as loading and unloading very heavy loads in ports efficiently by minimizing the action time. Certainly its use in controlling pH is feasible. This is due two reasons:

1. The fuzzy control does not require any transfer function, nor any tedious mathematical analysis. So there is no need to model the system continuously, with each pH space, so the change of the pH characteristic does not influence the control strategy.

2. The membership space of the pH is restricted between zero and fourteen where pH between zero and seven is acid and between seven and fourteen is base. This space is divided into a limited number of memberships, and the control for each membership could be easily tuned separately. To apply this strategy we had to look for the best possible solution. And luckily, we find the solution in MATLAB, through SIMULINK fuzzy control blocksets. The choice of SIMULINK fuzzy control blocksets was considered very carefully for several reasons.

    1. The huge number of rule one could implement. In fact, we have currently applied more than 125 rules and still the margin is open.

    2. The simplicity of MATLAB fuzzy control, where the SIMULINK blocksets could be used directly. This saves a lot of computing time. On top of that, those blocksets are already optimized.

    3. Though MATLAB was originally designed as a simulator platform, for the last few years, several companies have developed several interfacing cards to interface online different processes to the MATLAB platform, such as HUMUSOFT MF 624 multifunction I/O card and National Instrument card NI PCI-6221 data acquisition card. Hardware interface to the process in question, real time, where this has been done with a relative ease thank's to National Instrument NI PCI- 6221 data acquisition card.

But before discussing how SIMULINK is used, we first have to highlight the pH apparatus used. Luckily, we found an obsolete pH control apparatus made by ARMFIELD UK (PC5 PH control RIG) which was made back in the early eightees, with the following components: framework assembly complete with pump set, two storage tanks, two flow meters, with a completely irreparable pH probe, pneumatically operated valve driven with a current to pressure converter, air filter regulator, glass vessel, clamps , stirrer together with obsolete three term PID electronic controller, slide indicator and chart recorder. The control was developed around a dedicated classical PID controller where the user only sets up the PID parameters through a number of knobs. The response is either given through slide indicator or chart recorder. (see figure (1)). This procedure was no use, where advanced control is not possible. So this controller was completely isolated and replaced by a modern SIMULINK based controller built for this purpose. The process is as follows. Two tanks are used ; one filled with an acidic liquid and the other with base liquid. The acidic liquid is controlled manually and the base liquid is controlled through a 3 to 15 PSI proportional control valve. The pressure is generated by controlling a pressure gauge through a current to pressure converter. Unfortunately, the output from MATLAB to the acquisition card is only in volts, whereas the valve driving signal is in milliamperes. This has lead to the design of a 0 - 5V voltage to 4-20mA current converter to drive the valve. The control voltage is generated by SIMULINK as a result of the control strategy developed around the fuzzy control blocksets. The control signal produced by the blockset is outputted through the NI card to the hardware. The beauty of this control is that the process could be monitored through MATLAB virtual instrument online.

1.1. PH control

PH is an important variable in production fields such as chemical and petrochemical industries where tons of toxic products are pumped into environment due to contaminated chemical waste. Most of those product wastes are mainly alkaline. This will certainly harms the environment in particular sea life as well as agricultural products which in turn reflects on the human life quality. So it is essential to treat those wastes to neutralize their pH to an acceptable level, ideally around 7. So what is pH. The PH of a solution is defined as the negative of the logarithm to the base of 10 of the hydrogen ion concentration.

$$PH = -\log 10 \left[H + \right]$$

Most of the factories waste is mainly alkaline; this certainly harms the environment by poisoning life onshore or offshore, including humans either through contaminated food and water or through breathing. This is witnessed by the increased rate of cancer cases in the world. So it is a must to neutralize the industry waste by neutralizing the pH. This is quantitavely done by bringing the pH to around the magic value of seven. In industry, the pH could vary between any value between 2 and 10. Here in our lab, we are using PC5 Armfield obsolete PH control apparatus. Its PI & D diagram is shown in figure(1).

The neutralization process basically follows the following reaction:

$$(NCL + NAOH \rightarrow NACL + H_2O)$$

This reaction results in salt and water which do not present any harm to nature. (The process system is shown in figure(2)). The system basically consists of two liquid circuits; one feeding the acidic substance and the other feeds the base liquid. The added liquid is controlled by a proportional control valve whereas the base liquid is manually operated.

To make the mixture homogeneous, a variable speed mixer is used. The pH is picked up with the aid of a probe placed into the mixing vessel close to the outlet. Unlike the PID controller where many restrictions are imposed, fuzzy controller only requires the probe to be out off the flow turbulence way next the outlet. The probe reading is conditioned and fed to the controller through the NI PCI-6221 card of the E series, and at the same time, fed to the pH meter for confirmation. The card has 16 analogue input channels which could be connected as differential or single ended, sixteen bit resolution and two output analogue channels. The signal conditioning is no more than an instrumentation amplifier (figure(3)) of type INA114. This type of amplifier is very precise. The output of the amplifier is then fed to

NI card, to be read into SIMULINK to be analyzed using the fuzzy controller. Once the signal has been treated, the resulting control variable is outputted through the output port of the NI card to drive the control valve. Unfortunately this output is in volts, whereas the driving signal required by the control valve is in milliamperes(current). This requires the design of a voltage to current converter. It should be mentioned here that the control valve used is of proportional type where it closes linearly from fully closed to fully open by using a current to pressure converter which converters a 4-20mA to 3-15PSI pressure. The Valve controls the acid flow rate of type HCL. So by varying the valve opening, the flow rate changes so does the pH. The base flow is manually controlled. The output of the pH sensor is fed to an instrumentation amplifier as mentioned earlier, to condition it, and at the same time to the NI6221 acquisition card, through which it is read into the SIMULINK fuzzy controller. The output of the controller is applied to the voltage to current converter, which in turn drives the current to pressure converter. This action adjusts the flow rate of the HCL, thus the input to the controller is the pH reading of the waist (NAOH) which is compared against the required set point. At the same time the output obtained from the controller is used to control the valve. (1- convert the output voltage to current. 2- convert the current to pressure which drives the valve) and the valve in turn controls the percentage the valve opening to control the HCL flow rate. This output tends to maintain the pH value of the waist (NAOH) to a target value.

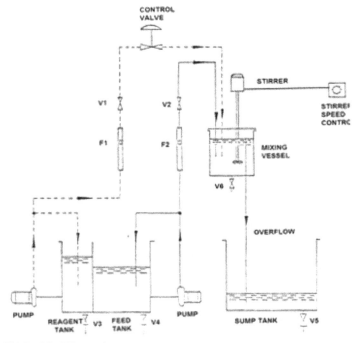

Figure 1. PI & D of the PH control system

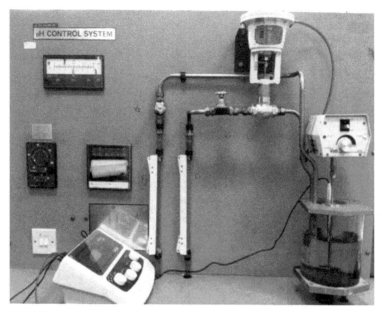

Figure 2. The PH control system

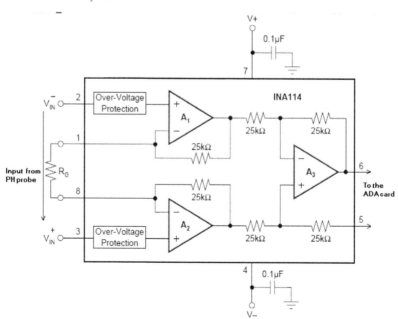

Figure 3. Signal amplifier of type INA114

2. Data acquisition

The National Instrument Data Acquisition Toolbox™ provides functions for connecting MATLAB® to data acquisition hardware. The toolbox supports a variety of DAQ hardware.

With it, one could configure data acquisition hardware to read data into MATLAB or SIMULINK for immediate analysis. One can also send out data over analogue or digital output channels provided by data acquisition hardware. Depending on which card is used, one can configure several channels, as input or output, digital or analogue. The card is interfaced to the process through a screw type connectors SCB-68 Quick Reference Label. Figure(4) shows the real connector board.

Figure 4. Interfacing connecting card to PCI 6221

Data Acquisition Toolbox lets you make a variety of measurements directly to MATLAB or SIMULINK, without the need to convert the data, so one can directly read the pH from the probe through the signal conditioning circuitry. In our case, only analogue input channel0 and output channel0 are used.

2.1. Voltage to current converter "V/I" circuit

A voltage to current converter is basically a circuit which delivers a constant current with a variable voltage. The voltage changes with the change of load. The circuit used here is the XTR105 from Texas Instruments, which converts the 0 to 5 volts to a 4 to 20 milliamperes through the setting of the gain resistor R_G. This is the perfect signal to drive the control valve. R_G, the gain resistor is given by:

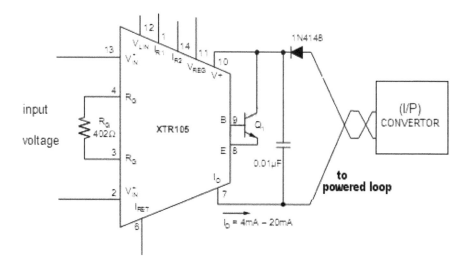

Figure 5. Voltage to current circuit

$$R_G = \frac{2R_1\left(R_2 + R_Z\right) - 4\left(R_2 R_Z\right)}{R_2 - R_1}$$

And the load current I_0 is given by:

$$I_O = 4mA + V_{IN} \times \left(40/R_G\right)$$

Where V_{IN} is the input differential voltage in volts applied between pin 13 and pin2 and R_G is the gain resistor in Ohms. It could be noticed that with no input voltage, the output current is 4mA. Transistor Q_1 conducts the majority of the signal dependent 4-20mA loop current. Using an external transistor isolates the majority of the power dissipation from the precision input and reference circuitry of the XTR105, maintaining excellent accuracy.

The output current of the XTR105 is directly fed to current to pressure converter (I/P) which in turn controls the opening and closing of the control valve.

2.2. Control valve

The valve is opened and closed according to controlling action according to the added desirable HCL solution. The calibration of the valve opening to the input current is shown in table(1); and Its behavior is shown in figure (6). It is clear that the relationship is linear.

Voltage	Current	Opening Valve (%)
0	-1	100 %
:	7.2	80 %
2	10.4	50 %
3	13.6	40 %
4	16.8	20 %
5	20	0 %

Table 1. Output current in terms of input voltage

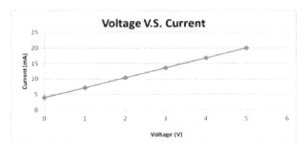

Figure 6. Voltage to current conversion

2.3. Software

After discussing the hardware required and the calibration of the equipment, we devote the rest of this chapter to the software development. In this project we develop the pH control strategy using SIMULINK fuzzy controller and compare it with the PID controller using different currently available tuning techniques. But before going into that, let's see first the behaviour of the pH.

2.3.1. PH behaviour

Before the fuzzy controller is discussed, a major problem inherent into the pH is highlighted. That is the severe non linearity inherent into the pH . Though the PH changes linearly from zero to two and from nine to fourteen, but unfortunately, it oscillates between two and nine. This is known as titration curve. This renders any linear control strategy inefficient, including the three term controller. This explains the complete deficiency of the PID controller, no matter how small is the gain chosen. (See figure (7)).

Figure (8) shows online titration curve. When reagent flow first starts, the pH only changes minimally. This results in a low process gain. But, as more reagent is added, the pH suddenly changes by a large amount, resulting in a high process gain. This titration curve shows the degree of difficulty of controlling the pH . So due to this high non linearity, it is extremely difficult to use any linear technique to control the pH . This has open the door to look at other alternatives, one of them is the use of fuzzy control as it was mentioned earlier.

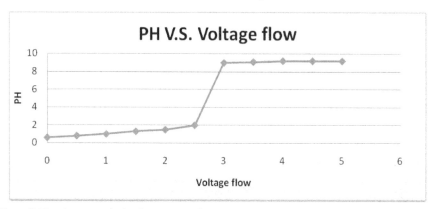

Figure 7. Titration curve obtained experimentally

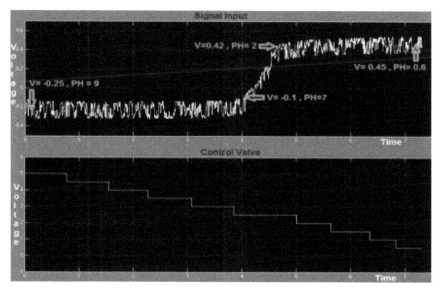

Figure 8. Titration curve test online

It is also worth mentioning here that the relationship between the output voltage and the pH is linear, where a cretin voltage corresponds to a cretin pH level. This is shown in figure (9). This curve has been obtained experimentally. It shows that the output voltage varies between -0.5V and 0.5V for full pH swing. The relationship is given by:

$$Y = -0.0126X + 7.0119$$

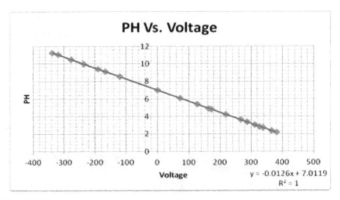

Figure 9. PH vs. Voltage

2.4. MATLAB

MATLAB is a high-performance language for technical computing where it integrates computation, visualization, and programming in an easy-to-use environment where problems and solutions are expressed in familiar mathematical notation. In Addition it has easy to use drivers to interface applications through standard interfacing cards such as NI-PCI 6221 card. On top of that the MATLAB SIMULINK platform incorporates a wide range of signal processing tools. This include easy to use fuzzy control block sets.

2.5. Configuration of acquisition card NI-PCI 6221 using SIMULINK

After MATLAB is installed, together with NI DAQmax drivers, the data acquisition card is configured. This is summarized as shown in the following slides. (Refer to figures from 10.a to 10.c).

A

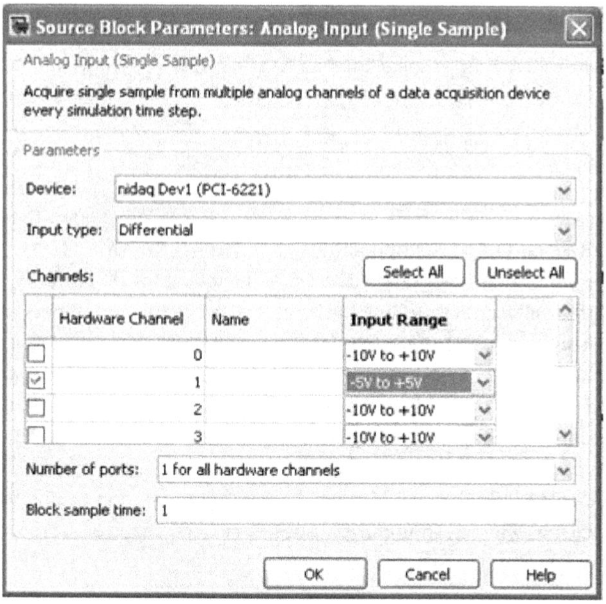

B

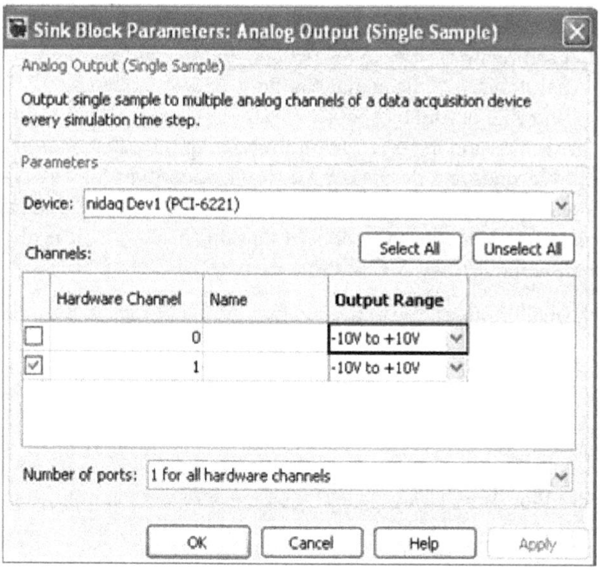

C

Figure 10. a: configure Parameters, b: configure input, c: configure output

2.5.1. PID control

The three term controller (Proportional-Integral-Deriavative) is well defined as:

$$u(t) = K\left(e(t) + \frac{1}{T_i}\int_0^t e(\tau)d\tau + T_d \frac{de(t)}{dt} \right)$$

Where e(t) is the error signal, which represents the difference between the desired value known a set point SP and the measured variable MV. So e(t) =SP –MV. T_i is the integral time constant, T_d is the derivative time constant and K is the loop gain. So basically the role of this controller is to force the output to follow the input, as fast as the parameters permit, with an acceptable overshoot and without steady state error. This requires very careful choosing of the parameters (known as tuning) with a considerable gain without driving the system into non stability. The PID controller algorithm is used for the control of almost all loops in the process industries, and is also the basis for many advanced control algorithms and strategies. In order for control loops to work properly, the PID loop must be properly tuned. Standard methods for tuning loops and criteria for judging the loop tuning have been used for many years such as Ziegler, though new ones have been reported in recent literature to be used on modern digital control systems.

2.5.1.1. PID tuning

- When one wants to find the parameters of PID control he needs first the transfer function for his process. G. Shinskey and J. Gerry (6) have described the pH tuning technique after setting up a series of restrictions summarized as follows((figure(11)):
- Let the pH signal stabilize in the manual mode
- Decrease the controller output by about 10%
- Wait about 15 seconds and increase the controller output by 20% of its original value.
- Wait another 15 seconds and decrease the controller output by 10% of its original value.
- Let the pH signal re-stabilize. Analysis software processes the data to optimal PID tuning variables. It could be clearly noticed that this method is near to an offline more than to online technique.

This results in the smallest upset due to the fact that the net change in the amount of reagent added is zero.

From figure(11), by reducing the control valve opening by 30% (step response), the pH response could be represented by a first order system plus a time delay model (FOPTD). The following could be noticed:

For this First Order Plus Time Delay (FOPTD) model, we note the following characteristics of its step response:

1. The response attains 63.2% of its final response at time, $t = \tau + \theta$.
2. The line drawn tangent to the response at maximum slope $(t = \theta)$ intersects the y/KM=1 line at $(t = \tau + \theta)$.

3.   The step response is essentially complete at t=5τ. In other words, the settling time is
     t$_s$=5τ.

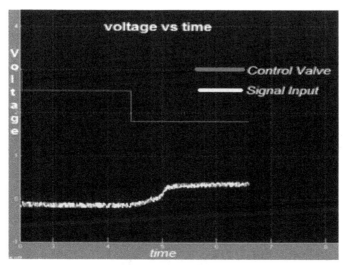

Figure 11. PH with small disturbance on the flow rate

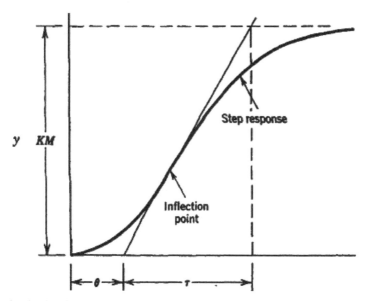

Figure 12. Graphical analysis of to pbtain parameters of FOPTD

From pervious steps the transfer function is:

$$TF = \frac{-4.67e^{-0.916}}{0.4s+1}$$

In the next section, we discuss different tuning methods to determine the PID parameters.

2.5.1.2. ITEA technique

Integral of the time –weighted absolute error (ITEA). ITEA criterion penalizes errors that persist for long period of time.

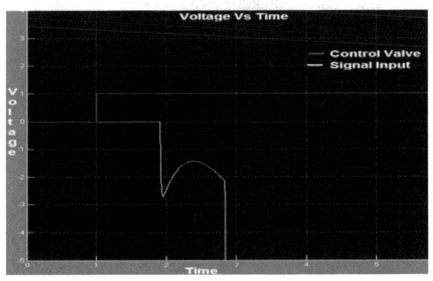

Figure 13. ITEA SIMULINK test

PROPOTIONAL:

$$Y = A\left(\frac{\theta}{\tau}\right)^B = 0.965\left(\frac{0.916}{0.41}\right)^{-0.85} = 0.488$$

$$KK_C = 0.488$$

$$K_C = \frac{0.488}{0.476} = -0.1045$$

INTEGRAL:

$$Y = A + B\left(\frac{\theta}{\tau}\right) = 0.796 - 0.1465\left(\frac{0.916}{0.41}\right) = 0.469$$

$$\frac{\tau}{\tau_I} = 0.469 \tau_I = \frac{0.4}{0.469} = 0.876$$

DERIVATIVE:

$$Y = A\left(\frac{\theta}{\tau}\right)^B = 0.308\left(\frac{0.916}{0.41}\right)^{0.929} = 0.649$$

$$\frac{\tau_D}{\tau} = 0.649$$

$$\tau_D = 0.649 \times 0.4 = 0.267$$

PID equation is:

$$PID = -0.1045\left(1 + \frac{1}{0.876s} + 0.267s\right)$$

2.5.1.3. IMC

More comprehensive method model design is the Integral Model Control (IMC).

PROPOTIONAL:

$$KK_C = \frac{\tau + \dfrac{\theta}{2}}{\tau_c + \dfrac{\theta}{2}} = \frac{0.4 + \dfrac{0.916}{2}}{1 + \dfrac{0.916}{2}} = 0.588$$

$$K_C = \frac{0.858}{-4.67} = -0.126$$

INTEGRAL:

$$\tau_I = \tau + \frac{\theta}{2} = 0.4 + \frac{0.916}{2} = 0.858$$

DERIVATIVE:

$$\tau_D = \frac{\tau\theta}{2\tau + \theta} = \frac{0.4 \times 0.916}{2 \times 0.4 + 0.916} = 0.2136$$

PID equation is:

$$PID = -0.126\left(1 + \frac{1}{0.858s} + 0.2136s\right)$$

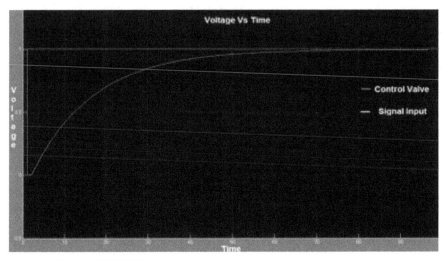

Figure 14. IMC using SIMULINK test

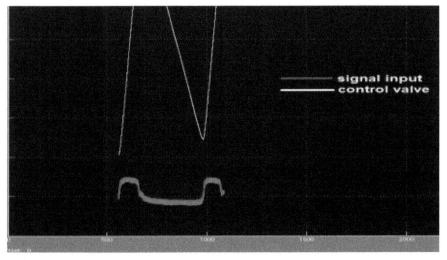

Figure 15. IMC online test

2.5.1.4. Self tuning

The SIMULINK is used to tune the PID (refer to figure(16)). The following transfer function of the self tuning PID was obtained:

$$PID = -0.16877\left(1 + \frac{1}{-0.1335s} + 0.0329s\right)$$

From figure (13-18), it could be easily noticed that neither technique, when applied to the real system, they have all produced unsatisfactory result. In fact, the best one is the self tuning, yet it has produced an oscillatory response. This has been reflected on the valve opening. (Refer to fig(18)). This is due to the fact that there are three gains. So any small change in the input results in a large change in the output. And this explains the behaviour of the titration curve. This has lead us to look for a non linear controller to control the system. This is the fuzzy logic control which is the subject of the next part.

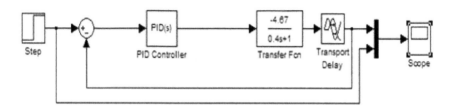

Figure 16. SIMULINK for Parameters

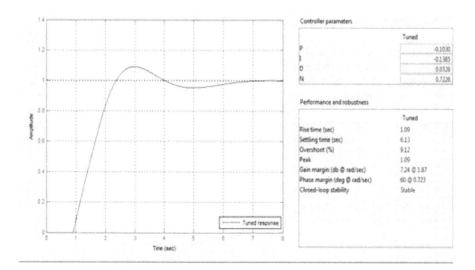

Figure 17. Self turning using SIMULINK simulation

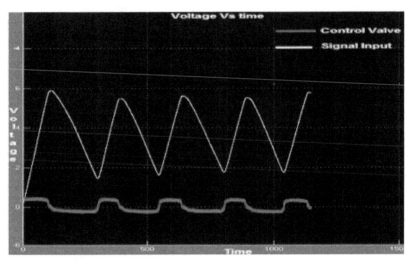

Figure 18. Self tunung online test

3. Fuzzy logic control

3.1. Introduction

In any standard book on fuzzy control, fuzzy logic control is defined to be a practical alternative for a variety of challenging control applications since it provides a convenient method for constructing non-linear controllers via the use of heuristic information. Since heuristic information may come from an operator who has acted as "a human in the loop" controller for a process. In the fuzzy control design methodology, a set of rules on how to control the process is written down and then it is incorporated into a fuzzy controller that emulates the decision making process of the human. In other cases, the heuristic information may come from a control engineer who has performed extensive mathematical modelling, analysis and development of control algorithms for a particular process. The ultimate objective of using fuzzy control is to provide a user-friendly formalism for representing and implementing the ideas we have about how to achieve high performance control. Apart from being a heavily used technology these days, fuzzy logic control is simple, effective and efficient. In this section, the structure, working and design of a fuzzy controller is discussed in detail through an in-depth analysis of the development and functioning of a fuzzy logic pH controller.

The general block diagram of a fuzzy controller is shown in figure (19). The controller is composed of four elements:

- A Rule Base
- An Inference Mechanism
- A Fuzzification Interface
- A Defuzzification Interface

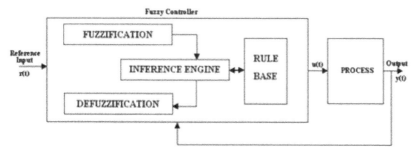

Figure 19. Fuzzy Controller

RULE BASE

This is a set of "If ……..then….." rules which contains a fuzzy logic quantification of the expert's linguistic description of how to achieve good control.

INFERENCE MECHANISM

This emulates the expert's decision making in interpreting and applying knowledge about how best to control the plant.

FUZZIFICATION INTERFACE

This converts controller inputs into information that the inference mechanism can easily use to activate and apply rules.

DEFUZZIFICATION INTERFACE

It converts controller inputs into information that the inference mechanism converts into actual inputs for the process.

SELECTION OF INPUTS AND OUTPUTS

It should be made sure that the controller will have the proper information available to be able to make good decisions and have proper control inputs to be able to steer the system in the directions needed to be able to achieve high-performance operation.

The fuzzy controller is to be designed to automate how a human expert who is successful at this task would control the system. Such a fuzzy controller can be successfully developed using high-level languages like C, Fortran, etc. Packages like MATLAB® also support Fuzzy Logic.

Fuzzy Sets and Membership Function

Given a linguistic variable Ui with a linguistic value Aij and membership function μ Aij(Ui) that maps Ui to [0,1], a 'fuzzy set is defined as

$$Aij = \left\{ \left(Ui, \mu \, Aij \left(Ui \right) \right); Ui \, \varepsilon \, \upsilon i \right\}$$

The above written concept can be clearly understood by going through the following example. Suppose we assign Ui="PH" and linguistic value A11="base", then A11 is a fuzzy set whose membership function describes the degree of certainty that the numeric value of the temperature, Ui ε υi, possesses the property characterized by A11. This is made even clearer by the fig (20).

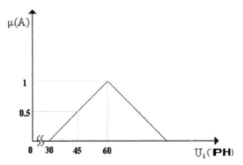

Figure 20. Membership Function

In the above example, the membership function chosen is of triangular form. There are many other membership functions like Gaussian, Trapezoidal, Sharp peak, Skewed etc. Depending on the application and choice of the designer, one could choose the shape which suits his application. Figure(21) shows just few.

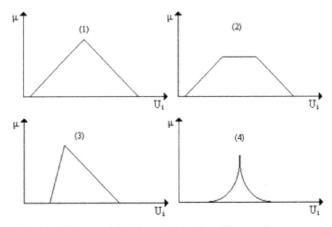

Figure 21. 1)Triangular, 2)Trapezoidal, 3)Skewed triangular, 4)Sharp peak

In the project in hand, the fuzzy controller has two inputs, the first one is the signal from the pH transmitter and the other one is the set point. The controller has a single output which goes through saturation, Quantizer and Weighted moving average. The saturation limiter is used to protect against over range of control valve and the Quantizer and Weighted moving average are used to hold the control valve(figure (22)).

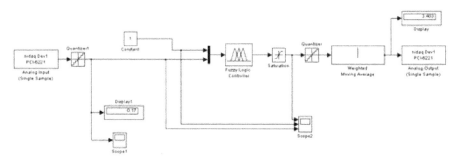

Figure 22. SIMULINK block diagram of the PH controller

A detailed description of the design and functioning of the fuzzy controller is given in the following section. The different sections in the fuzzy controller used in this PH controller are:

- Fuzzification Section
- Rule Base
- Inference Mechanism
- Defuzzification Section

3.2. Fuzzification section

The variables pH, set point and percentage of opening are selected for Fuzzification. In this section, the action performed is obtaining a value of the input variable and finding the numerical values of the membership function defined for that variable. As a result of Fuzzification, the situation currently sensed (input) is converted into such a form that, it can be used by the inference mechanism to trigger the rules in the rule base.

After fuzzification, the fuzzy sets obtained are labelled using the following term set, T={**LAD, MAD, SAD, SP, SAL, MAL, LAL, FULLY CLOSED, 3Q, M, Q, FULLY OPEN ,** #**N0,** }

3.2.1. Input 1

- S.acid = large acidic
- M.acid = medium acidic
- L.acid = small acidic
- natural = set point PH
- L.alk = law alkaline
- M.alk = medium alkaline
- S.alk = strong alkaline

3.2.2. Input 2

- #N0(1-14 PH) = SETPOINT

3.2.3. Output

- Fullyopen = 100% opening
- 3Q = 75% opening
- M = 50% opening
- Q = 25% opening
- Fullyclose = 0% opening

The membership functions of input variables PH and output variable percentage opening shown in figures 23, 24 and 25 respectively. μ_i is the membership function of output. In the current work the triangular membership is chosen.

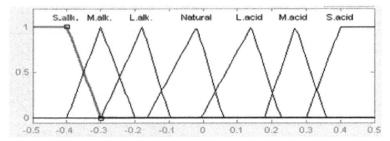

Figure 23. membership Function of input of PH

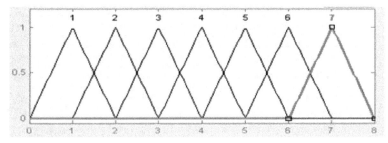

Figure 24. Membership Function of set point (input2)

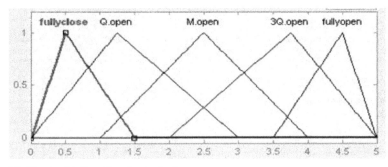

Figure 25. Membership Function of output pH

As a result of Fuzzification, we get the names of fuzzy sets to which the input belongs and to what extent they belong to these sets, their membership functions.

3.3. Rule base

Rule base stores the different rules that are to be fired or used according to the inputs. These rules are either gathered from experienced human operator or from careful study of existing PH systems. The base represents the control strategy employed in the PH control.

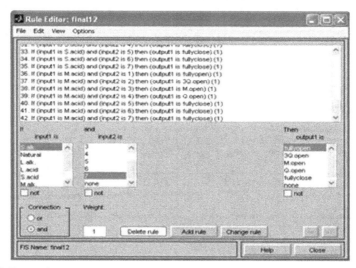

Figure 26. Fuzzy rule

The rules used have been designed based on the expertise. Those rules are carefully chosen to make the system as accurate as possible. They have been entered through the MATLAB editor. After rigoreous testing and trial, near optimum rules have been obtained. Table above gives the set of fuzzy action rules related to the application in hand.

3.4. Inference mechanism

The inference mechanism employed in pH control is based on individual rule firing. In this scheme, contribution of each rule is evaluated and overall decision is derived.

During inference process, each rule that is fired by a crisp value of pH is summed up after giving the weightages decided by the fuzzification unit. This weightage is called degree of satisfaction (DoS). DoS is decided by the fuzzification module.

In the inference mechanism, depending on which all fuzzy sets the input belongs to, the corresponding rules are fired. This describes the functioning of the three out of four blocks in the fuzzy controller. Now comes the defuzzification section.

	PH 1	PH 2	PH 3	PH 4	PH 5	PH 6	PH 7
S.acid	FULLY CLOSE	Q OPEN	M OPEN	M OPEN	M OPEN	3Q OPEN	3Q OPEN
M.acid	FULLY OPEN	3Q OPEN	M OPEN	Q OPEN	FULLY CLOSE	FULLY CLOSE	FULLY CLOSE
L.acid	FULLY OPEN	FULLY OPEN	3Q OPEN	M OPEN	M OPEN	FULLY CLOSE	FULLY CLOSE
Natural	M OPEN	M OPEN	Q OPEN	Q OPEN	Q OPEN	Q OPEN	FULLY CLOSE
L.alk.	3Q OPEN	3Q OPEN	3Q OPEN	3Q OPEN	M OPEN	M OPEN	M OPEN
M.alk.	3Q OPEN	3Q OPEN	3Q OPEN	M OPEN	M OPEN	Q OPEN	Q OPEN
S. .alk.	FULLY OPEN	FULLY OPEN	FULLY OPEN	FULLY OPEN	3Q OPEN	3Q OPEN	3Q OPEN

The Rule Base

3.5. Defuzzification

This section performs the task of converting the output of inference mechanism, the rules that are fired, and the DoS given by the fuzzification module into a signal to the control valve. For this, it uses "height defuzzification" which is computationally simple and fast.

4. Discussion and conclusions

Finally, let's conclude this chapter by discussing a real online example where it is required to bring the pH from 3 to 7. This example was chosen to show how the fuzzy controller has successfully solved oscillation due to titration curve mentioned earlier. Using all the expertise to set the membership functions as well as the rules, plus a fine tuning process, the membership function is shown in figure (27), and the pH response is shown in figure (28). It is clear that the pH has been brought from 3 to 7 in a very smooth manner. This value has been confirmed through the pH meter reading.

As a general conclusion, due to non linearity inherent in the chemical waist, the study presented here has shown that using fuzzy logic control is probably best suited to control the pH of industrial waist, despite the expertise required to fine tune the controller as well as the time required. It has also been shown that no matter how the linear controllers are tuned especially PID, including the many restrictions, plus the delays and settling time for each disturbance, their action was not satisfactory. Finally, the study has also shown that implementing the fuzzy control technique, by careful selection of memberships and setting the right rules, it is possible to bring any waist pH to neutrality smoothly in an acceptable time, regardless if the waist is strong base nature or strong acidic or not.

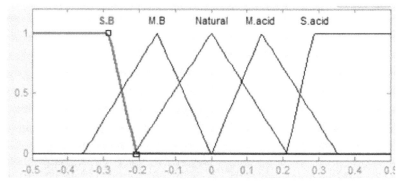

Figure 27. First membership function

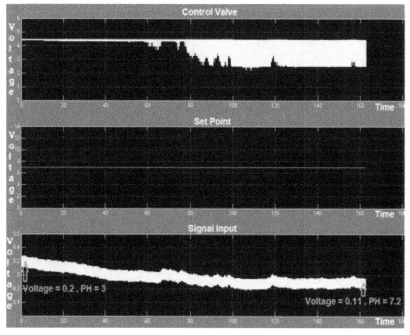

Figure 28. First test online at set point 7

Author details

Mostefa Ghassoul

Chemical Engineering, University of Bahrain, Bahrain

5. References

[1] faolex.fao.org/docs/pdf/mal13278.pdf.

[2] www.skcct.com/EQA%20Summary.htm.

[3] http://aabi.tripod.com/notes/modeling_control_neutralization_wswater.pdf.

[4] https://boc.com.au/boc_sp/.../BOC_Carbon_Dioxide_for_Water.pdf.

[5] Zadeh, L., Fuzzy sets, Information Control 8, 338–353, 1965

[6] http://www.mathworks.com/products/daq/index.html.

[7] www.eusflat.org/publications/.../295_Nortcliffe.pdf.

[8] http://discuss.itacumens.com/index.pHp?topic=27299.0

[9] Salehi S., Shahrokhi M. And Nejati M. "Adaptive nonlinear control of pH neutralization process using fuzzy approximators" Control Engineering Practice 17, (2009) 1329-1337

[10] Duan S., Shi P., Feng H., DUan Z. And Mao Z. "An on-line Adaptive Control Based on DO/pH measurements and ANN Pattern Recognition Model For Fed-Batch Cultivation" Biochemical Engineering Journal, 30 (2006) 88-86

Chapter 11

A New Modeling of
the Non-Linear Inductances in MATLAB

M. Ould Ahmedou, M. Ferfra, M. Chraygane and M. Maaroufi

Additional information is available at the end of the chapter

1. Introduction

In this chapter, we present a new approach for modeling the non-linear inductances by an analytic expression under the MATLAB-SIMULINK® code.

The current representation of these nonlinear inductances under MATLAB-SIMULINK® based on the introducing point by point (by a Lookup Table bloc in SIMULINK) [3]-[7] the values of Φ (i) deduced from the values of the magnetizing curve B-H and the geometric parameters of the corresponding portion of the magnetic circuit.

This new approach is based on a determination of analytic expressions of the non liner inductances deduced by a new analytic fitting of the nonlinear B-H curve. We have validate this new approach using the high voltage circuit of the power supply for magnetrons simulated by MATLAB-SIMULINK® code at the nominal state using the ferromagnetic material SF19. The comparison between experimental and simulated currents and voltages shows that the simulation curves match nearly with the experimental measurements (an error approximately one percent: 1%) [6].

This approach allowed us to give a general equivalent model for an eventual HV power supply (single and three phases) of the microwaves generators with N magnetrons (N = 1, 2,... ….10) for the industrial applications. In other words, we were able to modeling a HV transformer (single and three phases) with magnetic shunts able to supplying N magnetrons on its secondary. Thus, to define a general strategy for multicriteria optimization of this HV power supply with N magnetrons. This approach can also solve many problems of modeling, simulation and optimization of the electrics machines in general [8].

To summarize, this chapter is organized as follows. In the second section, we remind of the actual modeling of the nonlinear inductances under MATLAB-SIMULINK code. Section III presents the new model based on a hybrid method of fitting the magnetizing curve B-H in order to derive analytic expressions of the nonlinear inductances. In the last one a conclusion.

2. Actual modelling of the nonlinear inductances under MATLAB-SIMULINK code

In the following of this chapter, we take as example the equivalent circuit of the HV power supply of microwaves generators used for the industrial applications. The three nonlinear inductances (primary, secondary and shunt) of the special HV power transformer of this alimentation (model in Fig.1) are function of the reluctances of the magnetic circuit portion which it represents. Each one of them is represented by its characteristic Φ (i) outcome of the relation, $L(i) = (n_2 \Phi(i) / i)$ which can be determined from the magnetization curve B (H).

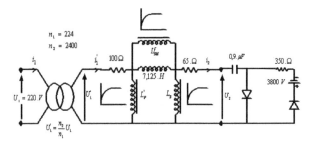

Figure 1. Equivalent circuit of HV power supply for microwaves generators

Not having analytical expression representing this B (H) curve for high values of the magnetic field H, we have introduced point by point the values of this curve using a linear interpolation between two consecutive points in the iterations of the code under SIMULINK. However, this method of interpolation can lead in case of temporal simulations including the traditional models of transformers to a numerical instability as quoted in [1]-[9]. A specific routine was elaborated in MATLAB to deduce the values couple (i, Φ) from those (H, B) and geometrical data of three inductances. The implementation of each nonlinear inductance of this circuit under SIMULINK software was realized by using the following blocks (Fig. 2):

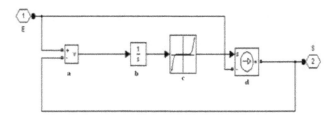

Figure 2. Implementation of each nonlinear inductance under SIMULINK, a: Voltage measurement, b: Integrator, c: Lookup Table, d: current source

- An integrator to derive the flux from the voltage.
- A Lookup Table function, which contains a big number of N points (N=100 points) relating to flux and currents deduced from the code previously quoted.
- A source of current imposed.

To ensure the convergence of nonlinear model simulation under SIMULINK, the simulation steps which is a crucial problem in the numerical simulations has been appropriately chosen Te= 0.01 ms after many trials.

We superimpose in Fig.3A, Fig.3B the simulation results obtained by SIMULINK code with those simulated by EMTP under the same conditions. These shapes resulting from the two codes under nominal operation (U1=220 V et f=50 Hz) are consistent with those obtained in

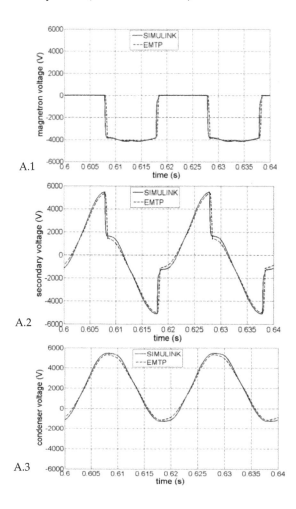

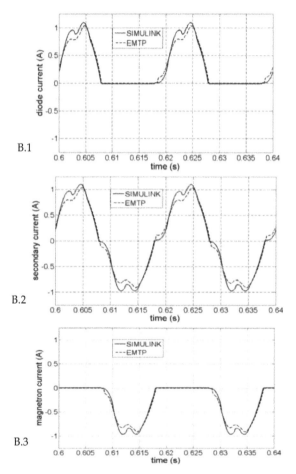

Figure 3. A. Simulation with EMTP and SIMULINK code: Forms of voltage waves (at the nominal operation); B. Simulation with EMTP and SIMULINK code: Forms of current waves (at the nominal operating)

practice (Fig.7), especially the magnetron current curves which respect the maximum current magnetron constraint (I_{peak}<1.2A) recommended by the manufacturer. Precisely, the current patterns resulting from SIMULINK are closer to practice than EMTP current patterns. Indeed, The current magnetron peak value reaches approximately -0.96 A (Fig.3.B.3) using SIMULINK code which is near -1 A from experimental results (Fig.7) while the peak value obtained from EMTP code equals -0.92 A. In general, between peak to peak values (Fig.3.A, Fig.3.B, Fig.7), the relative variations never exceed 8 % for EMTP code while those resulting from SIMULINK do not exceed 4%. The accuracy of the outcome resulting from SIMULINK can be justified by the large number of points

N=100=2x50 (including the negative values) used to feature B (H) in the table (see lookup table in Fig.2) while in our EMTP code version [18], we were limited to use a restricted number N=17. Taking into account the precision of the various data and acceptable tolerances on operation of the magnetron, modelling was considered to be satisfactory with the two codes.

3. New modelling of the nonlinear inductances

The field problem solution involving ferromagnetic materials is complicated by the nonlinear relationship between B and H. One of the problems encountered is the absence of single mathematical expression, to represent the magnetization curve characteristic over a wide range of magnetic fields, having a smooth variation of the incremental permeability. As well, in our previous works [2]-[3], the B-H curve introduced in the π old model of this special transformer of the HV power supply for magnetrons and based on a set of measurement data, is approximated under software tools (EMTP and SIMULINK) by several straight line segments connecting the points of measurements. However, the B-H curve obtained is not smooth at the joints of the segments and the slopes of the straight lines representing the permeability are discontinuous at these joints [4]-[5]. Hence, the accuracy of permeability computed using such an approximation of the B-H curve is limited by the number of the straight-line segments. In order to improve this π model of this special transformer, we present a more accurate modelling of the nonlinear B-H curve of ferromagnetic material used for fabrication (SF19). In fact, the nonlinear B-H curve is represented by analytic expressions considering two parts of this curve: the first one is the linear region which is fitted by a non integer power series and the second one representing the saturation region is approximated by polynomial representation.

3.1. Fitting H-B curve by a hybrid method

A set of N discrete measurements data In and Φn or Hn-Bn of this special transformer (n=1,2,3,...N=100) is given as depicted in Fig.4. Two parts are considered for this analytic representation:

• The linear region is fitted by a non-integer power series [1]. It is based on selected powers of B (not generally integer) with positive coefficients giving a power series. This linear part of this curve can be expressed by the power curve :

$$H = \sum_i k_i B^{n_i} \quad \text{with } k_i{>}0,\ n_i{>}0 \text{ , for all i.} \tag{1}$$

An adequate procedure of determining initial ki and ni values from logarithmic plots is adopted ensuring that these initial estimates of the parameters will be positive. Once an initial estimate of parameters (ki, ni) has been obtained, the parameters are optimized using regression analysis to get the best fit which is defined as corresponding to the minimum sum of squares of absolute errors. The resulting analytic expression of H is given by:

$$\text{for} H \leq H_{18} \quad H(B) = 220.65B^{0.96} + 19.5B^{11} \tag{2}$$

- The saturation region is fitted by a polynomial representation based on the method of least squares [5]-[1].

$$\text{for } H > H_{18}$$

$$H = a_1.B + a_3.B^3 + a_5.B^5 \ldots .+a_{2p+1}B^{2p+1} \tag{3}$$

Using the 'polyfit' function in MATLAB boxes, we determine all parameters ai. The best fit is obtained by choosing p=3.The resulting expression of H is given as follows:

$$H(B) = 62967B - 59157B^3 + 17475B^5 - 1409B^7 \tag{4}$$

The choice of a hybrid method consisting of two analytic expressions is more adequate than only one analytic expression for fitting the whole magnetizing curve of this material, according to our attempts to estimate these coefficients. It is due to the fact that the fitting is better and uses a small number of terms in analytic expressions to be identified. To illustrate the accuracy of this procedure for modelling nonlinear characteristic of this ferromagnetic material (SF19), we superpose in Fig.4 the simulate curve B-H obtained by the two analytic expressions and data measurements. It shows no discrepancies between the two curves.

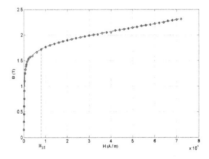

Figure 4. Magnetization curve SF19: ° ° ° data measurements, ⸺ curve represented by non integer power series, - - - - curve represented by polynomial function.

3.2. Analytic expressions of inductances

Finally, we determine the analytic expressions of inductances from this analytic approach for modelling the nonlinear characteristic B-H and the transformer data. Two analytic expressions deduced for each inductance of this new model are given using the formulae:

For B ≤ 1.7225 T

$$L'_p = L_S = \frac{n_2 \Phi_P}{i_P} = \frac{n_2^2 B S_1}{H l_P} = \frac{n_2^2 S_1}{l_P} \cdot \frac{B}{H(B)}$$

$$L'_p = L_S = 106338{,}46 \frac{B}{220.65B^{0.96}+19.5B^{11}} \tag{5}$$

For B ≥ 1.7225 T

$$L'_p = 106338,46 \frac{B}{62967B - 59157B^3 + 17475B^5 - 1409B^7}$$

It is the same for the shunt inductance

For B ≤ 1.7225 T

$$L'_{Sh} = \frac{n_2 \Phi_3}{i'_{Sh}} = \frac{n_2. \, 2. \, \Phi_{Sh}}{Hl_{Sh}} = \frac{n_2. \, 2(B. \, S_3)}{Hl_{Sh}} = \frac{2n_2 B. \, S_3}{Hl_{Sh}}$$

$$L'_{Sh} = 138693 \frac{B}{H(B)}$$

$$L'_{Sh} = 138693 \frac{B}{220.65B^{0.96} + 19.5B^{11}} \tag{6}$$

For B ≥ 1.7225 T

$$L'_{Sh} = 138693 \frac{B}{62967B - 59157B^3 + 17475B^5 - 1409B^7} \tag{7}$$

In the simulation of new model, the three nonlinear inductances (primary, secondary and shunt) are function of induction or flux. The implementation of each nonlinear inductance with its analytic expressions under SIMULINK software was realized by using the blocks shown in Fig.5. This model (or bloc) is valid for any nonlinear inductance. It is validated in [14], and shows a good agreement with the experimental results.

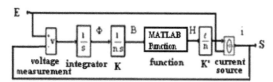

Figure 5. Implementation of the nonlinear inductance under MATLAB-SIMULINK

We superpose in Fig.6A and Fig.6B the simulation results of this new modelling, obtained by SIMULINK code with those obtained from old one by EMTP under the same conditions. These shapes resulting from the two codes under nominal operation (U1=220 V, f=50 Hz) are consistent with those obtained in practice (Fig.7), especially the magnetron current curves which respect the maximum current magnetron constraint (I_{peak} < 1.2A) recommended by the manufacturer. Precisely, the current patterns resulting from the new modelling under SIMULINK are closer to practice than EMTP current patterns issues from old modelling (Fig.2). Indeed, The current magnetron peak value reaches approximately -1 A (Fig.6.B.3) using SIMULINK code which is identical to experimental results (Fig.7) while the peak value obtained from EMTP code equals -0.92 A. In general, between peak to peak values (Fig.6.A, Fig.6.B, Fig.7), the relative variations never exceed 8 % for EMTP code (with old model) while those resulting from SIMULINK with the new model do not exceed 1%. The accuracy of the outcome resulting from SIMULINK can be justified by determining analytic inductances of this model. It leads to continuous slopes representing permeability while with the old model under EMTP introducing the B-H curve point by point and approximating it by several straight line segments, the slopes representing the permeability are discontinuous at the joints. Taking into account the precision of the various data (software) and acceptable tolerances in the operation of the magnetron, the validation of this improved modelling based on analytic inductances is considered to be more satisfactory than the old one.

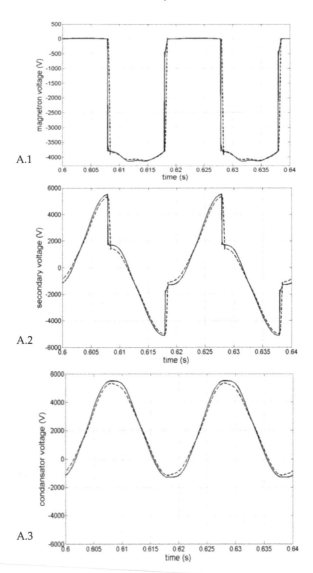

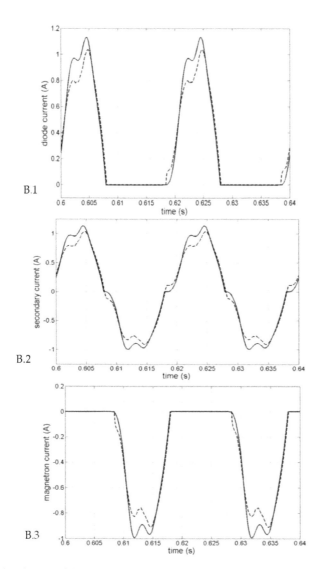

Figure 6. A. Simulation with EMTP (- - -) and SIMULINK ( ) code: Forms of voltage waves (nominal operation); B. Simulation with EMTP(- - -) and SIMULINK( ) code: Forms of current waves (nominal operating)

4. Experimental results

We sought to integrate the transformer new model (with analytic expressions of inductances) in the circuit of the HV supply from the source to the magnetron (Fig. 1), where we represented the tube microwave by the equivalent diagram deduced from its electric characteristic [2]-[3]-[6] which is formally similar to that of a diode of dynamic resistance $R = \frac{\Delta U}{\Delta I}$ neighbor of 350 Ohms and threshold voltage E of about 3800 Volts. We validate this new model by carrying out tests that have been set up previously [2] on generator microwaves composed of the following elements (Fig.1):

- A high voltage transformer with magnetic shunt ratings: f=50 Hz, S=1650 VA, U_1=220 V, and, no-load U_2=2330 V (r'_1 =100 Ω and r_2=65 Ω, for n1=224 and n2=2400 turns).
- A cell composed of a condenser, its capacity C=0,9 μF and a diode high voltage DHV.
- A magnetron designed to operate under an approximate voltage of 4000 V. To obtain its nominal power, it needs an average current Imoy=300 mA, but without exceeding the peak current which might destroy it (Imax<1,2 A). The experimental curves are presented in Fig.6. The first three curves represent the shapes of voltage quantities while the last ones represent current patterns.

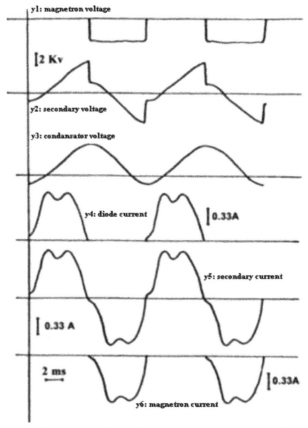

Figure 7. Experimental forms curves of the voltages and currents waves (nominal operating)

5. Conclusion

From the Simulink block modelling a non-linear inductance by introducing point by point its values, we performed a new model in two steps:

Step 1. A program M-file was developed and gives us the final results of the B-H curve fitting.

Step 2. By performing a function 'MATLAB Function' that replace us the nonlinear inductance of the current passing through this inductance as shown in Fig.4.

This approach can solve many problems of modeling, simulation and optimization of the electrical networks and electric machines also [7].

Thus, an improved procedure for modeling the nonlinear characteristic B-H of the ferromagnetic materiel (SF19) of this special transformer supplying one magnetron has been presented. Starting with a discrete set of measurement data of B and H, we have obtained two analytic expressions of B-H curve in terms of non-integer power series for the linear part of this curve and polynomial representation for the saturation region. Then, these expressions have been used for improving the old modelling of nonlinear inductances into the new one based on the determination of analytic expressions of each inductance. We validate the new π model (with three nonlinear inductances) of the transformer with magnetic shunts, used in HV supply for magnetron by MATLAB-SIMULINK code in nominal mode. A comparison between the numerical results and experimental ones has shown a significant agreement.

Author details

M. Ould Ahmedou, M. Ferfra and M. Maaroufi
Mohammadia School of Engineering (Mohamed V University), Rabat, Morocco

M. Chraygane
Ibn Zohr University, Agadir, Morocco

6. References

[1] J. R. Lucas, representation of magnetization curves over a wide region using a non-integer power series, international J. Elect. Enging. Edduc – vol. 25. pp. 335 – 340. Manchester U.P. 1988. Printed in Great Britais.

[2] Chraygane M., ferfra M. & Hlimi B., Modeling of a high voltage power for microwave generators industrial in one magnetron, 3EI journal, Paris, France, vol. 41, 2005, pp. 37-47.

[3] M.Ould.Ahmedou, M.Chraygane, M.Ferfra, New π Model Validation Approach to the Leakage Flux Transformer of a High Voltage Power Supply Used for Magnetron for the Industrial Micro-Waves Generators 800 Watts. International Review of Electrical Engineering (I.R.E.E.), Vol. 5. n. 3. May-June.2010. pp. 1003-1011.

[4] B. Kawkabani, J.-J. Simond, Improved Modeling of Three-Phase Transformer Analysis Based on Magnetic Equivalent Circuit Diagrams And Taking Into Account Nonlinear B-H Curve, Journal Electromotion, Volume 13, Number 1, January-March 2006, pp. 5-10.

[5]   Guanghao Liu, Xiao-Bang Xu, Improved Modeling of the Nonlinear B–H Curve and Its Application in Power Cable Analysis, IEEE Transaction on Magnetics, vol. 38, NO. 4, July 2002.

[6]   Ahmedou, M.Ould., Ferfra, M., Nouri, R., Chraygane, M, "Improved π model of the leakage flux transformer used for magnetrons", 2011 International Conference on Multimedia Computing and Systems -Proceedings , art. no. 5945710

[7]   MATLAB Tool Books.

[8]   M.Ould.Ahmedou, M.Ferfra, N.El Ghazal, M.Chraygane, M.Maaroufi, 'Implementation And Optimization Under Matlab Code Of A Hv Power Transformer For Microwave Generators Supplying Two Magnetrons', Journal of Theoretical and Applied Information Technology pp 227 - 238 Vol 33. No. 2 – 2011.

[9]   Ferfra. M, Chraygane. M, Fadel. M, Ould Ahmedou. M. "Non linear modelling of an overall new high voltage power supply for N=2 magnetrons for industrial microwave generators | [Modelisation non lineaire d'une nouvelle alimentation haute tension globale de N=2 magnetrons pour generateurs micro-ondes industriels]" Physical and Chemical News 54 , pp. 17-30, 2010.

[10] Aguili T & Chraygane M., An original power generators for microwave, General Review of Electric - France, GRE 5 (1990) 49-51.

[11] Chraygane M, Modeling and optimization of a transformer with shunt of the high voltage power supply for magnetron used as microwave generators2450MHz 800W for industrial applications, Thesis of doctorate, Claude Bernard University-Lyon I, France, n° 189 (1993).

[12] Chraygane M, Teissier M., Jammal A. et Masson J.P , Modelling of a transformer with shunts used in the HV power supply of a microwave generator in a magnetron, publication, physic III journal, France, (1994) 2329-2338.

[13] M. Chraygane, M. El Khouzaï, M. Ferfra, & B. Hlimi, Analytical study of the repartition of flux in the leakage transformer used in a power supply for magnetron 800 Watts at 2450Hz, Physical and Chemical News, PCN journal, vol. 22, 2005, pp. 65-74.

[14] M. Chraygane, M. Ferfra, & B. Hlimi, Analytical and experimental study of the distribution of flux in the transformer with shunts of a high voltage power supply for magnetron 800 Watts at 2450Hz, article, journal Physical and Chemical News, PCN, vol. 27,2006, pp. 31-42.

[15] M. Chraygane, M. Ferfra, B. Hlimi, Analytic determination of the flux and the currents of the leakage flux transformer of a high voltage power supply for magnetron used for the industrial micro-waves generators 800 Watts – 2450 Mhz. Phys. Chem. News, PCN, vol. 40, 2008, pp. 51-61.

[16] Mukerji, Saurabh Kumar; Goel, Sandeep Kumar; Basu, Kartik Prasad, Experimental determination of equivalent-circuit parameters for transformers with large series-branch impedances, International Journal of Electrical Engineering Education, vol 43, November 2006 , pp. 352-357.

[17] Jouni Pylvänäinen, Kirsi Nousiainen, Pekka Verho Studies to Utilise Calculated Condition Information and Measurements for Transformer Condition Assessment. International Review of Electrical Engineering (I.R.E.E.). Vol. 4. n. 4. june.2009. pp. 684-689.

[18] Mustafa. Kizilcay and Laszlo Prikler, "ATP-EMTP Beginner's Guide for EEUG Members, European EMTP-ATP Users Group e.V", June (2000).

Chapter 12

An Advanced Transmission Line and Cable Model in Matlab for the Simulation of Power-System Transients

Octavio Ramos-Leaños, Jose Luis Naredo and Jose Alberto Gutierrez-Robles

Additional information is available at the end of the chapter

1. Introduction

The design and operation of power systems, as well as of power apparatuses, each time depends more on accurate simulations of Electromagnetic Transients (EMTs). Essential to this is to count with advanced models for representing power transmission lines and cables. Electromagnetic Transients Program (EMTP), the most used EMT software, offer various line models. Among these, the most important ones are: 1) the Constant Parameters Line model (CP), 2) the Frequency Dependent or J. Marti Line model (FD) and 3) the Universal Line Model (ULM). The CP Line model is the simplest and most efficient one from the computational point of view. Nevertheless, it tends to overestimate the transient phenomena as it considers that line parameters are constant. Thus, it is recommended only for modeling lines on zones distant to an area where a transient event occurs. The FD Line model (Marti, 1982) evaluates multi–conductor line propagation in the modal domain and takes into account effects due to frequency dependence of the line parameters. Nevertheless, as the transformations between the modal and the phase domains are approximated by real and constant matrices, its accuracy is limited to cases of aerial lines which are symmetric or nearly symmetric. The FD model tends to underestimate the transient phenomena. ULM (Morched et al., 1999) takes into account the full-frequency dependence of line parameters. ULM works directly in phase domain, thus avoiding simplifying assumptions regarding modal–to–phase transformations. So far it is the most general model, capable to accurately represent asymmetric aerial lines as well as underground cables.

The development of ULM is fairly recent and these authors consider that it still is a subject for further research and development. The authors believe also that researchers and power system analysts will benefit considerably from the full understanding of the theoretical basis of the ULM, as well as from counting with a ULM–type code that is easy to understand and modify. One problem with this is that the theoretical basis of ULM includes various topics and subjects that are scattered through several dozens of highly specialized papers. Another difficulty with this is the high complexity of the code for a ULM–type model. This chapter aims at providing a clear and complete description of the theoretical basis for this model. Although this description is intended for power engineers with an interest in electromagnetic transient phenomena, it can be of interest also to electronic engineers involved in the analysis and design of interconnects. The chapter includes as well the description of Matlab program of a ULM–type model, along with executable code and basic examples.

2. Multi-conductor transmission line analysis

2.1. Telegrapher's Equations

Electromagnetic behavior of transmission lines and cables is described by the Modified Telegrapher Equations, which in frequency domain are expressed as follows:

$$-\frac{d\mathbf{V}}{dx} = \mathbf{ZI}. \tag{1}$$

$$-\frac{d\mathbf{I}}{dx} = \mathbf{YV}. \tag{2}$$

where V is the vector of voltages, I is the vector of currents, Z and Y are the $(N \times N)$ per unit-length series impedance and shunt admitance matrix of a given line with N conductors, repectively. To solve equations (1) and (2), let equation (1) be first differentiated with respect to x; then, (2) is used to eliminate the vector of currents at the right hand side. The resulting expression is a second order matrix ODE involving only unknown voltages:

$$\frac{d^2\mathbf{V}}{dx^2} = \mathbf{ZYV}. \tag{3}$$

In the same way, equation (2) can be differentiated with respect to x and (1) can be used to eliminate the right-hand-side voltage term. The resulting expression involves unknown currents only:

$$\frac{d^2\mathbf{I}}{dx^2} = \mathbf{YZI}. \tag{4}$$

Solution to (4) is:

$$\mathbf{I}(x) = \mathbf{C}_1 e^{-\sqrt{\mathbf{YZ}}x} + \mathbf{C}_2 e^{\sqrt{\mathbf{YZ}}x}, \tag{5}$$

where C_1 and C_2 are vectors of integration constants determined by the line boundary conditions; that is, by the connections at the two line ends. In fact, the term including C_1 represents a vector of phase currents propagating forward (or in the positive x–direction) along the line, whereas the one with C_2 represents a backward (or negative x–direction) propagating vector of phase currents. Expression (5) is an extension of the well–known solution for the single–conductor line. Note that this extension involves the concept of matrix functions. This topic is explained at section 2.2.

The solution to (3) takes a form analogous to (5) and it is obtained conveniently from (5) and (2) as follows:

$$V(x) = -Y^{-1}\frac{dI}{dx} = Z_C\left[C_1 e^{-\sqrt{YZ}x} - C_2 e^{\sqrt{YZ}x} \right]$$

(6)

where, $Z_C = Y^{-1}\sqrt{YZ}$ is the characteristic impedance matrix and its inverse is the characteristic admittance matrix $Y_C = \sqrt{YZ}Z^{-1}$.

2.2. Modal analysis and matrix functions

Matrix functions needed for multi-conductor line analysis are extensions of analytic functions of a one–dimensional variable. Consider the following function and its Taylor expansion:

$$f(x) = \sum_{k=0}^{\infty} a_k x^k$$

(7)

The application of $f()$ to a square matrix A of order $N \times N$ as its argument is accomplished as follows:

$$f(A) = \sum_{k=0}^{\infty} a_k A^k,$$

(8)

where A^0 is equal to U, the $N \times N$ unit matrix. Consider now the case of a diagonal matrix:

$$\Lambda = \begin{bmatrix} \lambda_1 & 0 & \cdots & 0 \\ 0 & \lambda_2 & \cdots & 0 \\ \vdots & \vdots & \ddots & \vdots \\ 0 & 0 & \cdots & \lambda_N \end{bmatrix}.$$

(9)

Application of (8) to Λ yields:

$$f(\Lambda) = \sum_{k=0}^{\infty} a_k \Lambda^k = \begin{bmatrix} \sum_k a_k \lambda_1^k & 0 & \cdots & 0 \\ 0 & \sum_k a_k \lambda_2^k & \cdots & 0 \\ \vdots & \vdots & \ddots & \vdots \\ 0 & 0 & \cdots & \sum_k a_k \lambda_N^k \end{bmatrix} = \begin{bmatrix} f(\lambda_1) & 0 & \cdots & 0 \\ 0 & f(\lambda_2) & \cdots & 0 \\ \vdots & \vdots & \ddots & \vdots \\ 0 & 0 & \cdots & f(\lambda_N) \end{bmatrix}$$

(10)

This expression thus shows that the function of a diagonal matrix is simply obtained applying the one–dimensional form of the function to the matrix nonzero elements. Consider next the function of a diagonalizable matrix A; that is, a matrix A that is similar to a diagonal one Λ:

$$A = M \Lambda \, M^{-1}. \tag{11}$$

where M is the nonsingular matrix whose columns are the eigenvectors of A, while Λ is the matrix whose diagonal elements are the eigenvalues of A (Strang, 1988).

Application of $f()$ as in (10) to A yields:

$$f(A) = \sum_{k=0}^{\infty} a_k (M \Lambda M^{-1})^k = M \left(\sum_{k=0}^{\infty} a_k \Lambda^k \right) M^{-1} = Mf(\Lambda) M^{-1} \tag{12}$$

Therefore, the function of a diagonalizable matrix is conveniently obtained first by factoring A as in (10), then by applying the function to the diagonal elements of Λ and, finally, by performing the triple matrix product as in (11) and (12).

It is clear from subsection **2.1**, that multi-conductor line analysis requires evaluating matrix functions of **YZ**. To do so, it is generally assumed that **YZ** always is diagonalizable (Wedephol, 1965; Dommel, 1992). Although there is a possibility for **YZ** not being diagonalizable (Brandao Faria, 1986), occurrences of this can be easily avoided when conducting practical analysis (Naredo, 1986).

3. Line modelling

Figure 1 shows the representation of a multi-conductor transmission line (or cable) of length L, with one of its ends at $x = 0$ and the other at $x = L$. Let I_0 be the vector of phase currents being injected into the line and V_0 the vector of phase voltages, both at $x=0$. In the same form, I_L and V_L represent the respective vectors of injected phase currents and of phase voltages at $x=L$. Line equation solutions (5) and (6) are applied to the line end at $x=0$:

$$I_0 = I(0) = C_1 + C_2 \tag{13}$$

$$V_0 = V(0) = Z_C[C_1 + C_2]. \tag{14}$$

Then, the value of C_1 is determined from (13) and (14):

$$C_1 = \frac{I_0 + Y_C V_0}{2}. \tag{15}$$

Expressions (5) and (6) are applied to the line end conditions at $x = L$:

$$I_L = -I(L) = -C_1 e^{-\sqrt{YZ}L} - C_2 e^{\sqrt{YZ}L} \tag{16}$$

and

$$V_L = V(L) = Z_C \left[C_1 e^{-\sqrt{YZ}L} - C_2 e^{\sqrt{YZ}L} \right]. \tag{17}$$

After doing this, (17) is pre–multiplied by Y_C and subtracted from (16) to obtain:

$$I_L - Y_C V_L = -2C_1 e^{-\sqrt{YZ}L}. \tag{18}$$

Finally, (15) is introduced in (18) rendering

$$I_L - Y_C V_L = -e^{-\sqrt{YZ}L} \left[I_0 + Y_C V_0 \right] \tag{19}$$

Expression (19) establishes the relation among voltages and currents at the terminals of a multi-conductor line section. Its physical meaning follows from realizing that the term $I_0{+}Y_CV_0$ at its right hand side represents a traveling wave of currents leaving the line end at $x = 0$ and propagating in the positive x–axis direction, whereas $I_L{-}Y_CV_L$ at the left hand side is the traveling wave of currents leaving the line end at $x = L$.

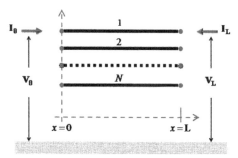

Figure 1. Multi-conductor line segment of length L.

By a similar process as the previous one for deriving (19), it is possible to show also that the following relation holds as line equation solutions (5) and (6) are applied to line end conditions at x=0:

$$I_0 - Y_C V_0 = -e^{-\sqrt{YZ}L} \left[I_L + Y_C V_L \right] \tag{20}$$

Note however that this relation can also be obtained by simply exchanging at (19) sub–indexes 0 and L. This exchange is justified by the input/output symmetry of the line section. Expressions (19) and (20) provide a very general mathematical model for a multi-conductor transmission line. This is a model based on traveling wave principles. Let (19) and (20) be rewritten as follows:

$$I_L = I_{sh,L} - I_{aux,L} \tag{21}$$

where, $I_{sh,L} = Y_C V_L$ is the shunt currents vector produced at terminal L by injected voltages V_L. $I_{aux,L} = H I_{rfl,0}$ is the auxiliary currents vector consisting of the reflected currents at terminal 0, $I_{rfl,0} = I_0 + Y_C V_0$ and the transfer functions matrix $H = e^{-\sqrt{(YZ)}L}$.

In the same way as it has been previously done for (19), expression (20) is conveniently represented as follows:

$$\mathbf{I}_0 = \mathbf{I}_{sh,0} - \mathbf{I}_{aux,0} \tag{22}$$

with, $I_{sh,0} = Y_C V_0$, $I_{aux,0} = HI_{rfl,L}$, and $I_{rfl,L} = I_L + Y_C V_L$.

Expressions (21) and (22) constitute a traveling wave line model for the segment of length L depicted in figure 1. The former set of expressions represents end L of the line segment, while the latter set represents end 0. A schematic representation for the whole model is provided by figure 2. Note that the coupling between the two line ends is through the auxiliary sources $I_{aux,0}$ and $I_{aux,L}$.

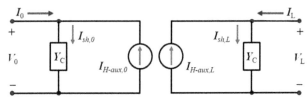

Figure 2. Frequency domain circuit representation of a multi-conductor line.

The line model defined by expressions (21) and (22) is in the frequency domain. Power system transient simulations require this model to be transformed to the time domain. For instance, the transformation of (21) to the time domain yields:

$$\mathbf{i}_0 = \mathbf{i}_{sh,0} - \mathbf{i}_{aux,0} \tag{23}$$

with

$$\mathbf{i}_{sh,0} = \mathbf{y}_C * \mathbf{v}_L \tag{24}$$

and

$$\mathbf{i}_{aux,0} = \mathbf{h} * \mathbf{i}_{rfl,0} \tag{25}$$

Note that at (23), (24), (25) the lowercase variables represent the time domain images of their uppercase counterparts at (22) and that the symbol * represents convolution. Reflected currents can be represented as

$$\mathbf{i}_{rfl,L} = 2\mathbf{i}_{sh,L} - \mathbf{i}_{aux,L} \tag{26}$$

Expressions (23)-(26) constitute a general traveling–wave based time–domain model for line end 0. The model corresponding to the other end is obtained by interchanging sub–indexes "0" and "L" at (23)-(26). Equation (23) essentially provides the interface of the line–end 0 model to the nodal network solver that, for power system transient analysis, usually is the EMTP (Dommel, 1996). Expressions (24) and (25) require the performing of matrix–to–vector convolutions that are carried out conveniently by means of State–Space methods (Semlyen & Abdel-Rahman, 1982). State–Space equivalents of (23) and (24) arise naturally as Y_C and H are represented by means of fitted rational functions (Semlyen & Dabuleanu, 1975).

4. Phase domain line model

Since rational fitting and model solutions are carried out directly in the phase domain, the model described here is said to be a phase domain line model. Rational fitting for this model is carried out using the Vector fitting (VF) tool (Gustavsen, 2008). In the case of Y_C, the whole fitting process is done in the phase domain, whereas for H initial poles and time delays are first calculated in the modal domain.

4.1. Rational approximation of Yc

The following rational representation has been proposed for Y_C in (Marti, 1982) and (Morched et al., 1999):

$$\mathbf{Y}_C = \mathbf{G}_0 + \sum_{i=1}^{Ny} \frac{\mathbf{G}_i}{s - q_i} \tag{27}$$

where Ny is the fitting order, q_i represents the i–th fitting pole, G_i is the corresponding matrix of residues and G_0 is a constant matrix obtained at the limit of Y_C when $s=j\omega \to \infty$. Note in (27) that common poles are used for the fitting of all the elements of Y_C obtained by fitting the matrix trace and finally the fitting of the matrices of residues G_i and of proportional terms G_0 is done in the phase domain. Section 7 provides an overview of the VF procedure and further information is to be found in (Gustavsen & Semlyen, 1999) and (Gustavsen, 2008).

4.2. Rational approximation of H

Rational fitting of transfer matrix H is substantially more involving than the one of Y_C above. To attain an accurate and compact (low order) rational representation for H it is essential to factor out all terms involving time delays (Marti, 1982). The major difficulty here is that its elements could involve a mix of up to N different delay terms due to the multimode propagation on an N–conductor line (Wedepohl, 1965). Separation of matrix H into single-delay terms is obtained from the following modal factorization (Wedepohl, 1965):

$$\mathbf{H} = \mathbf{MH}_m\mathbf{M}^{-1} \tag{28}$$

where H_m is a diagonal matrix of the form

$$\mathbf{H}_m = diag[e^{-\gamma_1 L}, e^{-\gamma_2 L}, ..., e^{-\gamma_N L}] \tag{29}$$

and $\gamma=\sqrt{(YZ)}$ is the propagation constant of a conductor line (Wedepohl, 1965). As the triple product in (28) is performed by partitioning M in columns and M^{-1} in rows, the following expression is derived:

$$\mathbf{H} = \sum_{i=1}^{N} \mathbf{D}_i e^{-\gamma_i L} \tag{30}$$

where D_i is the rank–1 matrix obtained from pre–multiplying the i–th column of M by the i–th row of M^{-1}. Matrix D_i in fact is an idempotent (Marcano & Marti, 1997). The exponential factors at (30) can be further decomposed as follows:

$$e^{-\gamma_i L} = e^{-\tilde{\gamma}_i L} e^{-s\tau_i} ; i = 1, 2, \ldots, N \tag{31}$$

where $\exp\left(-\tilde{\gamma}_i L\right)$ is a minimum phase–shift function (Bode, 1945) and τ_i is the time delay associated to the velocity of the i–th mode. Hence:

$$\mathbf{H} = \sum_{i=1}^{N} \mathbf{D}_i e^{-\tilde{\gamma}_i L} e^{-s\tau_i} \tag{32}$$

The time delays in (32) can be initially estimated by applying Bode's relation for minimum phase complex functions (Bode, 1945) to the magnitudes of $exp(-\gamma_i L)$ in (30). Although (32) provides the desired separation of H as a sum of terms, each one involving a single delay factor, the following consideration is brought in for computational efficiency (Morched et al., 1999). Modal delays often occur in groups with almost identical values. Suppose that a number Ng of these groups can be formed and that (32) can be modified as follows:

$$\mathbf{H} = \sum_{k=1}^{Ng} \tilde{\mathbf{H}}_k e^{-s\tau_k} \tag{33}$$

where Ng is less or equal to N, and τ_k is the representative delay for the k–th group. Clearly, by comparing (33) and (32):

$$\tilde{\mathbf{H}}_k = \sum_{i=1}^{Ik} \mathbf{D}_i e^{-\tilde{\gamma}_i L} e^{-s\tau_i} k = 1, 2, \ldots, Ng \tag{34}$$

with Ik being the number of modal terms in the k–th group. To determine whether a set of exponential factors can be grouped or not, the maximum phase shifts associated to their time delays are compared. The set is grouped into a single delay group if the phase shift differences are below a pre-established value typically chosen at $10°$ (Morched et al., 1999). Each term $\tilde{\mathbf{H}}_k$ at (34) can now be considered free of delay factors and can be fitted as follows:

$$\tilde{\mathbf{H}}_k = \sum_{i=1}^{Nh(k)} \frac{\mathbf{R}_{k,i}}{s - p_{k,i}} k = 1, 2, \ldots, Ng \tag{35}$$

where $Nh(k)$ is the fitting order for the k–th term $\tilde{\mathbf{H}}_k$, $p_{k,i}$ represents its i–th fitting pole and $R_{k,i}$ is the corresponding matrix of residues. Note in (35) that common poles are being used to fit all elements at each matrix $\tilde{\mathbf{H}}_k$. As (35) is introduced in (33), the following rational form is obtained for H:

$$\mathbf{H} = \sum_{k=1}^{Ng} e^{-s\tau_k} \sum_{i=1}^{Nh(k)} \frac{\mathbf{R}_{k,i}}{s - p_{k,i}} \tag{36}$$

Initial estimates for the poles as well as time delays are obtained in the modal domain. The poles result from applying VF to the sum of the modal exponential factors conforming each delay group. The time delays proceed from Bode's formula as it has been said before. With all the poles $p_{k,i}$ and group delays τ_k of (36) being estimated in the modal domain, the overall fitting of H is completed in the phase domain by obtaining the matrices of residues $R_{k,i}$ and recalculating the poles (Gustavsen & Nordstrom, 2008). The fitting parameters so obtained can be taken as final or can be further refined by an iterative process. VF is applied throughout all these fitting tasks and detailed descriptions of these processes can be found in (Gustavsen & Nordstrom, 2008; Gustavsen & Semlyen, 1999).

4.3. State-space analysis

With the rational representation of Y_C and H state–space forms to evaluate $i_{sh,0}$ and $i_{aux,0}$ arise naturally. Consider first the case of $i_{sh,0}$. Taking (22) and introducing (27) yields

$$\mathbf{I}_{sh,0} = \mathbf{G}_0 \mathbf{V}_0 + \sum_{i=1}^{Ny} \mathbf{W}_i \tag{37}$$

where

$$\mathbf{W}_i = \frac{\mathbf{G}_i}{s - q_i} \mathbf{V}_0 \; i = 1, 2, ..., Ny \tag{38}$$

Application of the Inverse Laplace Transform to (37) and (38) gives the following continuous-time-state-space (CTSS) form for $i_{sh,0}$:

$$\mathbf{i}_{sh,0} = \mathbf{G}_0 \mathbf{v}_0 + \sum_{i=1}^{Ny} \mathbf{w}_i \tag{39}$$

and

$$\frac{d\mathbf{w}_i}{dt} = q_i \mathbf{w}_i + \mathbf{G}_i \mathbf{v}_0 \; i = 1, 2, ..., Ny \tag{40}$$

The CTSS form to evaluate $i_{aux,0}$, is derived now. On replacing the fitted form of H given by (36) into (22):

$$\mathbf{I}_{aux,0} = \sum_{k=1}^{Ng} \sum_{i=1}^{Nh(k)} \mathbf{X}_{k,i} \tag{41}$$

with

$$\mathbf{X}_{k,i} = \frac{R_{k,i}}{s - p_{k,i}} I_{rfl,L} e^{-s\tau_k}; \; \begin{matrix} i = 1, 2, ..., Ny \\ k = 1, 2, ..., Ng \end{matrix} \tag{42}$$

Application of the Inverse Laplace Transform to (41) and (42) renders the following CTSS form:

$$i_{aux,0} = \sum_{k=1}^{Ng} \sum_{i=1}^{Nh(k)} x_{k,i} \tag{43}$$

$$\frac{dx_{k,i}}{dt} = p_{k,i} x_{k,i} + R_{k,i} i_{rfl,L}(t - \tau_k); \quad \begin{matrix} i = 1,2,...,Ny \\ k = 1,2,...,Ng \end{matrix} \tag{44}$$

CTSS forms (39), (40), (43) and (44) provide the basis for a phase domain line model (Morched et al., 1999). Nevertheless, their solution by a digital processor requires the conversion to discrete–time state–space (DTSS). This is accomplished by applying a numerical differentiation rule to the CTSS forms. The one adopted here is the mid–point rule of differentiation, which is equivalent to the trapezoidal integration rule extensively used in EMTP (Dommel, 1969, 1992). Application of this rule to (44) with Δt as the solution time step results in:

$$x_{k,i} = a_{k,i} x'_{k,i} + \tilde{R}_{k,i} [i_{rfl,L}(t - \tau_k) + i'_{rfl,L}(t - \tau_k)]; \quad \begin{matrix} i = 1,2,...,Ny \\ k = 1,2,...,Ng \end{matrix} \tag{45}$$

where $a_{k,i} = (2+\Delta t p_{k,i})/ (2-\Delta t p_{k,i})$ and $\tilde{R}_{k,i} = (\Delta t R_{k,i})/ (2-\Delta t p_{k,i})$. $x_{k,i}$ are discrete-state variables and primed variables denote their value at one previous time step $x'_{k,i} = x_{k,i}(t-\Delta t)$. The discrete–time version of (43) maintains its original form:

$$i_{aux,0} = \sum_{k=1}^{Ng} \sum_{i=1}^{Nh(k)} x_{k,i}$$

Transmission line simulation of EMTs requires the use of time steps Δt smaller than any of the travel times τ_k in the line. Hence, (45) provides the update of state vectors $x_{k,i}$ using only past values of variables already available, either from initial conditions or from previous simulation time steps.

The differentiation mid–point rule is now applied to (40):

$$w_i = a_i w'_i + \tilde{G}_i (v_0 + v'_0); i = 1,2,...,Ny \tag{46}$$

where $a_i = (2+\Delta t q_i)/ (2-\Delta t q_i)$ and $\tilde{G}_i = (\Delta t G_i)/ (2-\Delta t q_i)$

Expression (46) is not a proper DTSS form, as w_i depends on the present–time value of v_0 which still is to be determined (Gustavsen & Mahseredjian, 2007). This problem is fixed here with the following redefinition of the state variable vector:

$$y_i = (\tilde{G}_i^{-1} w_i - v_0)/(a_i + 1); i = 1,2,...,Ny \tag{47}$$

Introducing (47) in (46) and (39) the following expressions are obtained:

$$y_i = a_i y'_i + v'_0; i = 1,2,...,Ny \tag{48}$$

$$i_{sh,0} = Gv_0 + i_{y-aux,0} \tag{49}$$

where

$$\mathbf{i}_{y-aux,0} = \sum_{i=1}^{Ny} \hat{\mathbf{G}}_i \mathbf{y}_i \; ; \; \hat{\mathbf{G}}_i = (a_i + 1)\tilde{\mathbf{G}}_i \; ; \; \mathbf{G} = \mathbf{G}_0 + \sum_{i=1}^{Ny} \tilde{\mathbf{G}}_i$$

Expression (48) is a proper DTSS form for the sequential evaluation of $i_{sh,0}$ at the phase domain line model.

Finally, the introduction of (43) and (49) in (23) results in:

$$\mathbf{i}_0 = \mathbf{G}\mathbf{v}_0 + \mathbf{i}_{hist,0} \tag{50}$$

with

$$\mathbf{i}_{hist,0} = \mathbf{i}_{y-aux,0} - \mathbf{i}_{aux,0} = \sum_{i=1}^{Ny} \hat{\mathbf{G}}_i \mathbf{y}_i - \sum_{k=1}^{Ng} \sum_{i=1}^{Nh(k)} x_{k,i}$$

Expression (50), along with (48) and (49), provides a discrete time–domain model for end 0 of the line segment at figure 1. The expressions for the model at end L are simply obtained by exchanging sub–indexes 0 and L at (48), (49) and (50). Obviously, state variables "y_i" and "$x_{k,i}$" of end L model are different from those of end 0. Figure 3 provides a discrete–time circuit–model for the line segment of length $x=L$. This model is based on expression (50) and its companion for line end L. Note that the model consists of parallel arrangements of shunt conductances and auxiliary sources of currents comprising historic terms of ends (or nodes) 0 and L. Figure 3 model is thus in an appropriate form for computer code implementation. In this chapter, the Matlab environment has been chosen for this end.

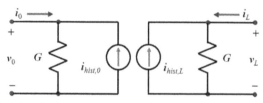

Figure 3. Discrete time domain circuit representation of a multi-conductor line.

5. Line model implementation in Matlab

The discrete–time line model depicted in figure 3 and defined by (50) has been programmed by these authors in Matlab as an M–code function (see Appendix). This function consists of two sub–blocks, one for each multi-conductor line end. This model is to be used with a nodal network solver, a complete explanation on the nodal solver can be found in (Dommel, 1969 & 1992). Expression (50) constitutes essentially the interface between the line model and the nodal solver. Each one of the two sub–blocks in the line model performs iteratively the six tasks that are described next for line–end 0 sub–block. Figure 4 provides the block diagram of the complete line/cable model, along with its interfacing with the nodal solver.

Step 1. State–variable and history–current values are assumed known, either from initial conditions or from previous simulation steps. These values are used by the nodal solver to determine line end (nodal) voltages v_0 and v_L.

Step 2. Shunt current due to the characteristic admittance of the line is calculated by (49) repeated here for convenience:

$$\mathbf{i}_{sh,0} = \mathbf{G}\mathbf{v}_0 + \mathbf{i}_{y-aux,0}$$

Step 3. Auxiliary current source value, due to the reflected traveling waves at the remote line end, is updated by (43):

$$\mathbf{i}_{aux,0} = \sum_{k=1}^{Ng} \sum_{i=1}^{Nh(k)} \mathbf{x}_{k,i}$$

Step 4. Vector of reflected currents at the local line–end (node) "$i_{rfl,0}$" is calculated for the present time by means of (26) being modified to suit line–end 0:

$$\mathbf{i}_{rfl,0} = 2\mathbf{i}_{sh,0} - \mathbf{i}_{aux,0}$$

This vector is delivered to end L sub–block through a delay buffer. Although branch current vector i_0 usually is not explicitly required, it is conveniently evaluated here by (50):

$$\mathbf{i}_0 = \mathbf{G}\mathbf{v}_0 + \mathbf{i}_{hist,0}$$

Step 5. Internal states inside the line model are updated by (48) and (45):

$$\mathbf{y}_i = a_i\mathbf{y}'_i + v'_0$$

$$\mathbf{x}_{k,i} = a_{k,i}\mathbf{x}'_{k,i} + \tilde{\mathbf{R}}_{k,i}[\mathbf{i}_{rfl,L}(t - \tau_k) + \mathbf{i}'_{rfl,L}(t - \tau_k)]$$

Step 6. The vector of history currents for end (node) 0 is updated by means of (50) and the update is delivered to the nodal-network solver.

Steps 1 to 6 are iterated N_t times until $N_t \Delta t$ spans the total simulation time of interest.

5.1. Handling of line-travel delays

It follows from expressions (43) and (45) that the calculation of $i_{aux,0}$ requires the reflected currents vector $i_{rfl,L}$ being evaluated with various time delays τ_1, τ_2 ..., τ_{Ng}. Recall that the delays are due to the travel time needed by a wave to travel from one line end to the other. Past values of $i_{rfl,L}$ can be obtained either from line initial conditions or from previous simulation steps; nevertheless, these values are given by samples regularly distributed Δt seconds apart. Since the involved travel times (or line delays) usually are not integer multiples of Δt, the required values of $i_{rfl,L}$ must be obtained by means of interpolations. The standard procedure for this is to interpolate linearly (Dommel, 1992) and this is adopted here.

Evaluation of the delayed values require a memory buffer spanning at least the largest travel time

$$\tau_{max} = \max\{\tau_1, \tau_2, ..., \tau_{Ng}\},$$ (51)

and buffer length N_b is calculated as follows:

$$N_b = \left\lfloor \frac{\tau_{max}}{\Delta t} \right\rfloor + 1$$ (52)

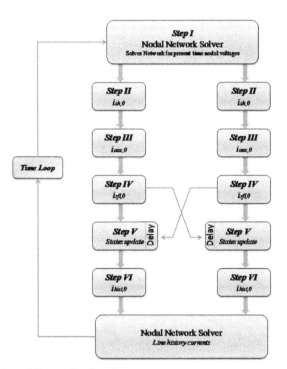

Figure 4. Line/Cable model's complete flow diagram.

If a propagation delay is an integer multiple of Δt, the required value of i_{rfl} can be readily retrieved from the memory buffer. This is illustrated by figure 5 where the simulation time step is Δt=0.03 ms and the travel time is τ=0.10 ms. It can be seen that at simulation time t= 0.24 ms the required history value at 0.09ms is available from the table.

On a multiphase system, nevertheless, it is highly improbable that all the propagation times can be made integer multiples of a single value of Δt suitable for transient simulations. Thus, the required values must be obtained through interpolation. Figure 6 illustrates this case, where a simulation time step $\Delta t=0.04$ ms is assumed instead of the $\Delta t=0.03$ ms one at figure 5. Notice that now the required history value, for a time delay of 0.09ms, is not readily available.

Suppose now that the required value $i_{rfl}(t-\tau)$ is between the k-th and the $(k+1)$-th stored samples of i_{rfl}. Let ζ be the fractional part of $\tau/\Delta t$, that can be obtained as follows:

$$\zeta = \frac{\tau}{\Delta t} - \left\lfloor \frac{\tau}{\Delta t} \right\rfloor, \tag{53}$$

with, $0 \le \zeta < 1$. The estimated value of $i_{rfl}(t-\tau)$ by linear interpolation is thus:

$$\mathbf{i}_{rfl,L}(t-\tau_k) \cong \mathbf{i}_{rfl,L}(t-r\Delta t) + \zeta[\mathbf{i}_{rfl,L}(t-k\Delta t) - \mathbf{i}_{rfl,L}(t-k\Delta t - \Delta t)]. \tag{54}$$

Figure 7 illustrates the memory buffer management, either for $i_{rfl,0}$ or for $i_{rfl,L}$. At the first simulation time step corresponding to time $t=0\times\Delta t$, calculated i_{rfl} is stored at memory 1, and so on until step N_b which is the buffer size limit. Beyond this limit, memory cells 1, 2, 3 and on, are overwritten as figure. 7 shows, since their previously stored values are not needed any longer.

$t(ms)$	$i_{rfl,0}$	$i_{rfl,L}$
0.0	*	*
0.03	*	*
0.09	*	*
0.12	*	*
0.15	*	*
0.18	*	*
0.21	*	*
0.24	*	*

Figure 5. Interpolation scheme: Δt integer multiple.

$t(ms)$	$i_{rfl,0}$	$i_{rfl,L}$
0.0	*	*
0.04	*	*
0.08	*	*
0.12	*	*
0.16	*	*
0.20	*	*
0.24	*	*

Figure 6. Interpolation scheme: Δt non integer multiple.

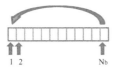

Figure 7. History buffer management.

Linear interpolation is an order 1 numerical procedure and the trapezoidal rule used for the rest of the line model is of order 2. The question arises as to whether or not the order 2 quadratic interpolation should be adopted instead. This has been investigated at (Gutierrez–Robles et al., 2011) and it has been found that the increase in accuracy is marginal.

6. Application examples

The simulation results presented as follows are obtained with the Matlab implementation of the model being described here. These results are compared against those from the phase domain line model in EMTP-RV. Two examples are presented next, first an aerial 9–conductor line and, finally, one for an underground cable. Also a basic m-code for the described phase domain line model is provided at the appendix. The code is given along with the companion routines to perform the first example presented in (Ramos- Leaños & Iracheta, 2010). The reader can readily modify the provided m-code for other applications of interest.

6.1. Aerial line case

The transversal geometry of this test case is shown in figure 8. Phase conductors are 1192.5 ASCR 54/19 and ground wires are 7 No 5 AWLD. This case consists of three coupled three–phase transmission lines. First line (or circuit 1) is composed of conductors 1 to 3, second line (or circuit 2) includes conductors 5 to 6 and the third line (or circuit 3) comprises conductors 7 to 9. The line length is 150 km. The test circuit is shown in figure 9 where the source is 169 kV, Y-grounded, source impedance is determined by its zero and positive sequence data in Ohms: R_0=2, R_1=1, X_0=22, X_1=15, and closing times are 0 s for phase a, 0.63 ms for phase b and 0.4 ms for phase c. The simulation time step is 5 µs.

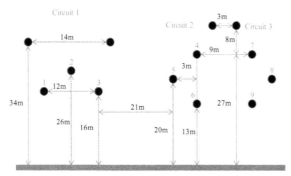

Figure 8. Aerial line transversal geometry.

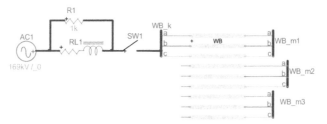

Figure 9. Test circuit for the case of a nine–conductor line.

Simulation results are presented in figure 10 where the receiving end voltage waveforms of circuit 1 are shown, those for phase a are in blue, those for phase b are in green and those for phase c are in red. A dashed line is used for waveforms obtained with EMTP-RV, while a solid line is used for the results with the line model in Matlab. Notice that the two sets of results overlap and not difference can be seen. Figure 10 provides the differences between the two sets of results. Note that the largest difference is around 3e-9.

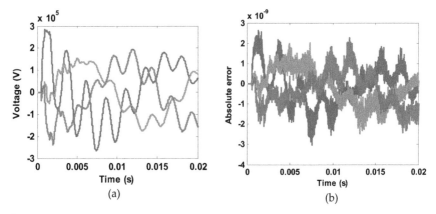

Figure 10. (a) Over voltages at receiving end for conductors 1, 2 and 3, (b) Differences between results with Matlab model and with EMTP–RV.

6.2. Underground cable case

The underground cable system used for this test consists of three single–phase coaxial cables, its transversal layout is shown in figure 11. The Corresponding connection diagram is provided in figure 12. Circuit parameters are given in table 1, the cable length is 6.67km and the time step used for the simulation is 1 µs. The applied excitation is by a 3ph 169kV ideal source.

The simulation experiment consists in the simultaneous energizing of the three cable cores. The results presented in figure 13 correspond to the core voltages at the far end. Phase a voltages are in blue, phase b voltages are in green and those for phase c are in red. A dashed line is used for the results obtained with EMTP-RV, while a solid line is used for the Matlab model results. Notice that both sets of results overlap and that no difference can be seen by eye. Figure 13 also shows the difference between the two sets of results which is around 4e-9. Compared to the 1.69e+5 amplitude of the excitation source, this difference shows the outstanding accuracy of the Matlab model.

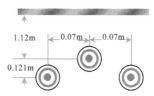

Figure 11. Cable layout.

Radius of inner solid conductor (m)	0.015
Resistivity nuclei/sheath (ohm/m)	4.25e-8/2.84e-8
Inner/Outer radius of sheath (m)	0.0258/0.0263
Relative permittivity of 1st & 2nd insulation	2.5

Table 1. Cable data.

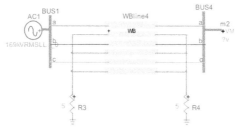

Figure 12. Cable test circuit.

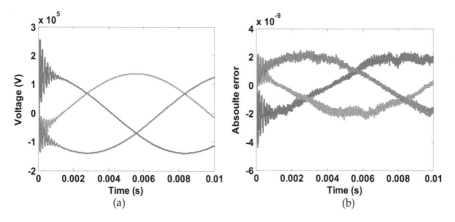

Figure 13. (a) Receivng end core voltages, (b) absolute error.

7. Vector fitting

The goal of VF is to approximate a complex function of frequency by means of a rational function; that is, a quotient of two polynomials of the frequency variable (Gustavsen & Semlyen, 1999). The function to be approximated could be trascendantal or could be specified by its values at a number of frequency points. The form of the approximation obtained with VF is that of a partial fraction expansion:

$$f(s) \cong \sum_{n=1}^{N} \frac{r_n}{s + \bar{p}_n} \tag{55}$$

VF estimates the system parameters by means of a two-stage linear least–squares procedure. First a set of initial poles for the partial fraction basis (55) is selected and relocated iteratively until a prescribed convergence criterion is attained. Then, convergence is tested by means of a second linear least–squares procedure in which the previously obtained poles are fixed and the corresponding residues are taken as the unknown parameters.

Consider the following relation (Gustavsen & Semlyen, 1999):

$$\sum_{n=1}^{N} \frac{\hat{r}_n}{s + \bar{p}_n} \cong f(s)\left(1 + \sum_{n=1}^{N} \frac{\tilde{r}_n}{s + \bar{p}_n}\right), \tag{56}$$

where, N is the order of approximation, $\bar{p}_n$ represents the unknown poles and $\hat{r}_n$ and $\tilde{r}_n$ are unknown residues. Poles are initialized by values distributed logarithmically over the frequency range of interest. Expression (56) is now rewritten as follows:

$$\left(\sum_{n=1}^{N} \frac{\hat{r}_n}{s + \bar{p}_n} - \left(\sum_{n=1}^{N} \frac{\tilde{r}_n}{s + \bar{p}_n}\right) f(s) \cong f(s). \tag{57}$$

An over–determined least squares equation–system is then obtained by evaluating (57) at a number M of specific frequencies, with $M > 2N$:

$$\mathbf{Ax = b}, \tag{58}$$

where A is the $M \times 2N$ matrix whose elements depend on the poles, x is the $2N$–dimension vector of unknown residues and b is the M–dimension vector with the values of the function to be approximated (Gustavsen & Semlyen, 1999). Special care is taken to accommodate next to each other those complex–conjugate pairs of pole–residues that can arise. Expression (58) is solved through an iterative process represented symbolically as follows:

$$\mathbf{A}^{(j-1)}\mathbf{x}^{(j)} = \mathbf{b}, \tag{59}$$

were (j–1) and (j) represent super–indexes and j is the iteration index. $A^{(0)}$ is obtained from the initial poles with logarithmic distribution over the frequency range of interest

(Gustavsen & Semlyen, 1999). As (59) is solved in the first iteration, a second step is to use the obtained residue values to recalculate new poles for the function to be fitted $f(s)$. This is accomplished by computing the eigenvalues of the following matrix Q (Gustavsen & Semlyen, 1999):

$$\mathbf{Q} = \mathbf{W} - \mathbf{g}\tilde{\mathbf{x}}^T, \tag{60}$$

where W is a diagonal matrix containing previously calculated poles $\bar{p}_n$, g is a vector of ones and $\tilde{x}$ is a vector containing the $\tilde{r}$ terms only. The reason for using (60) is explained next. Let (56) be rewritten as follows:

$$\frac{\displaystyle\sum_{n=1}^{N}\frac{\hat{r}_n}{s+\bar{p}_n}}{\displaystyle\sum_{n=1}^{N}\frac{\tilde{r}_n}{s+\bar{p}_n}+1} = \frac{\displaystyle\prod_{n=1}^{N'}(s+\hat{z}_n)}{\displaystyle\prod_{n=1}^{N}(s+\tilde{z}_n)} \cong f(s). \tag{61}$$

It is clear in (61) that the two polynomials containing the poles $\bar{p}_n$ cancel each other, and that the zeros $\tilde{z}_n$ become the poles of $f(s)$. Notice further that the denominator on the left–hand–side of (61) can be written as follows:

$$\sum_{n=1}^{N}\frac{\tilde{r}_n}{s+\bar{p}_n}+1 = \frac{\displaystyle\prod_{n=1}^{N}(s+\tilde{z}_n)}{\displaystyle\prod_{n=1}^{N}(s+\bar{p}_n)}. \tag{62}$$

Zeros $\tilde{z}_n$ are then obtained by finding the roots of (Gustavsen & Semlyen, 1999)

$$\sum_{i=1}^{N}\left(\tilde{r}_i\prod_{n=1,n\neq i}^{N}(s+\bar{p}_n)\right)+\prod_{n=1}^{N}(s+\bar{p}_n) = 0, \tag{63}$$

which is equivalent to finding the eigenvalues of Q in (60) (Gustavsen & Semlyen, 1999).

The newly found set of poles is replaced in (55) to determine a new set of residues r_n. This is again an over–determined linear system. The fitting error is tested at this stage for each available sample of $f(s)$. If the error level is not acceptable, the new poles are used to restart the procedure as with (56). If the desired error limit is not met after a pre-specified number of iterations, then, the order of approximation N is increased and the iterative procedure is restarted (Gustavsen & Semlyen, 1999).

Even in most cases where initial poles are not chosen adequately, VF is capable of finding a solution at the expense of more iterations. In some cases an iteration can produce unstable poles; these poles simply are flipped into the left–hand–side part of the complex plane (i.e., the stable part) and a new solution is searched (Gustavsen & Semlyen, 1999).

8. Conclusions

Proper design and operation of present-day power systems and apparatuses each time require accurate simulations of their electromagnetic transient performance. An important aspect of these simulations is the realistic representation of transmission lines by digital computer models. The ULM is the most general line model available today, mostly with EMTP–type programs. By being of relatively recent creation, this model still is a subject for substantial improvements in accuracy, stability and computational efficiency. It has been postulated in this work that, both, researchers and power system analysts will benefit considerably from the full understanding of the theoretical basis of the ULM, as well as from counting with a ULM–type code that is easy to understand and modify. It has been contended also that the best way to carry out ULM research and development is by providing a model version in an interpretive environment and Matlab has been the platform chosen for this. This chapter provides a comprehensive description of the theoretical basis of ULM, phase domain line model. In addition to this, full description of a ULM prototype in Matlab has been provided here, along with executable code and typical application examples.

Author details

Octavio Ramos-Leaños
École Polytechnique de Montréal, Canada

Jose Luis Naredo
Cinvestav-Guadalajara, Mexico

Jose Alberto Gutierrez-Robles
University of Guadalajara, Mexico

Appendix

CODE EXECUTION

The following code provides the line model described in the paper and it is embedded into an application example. It simulates the simultaneous energizing of a 150 km long aerial line. At the source side the three voltage sources have a 600 Ω Thevenin impedance. The program asks for the type of source (unit step or three phase sinusoids). At the load end the line is open. Figure 14 shows the geometry of the simulated line. Figure 15 shows the sending and receiving voltages for the unit step source, while Figure 16 shows the sending and receiving voltages for the sinusoidal source.

Note at Figure 15 that waveforms for phases A and C are equal and their plots are superposed. This is because the symmetry of the line and the excitation.

Main program

```
clear all
clc
% m file to set line data
LineData
% Per unit length parameters
[Zg,Zt,Zc,Yg,ZL,YL] = LineParameters(Mu,Eo,Rsu,Geom,Ncon,Ns,w);
% Modal Parameters
for k=1:Ns
   [Yc(:,:,k),Vm(k,:),Hm(k,:)] = ABYZLM(ZL(:,:,k),YL(:,:,k),lenght,w(k));
end
% Characteristic Admittance Fitting
[YcPoles,YcResidues,YcConstant,YcProportional] = YcFit(Yc,f,Ns,Ncon);
% Hk fit
[HkPoles,HkResidues,HkConstant,HkProportional,md] =
HkFitTrace(Hm,Vm,ZL,YL,f,Ns,lenght,Ncon);
% m file to execute simulation loop.
SimulationLoop
```

Code to Load LineData

```
% Line Geometry
% column 1—conductor number
% column 2-- x position of each cond in m
% column 3-- y position of each cod in m
% column 4-- radii of each conductor
% column 5-- number of conductor in bundle
% column 6-- distance between conductors in bundle
% column 7—conductor resistivity
% column 8—conductor relative permitivity
% column 9-- line lenght in m
 Geom=[1    0 20 0.0153 3 0.4 2.826e-8 1e3 150e3
        2  10 20 0.0153 3 0.4 2.826e-8 1e3 150e3
        3  20 20 0.0153 3 0.4 2.826e-8 1e3 150e3];
 lenght = Geom(1,9);          % Line lenght
 Ncon  = Geom(max(Geom(:,1)),1); % # of cond
 Rsu  = 100;              % Earth resistivity Ohm-m
 Mu   = 4*pi*1E-7;          % Henry's/meters
 Eo   = (1/(36*pi))*1E-9;  % Farads/meters
 Rhi  = 9.09E-7;  % Ohm-m resistivity of the iron.
 Ral = 2.61E-8;   % Ohm-m res of the aluminum.
 Rhg = 2.71E-7;  % Ohm-m  res of the sky wires.
 Ns  = 500;               % Number of samples
 f  = logspace(-2, 6, Ns);     % Vector of log spaced Frequencies
 w = 2*pi*f;  % Vector of freqs in radian/sec.
```

Function LineParameters

```
function [Zg,Zt,Zc,Yg,ZT,YT]=LineParameters (Mu,Eo,Rsu,Geom,Ncon,Ns,w)
% Function to compute the distances between conductor
[Dij,dij,hij]=Height(Geom);
```

```
Zg  = zeros(Ncon,Ncon,Ns);
Zt  = zeros(Ncon,Ncon,Ns);
Zc  = zeros(Ncon,Ncon,Ns);
Yg  = zeros(Ncon,Ncon,Ns);
Zcd = zeros(Ncon,Ns);
Zaf = zeros(Ncon,Ns);
P = (1./sqrt(j*w*Mu/Rsu));   % Complex depth
Pmatrix = log(Dij./dij);     % Potential Coeff. Matrix
Pinv    = inv(Pmatrix);      % Inverse of Pmatrix
% Loop to compute matrices at all frequencies
for kl = 1:Ns
   % Geometric impedance
   Zg(:,:,kl) = (j*w(kl)*Mu/(2*pi))*Pmatrix;
   % Earth impedance
   for km = 1:Ncon
     for kn = 1:Ncon
       if km == kn
         Zt(km,km,kl) = (j*w(kl)*Mu/(2*pi))*
         log(1+P(kl)./(0.5*hij(km,km)));
       else
         num  = hij(km,kn)^2 + 4*P(kl)*hij(km,kn) +
         4*P(kl)^2 + dij(km,kn)^2;
         den = hij(km,kn)^2 + dij(km,kn)^2;
         Zt(km,kn,kl) = (j*w(kl)*Mu/(4*pi))*
         log(num/den);
       end
     end
   end
   % Geometric admittance
   Yg(:,:,kl) = (j*w(kl)*2*pi*Eo)*Pinv;
end
% Conductor impedance
for kd = 1:Ncon;
  Rcon = Geom(kd,4);  % conductor radii in m.
  Nhaz = Geom(kd,5);  % # of conductor in bundle
  Rpha = Geom(kd,7);  % Resistivity in Ohm-m.
  Zcd(kd,:) = (1/Nhaz)*Rpha./(pi.*Rcon.^2);
  Zaf(kd,:) = (1/Nhaz)*(1+j).*(1./(2.*pi.*Rcon)) .*
  sqrt(0.5.*w.*Mu.*Rpha);
  Zc(kd,kd,:) = sqrt(Zcd(kd,:).^2 + Zaf(kd,:).^2);
end
% Outputs
ZT = Zg + Zt + Zc ;   % Total impedance
YT = Yg ;             % Total admittance
```

Function ABYZLM

```
function [Yc,Vm,Hmo] = ABYZLM(Z,Y,Lo,w)
 [M, Lm] = eig(Y*Z);   % Eigenvalues of YZ
Minv = inv(M);  % Inverse of eigenvectors matrix
Yc = inv(Z)*(M*sqrt(Lm)*Minv);  % Characteristic Admittance
```

```
Gamma   = sqrt(diag(Lm));          % Propagation constants.
Vm = w./imag(Gamma);     % Modal Velocities
Hmo = diag(expm(-sqrtm(Lm)*Lo));  % Modal propag. Matrix H
```

Function YcFit

```
function [YcPoles,YcResidues,YcConstant, YcProportional]=YcFit(Yc,f,Ns,Ncon)
% Trace of characteristic admittance matrix
for k = 1:Ns
   Ytrace(k,1) = trace(Yc(:,:,k));
end
Npol = 6;                     % Number of poles
[Ps] = InitialPoles(f,Npol);  % Set initial poles
s   = j*2*pi*f.';          % Vector of values of variable "s"
Ka=2; % 1.-Strictly proper, 2.-Proper, 3.-Improper
for khg=1:20
   % Fit the trace of Yc (Poles)
   [YcPoles]=Poles(Ytrace.',s,Ps,Ns,Ka);
   Ps=YcPoles;
end
% Residues and constant term for Yc from poles of trace of Yc
for k = 1:Ncon
   for l = 1:Ncon
     Hs(:,1) = Yc(k,l,:); % k-l term of admittance
     [C,D,E]=Residue(Hs.',s,YcPoles,Ns,Ka);
     YcResidues(k,l,:) = C;      % k-l residues term
     YcConstant(k,l)  = D;    % k-l constant term
     YcProportional(k,l)=E; %k-l proportional term
   end
end
```

Function HkFitTrace

```
function [HkPoles,HkResidues,HkConstant, HkProportional,md]=HkFit(Hm,Vm,ZL,YL,f,Ns,
lenght,Ncon);
   % Minimum phase of each mode
md = ModeDelay(Hm.',f,lenght,Vm.',Ns,Ncon);
% Computing Idempotents
for k=1:Ns
   % Function to calculate Idempotents of Y*Z
   [Hk] = HmIdem(ZL(:,:,k),YL(:,:,k),lenght,f(k), md,Hm(k,:));
   HkIdem(:,:,:,k) = Hk; % Idempotents
end
for m = 1:3
   for k=1:Ns
     TraceHk(m,k) = trace(HkIdem(:,:,m,k));
   end
end
s = j*2*pi*f.';      % Vector of the variable "s"
Ka =1;%1.-Strictly proper, 2.-Proper, 3.-Improper
Npol = 5;                     % Number of poles
[Ps] = InitialPoles(f,Npol); % Set the initial poles
```

```
for m = 1:3
  Hk = TraceHk(m,:);
  for khg=1:10
    [HkPol]=Poles(Hk,s,Ps,Ns,Ka);
    Ps=HkPol;
  end
  HkPoles(m,:)=Ps;
end
% Residues for Idempotent matrices of
% Hm from the poles of each trace.
for m = 1:3
  for k = 1:Ncon
    for l = 1:Ncon
      Hs(:,1) = HkIdem(k,l,m,:);   % k-l term
      [C,D,E]=Residue(Hs.',s,HkPoles(m,:),Ns,Ka);
      HkResidues(k,l,m,:)  = C;  % k-l-m term
      HkConstant(k,l,m)   = D;  % k-l-m constant
      HkProportional(k,l,m) = E;  % k-l-m prop
    end
  end
end
```

SimulationLoop program

```
Ts  = 0.016;          % Observation time
Nt  = fix(Ts/Dt);     % Number of time steps
t1  = fix(md./Dt);    % Delay of H in samples
t0  = fix(max(md)./Dt);   % Maximum time delay as expressed in
% number of samples
t   = (0:Dt:(Nt+t1)*Dt-Dt);   % Vector of time
Ks = menu('CHOOSE THE TYPE OF INPUT SOURCE' , '1 -unit step' , '2 -sinusoidal');
if Ks == 1 % unit step source
  Isr  = ones(Ncon,Nt+t0);
elseif Ks ==2 % sinusoidal source
  Isr(1,:) = sin(337*t);
  Isr(2,:) = sin(337*t+2*pi/3);
  Isr(3,:) = sin(337*t+4*pi/3);
end
NpYc = length(YcPoles); % Number of poles of Yc
NpH = length(HkPoles); % Number of poles for the first
% Idempotent matrix
Ng = 3;              %Number of groups
% Initialize the states for both nodes
ZA = zeros(Ncon,NpYc); % State variables
ZB = zeros(Ncon,NpYc); % State variables
YA = zeros(Ncon,NpH,Ng); % State variables
YB = zeros(Ncon,NpH,Ng); % State variables
IfarA = zeros(Ncon,t0+3); % Current at node A
IfarB = zeros(Ncon,t0+3); % Current at node B
VO = zeros(Ncon,1);   % Voltage at node A
Vi = zeros(Ncon,Nt+t0);   % Voltage at node A
```

```
VL  = zeros(Ncon,1);       % Voltage at node B
Vf = zeros(Ncon,Nt+t0);     % Voltage at node B
IO = zeros(Ncon,1);        % Current at node A
Ii  = zeros(Ncon,Nt+t0);      % Current at node A
IL  = zeros(Ncon,1);        % Current at node B
If  = zeros(Ncon,Nt+t0);      % Current at node B
Iri = zeros(Ncon,Nt+t0);      % Current at Y source
Irf = zeros(Ncon,Nt+t0);      % Current at Y charge
 IfarAint = zeros(Ncon,Ng);  % Current at node A
IfarBint = zeros(Ncon,Ng);    % Current at node B
% Constants for the state ZA and ZB
Ai(:,1) = (1+(Dt/2)*YcPoles)./(1-(Dt/2)*YcPoles);
Au(:,1) = ((Dt/2)./(1-(Dt/2)*YcPoles));
Bi(:,1) = (Ai+1).*Au;
Gy = zeros(Ncon,Ncon);
for nm = 1:NpYc
   Di(:,:,nm)   = YcResidues(:,:,nm)*Bi(nm);
   Gy  = Gy + YcResidues(:,:,nm)*Au(nm);
end
% Constants for the states YA and YB
for k = 1:Ng
   K1(:,k) = (1+(Dt/2)*HkPoles(:,k))./(1-(Dt/2)*HkPoles(:,k));
   Ka(:,k) = (((Dt/2))./(1-(Dt/2)*HkPoles(:,k)));
   Ku(:,k) = (K1(:,k)+1).*Ka(:,k);
end
for k = 1:Ng
   for nm = 1:NpH
   K2(:,:,nm,k) =  HkResidues(:,:,nm,k).*Ka(nm,k);
   K3(:,:,nm,k) = HkResidues(:,:,nm,k).*Ku(nm,k);
   end
end
Gy  = Gy + YcConstant;  % Admitance of the Ish
Yi  = diag(eye(3)*[1/600; 1/600; 1/600]);      % Admittance of the source, connected at node A
Gys = inv(Gy + Yi); % Impedance to calculate VO
Yr =diag(eye(3)*[1/1e6; 1/1e6; 1/1e6]);    % Admittance of load connected at node B
Gyr = inv(Gy + Yr); % Impedance to calculate VL
% Contants terms to perform the interpolation
tm =md - t1*Dt; % Time for the interpolation
% Linear interpolation constants
c1 = tm/Dt;
c2 = 1-c1;
c3 = ones(Ng,1);
% Pointers for the interpolation and the buffer
h1 = t1+1;
h2 = t1+2;
h3 = t1+3;
 for k = t0+2:Nt+t0-3
     IfarA(:,1) = IL + Gy*VL + sum(ZB(:,:),2);
     IfarB(:,1) = IO + Gy*VO + sum(ZA(:,:),2);
   % Linear interpolation
```

```matlab
for m = 1:Ng
   IfarAint(:,m) = c2(m)*IfarA(:,t1(m)) + c3(m)*IfarA(:,h1(m)) + c1(m)*IfarA(:,h2(m));
   IfarBint(:,m) = c2(m)*IfarB(:,t1(m)) + c3(m)*IfarB(:,h1(m)) + c1(m)*IfarB(:,h2(m));
end
IfarA(:,2:h3) = IfarA(:,1:h2);
IfarB(:,2:h3) = IfarB(:,1:h2);
for m = 1:NpYc
   ZA(:,m) = Ai(m)*ZA(:,m) + Di(:,:,m)*VO;
   ZB(:,m) = Ai(m)*ZB(:,m) + Di(:,:,m)*VL;
end
for l = 1:Ng
   for m = 1:NpH
      YA(:,m,l) = K1(m,l)*YA(:,m,l) + K2(:,:,m,l)*IfarAint(:,l);
      YB(:,m,l) = K1(m,l)*YB(:,m,l) + K2(:,:,m,l)*IfarBint(:,l);
   end
end
HistO = - sum(ZA(:,:),2) + sum(sum(YA(:,:,:),3),2);
HistL  = - sum(ZB(:,:),2) + sum(sum(YB(:,:,:),3),2);
VO = Gys*(Isr(:,k)+HistO);
VL = Gyr*HistL;
IO = Gy*VO - HistO;
IL = Gy*VL - HistL;
Vi(:,k) = VO;
Vf(:,k) = VL;
Ii(:,k) = IO;
If(:,k) = IL;
end
Iri = Yi*Vi;
Irf = Yr*Vf;
vt = (0:Dt:length(Vi(1,:)))*Dt-(t0+4)*Dt)';
N = length(vt);
a1 = t1+1;
a2 = Nt+t1-3;
figure(1),plot(vt,Vi(:,a1:a2),':',vt,Vf(:,a1:a2))
ylabel('Amplitude in volts')
xlabel('Time in seconds')
legend('Sending end phase A' , 'Sending end phase B' , 'Sending end phase C' , 'Receiving end phase A' ,
'Receiving end phase B' , 'Receiving end phase C')
```

Function Height

```matlab
function[Dij,dij,hij]=Height(Geom)
Ls  = Geom(max(Geom(:,1)),1);
Req = zeros(Ls,1);
% Equivalent bundle radii
k4 = sqrt(2*(Geom(:,6)/2).^2);
for nc = 1: Ls;
  if Geom(nc,5)==1
    Req(nc) = Geom(nc,4);
  else
    Req(nc) = (Geom(nc,4).*Geom(nc,5).*k4(nc).^
```

```
(Geom(nc,5)-1)).^(1./Geom(nc,5));
  end
end
% Direct and image distances among conductors
for xl = 1:Ls;
  for yl = 1:Ls;
    if xl==yl
      dij(xl,yl)=Req(xl);
      y1=Geom(yl,3);
      hij(xl,yl)=2*y1;
      Dij(xl,yl)=hij(xl,yl);
    else
      x=abs(Geom(yl,2)-Geom(xl,2));
      y=abs(Geom(yl,3)-Geom(xl,3));
      dij(xl,yl)=sqrt(x^2 + y^2);
      y1=Geom(xl,3);
      y2=Geom(yl,3);
      hij(xl,yl)=y1+y2;
      x=abs(Geom(yl,2)-Geom(xl,2));
      y=hij(xl,yl);
      Dij(xl,yl)=sqrt(x^2 + y^2);
    end
  end
end
```

Function InitialPoles

```
function [Ps]=InitialPoles(f,Npol)
 even  = fix(Npol/2); % # of complex initial poles
p_odd = Npol/2 - even; % Auxiliary variable to check if number
% of initial poles is odd
disc = p_odd ~= 0; %  0 for even Nr of initial poles  &  1 - for
% odd Nr.
% Set a real pole in case of disc == 1
if disc == 0    % Even Nr of initial poles
  pols = [];
else          % Odd Nr of initial poles
  pols = [(max(f)-min(f))/2];
end
% Set the complex initial poles
bet = linspace(min(f),max(f),even);
for n=1:length(bet)
  alf=-bet(n)*1e-2;
  pols=[pols (alf-j*bet(n)) (alf+j*bet(n)) ];
end
Ps = pols.'; % Column vector of initial poles
```

Function Poles

```
function [A]=Poles(Fs,s,Pi,Ns,Ka);
Np = length(Pi); % Length of vector containing starting poles
CPX = imag(Pi)~=0; % 0 for real pole and 1 for complex pole
```

```matlab
rp = 0;   % Initialize the index for real poles
cp = 0;   % Initialize the index for complex poles
RePole = [];   % Initialize the vector of real poles
CxPole=[];%Initialize the vector of complex poles
% Loop to separate real poles and complex poles
for k = 1:Np
  if CPX(k) == 0     % Real Pole
    rp = rp + 1;
    RePole(rp) = Pi(k);
  elseif CPX(k) == 1 % Complex pole
    cp = cp + 1;
    CxPole(cp) = Pi(k);
  end
end
Lambda = Pi.';
RePole = sort(RePole);      % Sort real poles
CxPole = sort(CxPole);      % Sort complex poles
Lambda = [RePole CxPole]; % Concatenate poles
I = diag(ones(1,Np));   % Unit matrix
A = [];            % Poles
B = ones(Ns,1);     % the weight factor
C   = [];         % Residues
D   = zeros(1);     % Constant term
E   = zeros(1);     % Proportional term
KQA   = ones(Ns,1);

cpx = imag(Lambda)~=0;   % 0 if pole is real and 1 if pole is
% complex.
dix = zeros(1,Np);      % Initializes vector of pole types
if cpx(1)~=0    % If the first pole is complex
  dix(1)=1;       % real part
  dix(2)=2;    % imag part
  k=3;          % continue dix for third position
else
  k=2;   % If the first pole is real continue dix for the second position
end
% complete the classification of the poles
for m=k:Np
  if cpx(m)~=0      % If the pole is complex
    if dix(m-1)==1
      dix(m)=2;   % If the previous position has the real part put 2
% to identifies the imag part
    else
      dix(m)=1;   % 1 for the real part of a complex pole
    end
  end
end
% Creates matriz A  divided in four parts A = [A1 A2 A3 A4]
% A1 = Dk
% A2 = B.*ones(Ns,1)
```

```matlab
% A3 = B.*s
% A4 = -Dk*Fs
Dk=zeros(Ns,Np);  % Initialize  matrix with zeros
for m=1:Np    % Iterative cycle for all poles
  if dix(m)== 0          % For a real pole
    Dk(:,m) = B./(s-Lambda(m));
  elseif dix(m)== 1  % For the real part
    Dk(:,m)=B./(s-Lambda(m)) +
            B./(s-Lambda(m)');
  elseif dix(m)== 2   % For the imag part
    Dk(:,m) = i.*B./(s-Lambda(m-1)) -
              i.*B./(s-Lambda(m-1)');
  end
end
% Creates work space for matrix A
A1 = Dk;
A2 = B.*ones(Ns,1);
A3 = B.*s;
for col = 1:Np
  A4(:,col) = -(Dk(:,col).*Fs.');
end
% Asigns values to A
if Ka == 1
  A = [A1 A4];  % Strictly proper rational fitting
elseif Ka == 2
  A = [A1 A2 A4];  % Proper rational fitting
elseif Ka == 3
  A = [A1 A2 A3 A4];  % Improper rational fitting
else
  disp('Ka need to be 1, 2 or 3')
end
% Creates matrix b = B*Fs
b = B.*Fs.';
% Separating real and imaginary part
Are = real(A);    % Real part of matrix A
Aim = imag(A);    % Imaginary part of matrix A
bre = real(b);    % Real part of matrix b
bim = imag(b);    % Imaginary part of matrix b
An = [Are; Aim];  % Real and imaginary part of A
bn = [bre; bim];  % Real and imaginary part of b
% Routine to applies the Euclidian norm to An
[Xmax Ymax] = size(An);
for col=1:Ymax
 Euclidian(col)=norm(An(:,col),2);
 An(:,col)=An(:,col)./Euclidian(col);
end
% Solving system
Xn = An\bn;
Xn = Xn./Euclidian.';
% Put the residues into matrix C
```

```matlab
if Ka == 1
  C = Xn(Np+1:Ymax);  % Strictly proper fitting
elseif Ka == 2
  C = Xn(Np+2:Ymax);    % Proper rational fitting
elseif Ka == 3
  C = Xn(Np+3:Ymax);% Improper rational fitting
else
  disp('Ka need to be 1, 2 or 3')
end
% C complex when the residues are complex
for m=1:Np
  if dix(m)==1
    alfa = C(m);  % real part of a complex pole
    betta = C(m+1);  % imag part of a complex pole
    C(m)   = alfa + i*betta;  % the complex pole
    C(m+1) = alfa - i*betta;  % the conjugate
  end
end
% Now calculate the zeros for sigma
BDA = zeros(Np);
KQA = ones(Np,1);
% Loop to calculate the zeros of sigma which are the new poles
for km = 1:Np
  if dix(km)== 0        % For a real pole
    BDA(km,km) = Lambda(km);
  elseif dix(km)==1  % For a cp with - imag part
    BDA(km,km)   = real(Lambda(km));
    BDA(km,km+1) = imag(Lambda(km));
    KQA(km)      = 2;
    Aux = C(km);
    C(km) = real(Aux);
  elseif dix(km)== 2 % For a cp with + imag part
    BDA(km,km)   = real(Lambda(km));
    BDA(km,km-1) = imag(Lambda(km));
    KQA(km)      = 0;
    C(km)  = imag(Aux);
  end
end
ZEROS = BDA - KQA*C.';
POLS  = eig(ZEROS).';
%Forcing (flipping) unstable poles to make them stable
uns  = real(POLS)>0;
POLS(uns) = POLS(uns)-2*real(POLS(uns));
 % Sort poles in ascending order. First real poles and then complex poles
CPX   = imag(POLS)~=0;  % Set to 0 for a real pole and  to1 for a
%complex pole
rp = 0;  % Initialize index for real poles
cp = 0;  % Initialize index for complex poles
RePole = [];  % Initialize the vector of real poles
CxPole = [];  % Initialize the vector of cp
```

```
% Loop to separate real and complex poles
for k = 1:Np
  if CPX(k) == 0     % Real Pole
    rp = rp + 1;
    RePole(rp) = POLS(k);
  elseif CPX(k) == 1 % Complex pole
    cp = cp + 1;
    CxPole(cp) = POLS(k);
  end
end
RePole = sort(RePole);     % Sort real poles
CxPole = sort(CxPole);     % Sort complex poles
%  For conjugate pairs store first the one with positive imag part
CxPole = (CxPole.')';
NewPol = [RePole CxPole];
A = NewPol.';     % Output
```

Function Residue

```
function [C,D,E]=Residue(Fs,s,Pi,Ns,Ka);
Np  = length(Pi);
CPX = imag(Pi)~=0;  % 0 for a rp and 1 for cp
rp    = 0;  % Initialize the index for real poles
cp    = 0;  % Initialize the index for complex poles
RePole = [];    % Initialize the vector of real poles
CxPole=[]; %Initialize the vector of complex poles
% Loop to separate real poles and complex poles
for k = 1:Np
  if CPX(k) == 0     % Real Pole
    rp = rp + 1;
    RePole(rp) = Pi(k);
  elseif CPX(k) == 1 % Complex pole
    cp = cp + 1;
    CxPole(cp) = Pi(k);
  End
end
RePole = sort(RePole);     % Sort real poles
CxPole = sort(CxPole);     % Sort complex poles
CxPole = (CxPole.')';
Lambda = [RePole CxPole];
I  = diag(ones(1,Np));  % Unit diagonal matrix
A    = [];         % Poles
B    = ones(Ns,1);     % weight factor
C    = [];         % Residues
D    = zeros(1);       % Constant term
E    = zeros(1);       % Proportional term
cpx = imag(Lambda)~=0;  % 0 for rp and 1 for cp
dix = zeros(1,Np);     % Vto identifies poles
if cpx(1)~=0       % If the first pole is complex
  dix(1)=1;        % put 1 in dix(1) for the real part
  dix(2)=2;        % put 2 in dix(2) for the imag part
```

```
  k=3;        % continue dix for the third position
else
  k=2;   % If the first pole is real continue dix for the second
% position
end
% complete classification of the poles
for m=k:Np
  if cpx(m)~=0      % If the pole is complex
    if dix(m-1)==1
      dix(m)=2;   % If the previous position has the real part, set to % 2 to identify the imag part
    else
      dix(m)=1;   % put 1 for the real part of a cp
    end
  end
end
% Output matrices:
Dk=zeros(Ns,Np);
for m=1:Np
  if dix(m)==0      % Real pole
    Dk(:,m) = B./(s-Lambda(m));
  elseif dix(m)==1    % Complex pole, 1st part
    Dk(:,m) = B./(s-Lambda(m)) + B./(s-Lambda(m)');
  elseif dix(m)==2    % Complex pole, 2nd part
    Dk(:,m) = i.*B./(s-Lambda(m-1)) - i.*B./(s-Lambda(m-1)');
  end
end
% Creates work space for matrices A and b
AA1=Dk;
AA2=B.*ones(Ns,1);
AA3=B.*s;
if Ka == 1
  AA = [AA1];   % Strictly proper rational fit
elseif Ka == 2
  AA = [AA1 AA2];   % Proper rational fit
elseif Ka == 3
  AA = [AA1 AA2 AA3];   % Improper fit
else
  disp('Ka must be 1, 2 or 3')
end
bb  = B.*Fs.';
AAre = real(AA);      % Real part of matrix A
AAim = imag(AA);   % Imaginary part of matrix A
bbre = real(bb);      % Real part of matrix b
bbim = imag(bb);      % Imaginary part of matrix b
AAn = [AAre; AAim];   % Real and imag part of A
bbn = [bbre; bbim];    % Real and imag part of b
 [Xmax Ymax] = size(AAn);
for col=1:Ymax
  Eeuclidian(col)=norm(AAn(:,col),2);
  AAn(:,col)=AAn(:,col)./Eeuclidian(col);
```

```
end
% Solving system  X
Xxn=AAn\bbn;
X=Xxn./Eeuclidian.';
% Putting residues into matrix C
C=X(1:Np);
% C is complex when the residues are complex
for m=1:Np
  if dix(m)==1
    alfa  = C(m);   % real part of a complex pole
    betta = C(m+1); % imag part of a complex pole
    C(m)  = alfa + i*betta;  % the complex pole
    C(m+1) = alfa - i*betta; % the conjugate
  end
end
% Outputs
if Ka == 1
  A  = Lambda.';   % Poles
  C  = C;        % Residues
  D  = 0;        % Constant term
  E  = 0;        % Proportional term
elseif Ka == 2
  A  = Lambda.';   % Poles
  C  = C;        % Residues
  D  = X(Np+1);  % Constant term
  E  = 0;        % Proportional term
elseif Ka == 3
  A  = Lambda.';   % Poles
  C  = C;        % Residues
  D  = X(Np+1);   % Constant term
  E  = X(Np+2);   % Proportional term
End
```

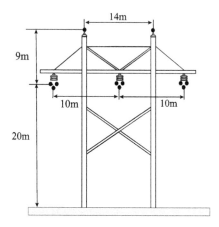

Figure 14. Transversal geometry of aerial line in example.

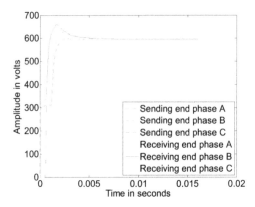

Figure 15. Voltage responses at sending and receiving ends. Unit step excitation.

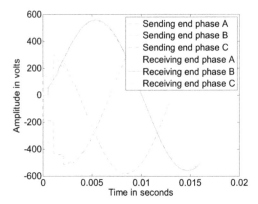

Figure 16. Voltage responses at sending and receiving ends. Sinusoidal excitation.

9. References

Bode, H. W. (1945). *Network Analysis and Feedback Amplifier Design*, D Van Nostrand Company, London, 1945.

Brandao Faria, J. A. & Borges da Silva, J. F. (1986). Wave Propagation in Polyphase Transmission Lines a General Solution to Include Cases Where Ordinary Modal Theory Fails, *Power Delivery, IEEE Transactions on*, vol.1, no.2, (April 1986), pp.(182-189).

Dommel H. W. (1969). Digital computer solution of electromagnetic transients in single and multiphase networks. *IEEE Trans. On Power App. Syst.*, Vol. 88, (July 1969), pp.(388).

Dommel, H. W. (1992). *EMTP Theory Book*, 2nd ed., Microtran Power System Analysis Corporation, Vancouver, Canada, 1992.

Gustavsen B. & Semlyen A.(1998). Simulation of transmission line transients using vector fitting and modal decomposition. *Power Delivery, IEEE Trans. On*, Vol.13, No.2,(April 1998), pp.(605-614).

Gustavsen, B., Semlyen, A. (1999). Rational approximation of frequency domain responses by vector fitting, *Power Delivery, IEEE Transactions on*, vol.14, no.3, (July 1999). pp.(1052-1061).

Gustavsen, B. & Mahseredjian, J. (2007). Simulation of Internal Overvoltages on Transmission Lines by an Extended Method of Characteristics Approach, *Power Delivery, IEEE Transactions on*, vol.22, no.3, (July 2007), pp.(1736-1742).

Gustavsen, B., Nordstrom, J. (2008). Pole Identification for The Universal Line Model Based on Trace Fitting, *Power Delivery, IEEE Transactions on*, vol. 23, no. 1, (January 2008), pp. (472–479).

Gustavsen, B. (2008). "User's Guide for vectfit3.m", Available at http://www.energy.sintef.no/Produkt/VECTFIT/index.asp, Aug. 2008.

Gutierrez-Robles, J. A., Snider, L. A., Naredo, J. L. & Ramos-Leaños (2011). An Investigacion of Interpolation Methods Applied in Transmission Line Models for EMT Analysis, *Proceedings of the International Conference on Power System Transients*, IPST, Delft, The Netherlands, Jun. 2011.

Marcano, F. J. & Marti, J. R. (1997). Idempotent Line Model: Case Studies, *Proceedings of the International Conference on Power System Transients*, IPST, Seattle, USA, Jun. 1997.

Marti, J. R. (1982). Accurate modeling of frequency dependent transmission lines in electromagnetic transient simulations. *IEEE Trans. On Power App. Syst.*, Vol. 101, No. 1, (January 1982), pp. (147-155)

Morched, A., Gustavsen B. & Tartibi M.(1999).A universal model for accurate calculation of electromagnetic transients on overhead lines and underground cables. *IEEE Trans. On Power Delivery*, Vol. 14, No. 3,(July 1999), pp. (1032-1038)

Naredo, J. L., Brandao Faria, J. A., Borges da Silva, J. F. (1986). Discussion to Wave Propagation in Polyphase Transmission Lines a General Solution to Include Cases Where Ordinary Modal Theory Fails, *Power Delivery, IEEE Transactions on*, vol.1, no.2, (April 1986), pp. (188-195)

Ramos-Leaños O. & Iracheta R. (2010). Wide-Band line model implementation in MatLab for EMT analysis. *Proceedings of the North American Power Symposium*, Arlington USA, September 2010.

Strang, G. (1988). *Linear Algebra and its Applications*. Third Edition, Harcourt College, 1988.

Semlyen A. & Dabuleanu A.(1975).Fast and accurate switching transient calculations on transmission lines with ground return using recursive convolutions. *IEEE Trans. On Power App. Syst.*, Vol. 94, No. 2,(April 1975), pp. (561-571)

Semlyen, A., Abdel-Rahman, M. (1982). A state variable approach for the calculation of switching transients on a power transmission line, *Circuits and Systems, IEEE Transactions on*, vol.29, no.9, (September 1982), pp. (624-633)

Wedepohl, L. M., (1965). Electrical characteristics of polyphase transmission systems with special reference to boundary-value calculations at power-line carrier frequencies, *Electrical Engineers, Proceedings of the Institution of*, vol.112, no.11,(November 1965), pp.(2103-2112)

Chapter 13

Dynamic Simulation of Electrical Machines and Drive Systems Using MATLAB GUI

Viliam Fedák, Tibor Balogh and Pavel Záskalický

Additional information is available at the end of the chapter

1. Introduction

Since the first appearance, the fields of electrical machine and drive systems have been continuously enriched by introduction of many important topics. Progress in power electronics, microcontrollers, new materials and advances in numerical modeling have led to development of new types of electrical machines and in field of electrical drives to realization of complex control algorithms. Their verification is usually done by simulation during system design, thus the effort is concentrated to development of simulation models.

MATLAB offers almost infinite possibilities for easy development of system models. MATLAB GUI (Graphic User Interface) in connection with Simulink and specialized toolboxes present a suitable and easy programmable tool for development of purpose-oriented virtual model of any dynamical system. Easy and comfortable change of parameters by control elements in MATLAB GUIDE (GUI Development Environment), such as push- and radio- buttons, text boxes, and easy visualization of results, enable to develop virtual models without deep knowledge of their substance nor without a tedious programming and debugging the models.

Well-elaborated models of electrical drives and machines available on-line were developed by (Riaz, n.d.). (Saadat, 2012) presented application of MATLAB GUI for electrical engineering subjects, available online and MATLAB GUI was utilized in (Petropol-Serb et al, 2007) for development of virtual model of induction machine.

Our contribution aims to present methodology and results in development of unified series of virtual models for electrical machines and drive systems using MATLAB GUI. The organization of the contribution is as follows: after brief description of tasks at virtual models design in GUI MATLAB (chapter 2) in the third chapter we describe development of few typical GUI oriented models of (more complex) electrical machines starting from a simple outline of mathematic model, following by simulation model. Emphasis is put on development of the virtual model itself and description of its features. The fourth chapter deals with CAD of drive controllers using GUI MATLAB. Finally, in the fifth chapter we share some experiences from development of the GUIs and their utilization for training of students. In conclusion we also present ideas for our future work.

2. Design methodology for virtual models of electrical machines and drives

2.1. Tasks in design of the GUI screen

The GUI providing human-computer interaction presents one of the most important parts when working with the system model. User interacts with the computer easily, intuitively, without need for derivation, design, development, composition, and debugging the simulation model; without necessity to learn its operation, and finally, he gets required information in transparent, well-arranged form. In the fact, such GUI presents a functional virtual model, where the user sets system parameters, chooses mode of operation and required outputs to observe results. Design of GUI starts with careful planning of the following tasks:

1. Derivation of system mathematical model
2. Getting, debugging, and verification of simulation model
3. Programming GUI
4. Determination of input parameters changes (editing boxes, sliders)
5. Determination of outputs in graphical and text form
6. Design of the screen (or a set of interconnected screens)
7. Choice of calculation modes and algorithm of their control
8. Final refining and verification of functionality of the designed GUI screen

2.2. Principles of ergonomics of the GUI screen

When designing a functional GUI screen for the technical systems, designer must understand principles of good interface and screen design. Generally, the rules are described in (Galitz, 2007). We have adapted and extended them for design of virtual model – of a GUI MATLAB screen. The most important principles, when designing the placement of objects on the GUI screen, are:

- *Legibility* — saying that information should be distinguishable.
- *Facitily* —how easy is the designed GUI screen intuitively usable.
- *Readability* — how information is identifiable and interpretable.
- *Attractivity* —to attract and call attention to different screen elements (placement of control elements and outputs, using colors, …).
- *Guiding the eye* — by placement and grouping command objects by visual lines/boxes.

Further, designer should deal with user considerations, as follows:

- Visually pleasing (user friendly) *composition of the screen*.
- *Organizing screen elements* (balance, symmetry, alignment, proportion, grouping).
- Screen navigation and flow.
- Choice of implicitly *pre-setting system parameters* and their range (so that virtual models can be generally used in larger range of parameter changes).
- *Changing system parameters* by sliders or by numerical values in editing boxes.
- Finally, designer has to maintain *ergonomic of the screen* where the control elements and outputs should be organized in a legible way.

3. Virtual models for analysis of dynamical properties of electrical machines

In background of every GUI MATLAB there is working a simulation model of the system derived from its mathematical model. The same procedure is applied at development of GUI for electrical machines and drives. Let's show the GUI MATLAB development procedure on few electrical machines – the AC induction machine (asynchronous motor) and the brushless DC motor.

3.1. AC drive with 3-phase asynchronous motor

The AC drive consists of an AC machine supplied by a converter. The variables of AC machine (an asynchronous motor in our case) like electrical quantities (supply voltages and currents), magnetic variables (magnetic fluxes), and mechanical variables (motor torque and rotor angular speed) are usually to be investigated in:

- Various *reference frames* (rotating coordinate systems). In case of asynchronous motor two basic reference frames are considered:
- $\{\alpha, \beta\}$ reference frame associated with stator, whose angular speed $\omega_k = 0$
- $\{x, y\}$ reference frame rotating by synchronous angular speed $\omega_k = \omega_1$
- Various modes of supply:
- harmonic (sinusoidal voltage)
- non-harmonic (stepped voltage), PWM

3.2. Asynchronous motor model

For dynamic properties investigation of asynchronous motor (influence of non-harmonic supply to properties of the AC drive, etc.) a dynamical model of AC machine is used. The AC machine is described by set differential equations. For their derivation some generally accepted simplifications are used (not listed here) concerning physical properties, construction of the machine, electromagnetic circuit, and supply source.

In order to simplify mathematical model of the squirrel cage motor, the multiphase rotor is replaced by an equivalent three-phase one and its parameters are re-calculated to the stator. Equations describing behavior of the machine are transformed from three- to two-phase system what yields to decreased number of differential equations. The quantities in equations are transformed into reference systems.

To derive dynamic model of asynchronous motor, the three-phase system is to be transformed into the two-phase one. In the fact, this transformation presents a replacement of the three-phase motor by equivalent two-phase one. The stator current space vector having real and imaginary components is defined by the equation:

$$\overline{i} = \frac{2}{3}(i_a + ai_b + a^2 i_c)$$

where

$$a = e^{j120^\circ} = -\frac{1}{2} + j\frac{\sqrt{3}}{2}, \quad a^2 = e^{j240^\circ} = -\frac{1}{2} - j\frac{\sqrt{3}}{2}$$

Basic equations of the AC machine with complex variables (denoted by a line over the symbol of the variable) in the reference frame rotating by general angular speed ω_k are:

$$\overline{u}_1 = R_1 \overline{i}_1 + \frac{d\overline{\Psi}_1}{dt} + j\omega_k \overline{\Psi}_1 \tag{1}$$

$$\overline{u}_2 = R_2 \overline{i}_2 + \frac{d\overline{\Psi}_2}{dt} + j(\omega_k - \omega)\overline{\Psi}_2 \tag{2}$$

$$\frac{J}{p}\frac{d\omega}{dt} = \frac{3p}{2} \operatorname{Im}(\overline{\Psi}_{1k}^c \overline{i}_{1k}) - m_z \tag{3}$$

where the nomenclature is as follows:

- u_1, i_1, R_1, L_1 – voltage, current, resistance and inductance of stator phase winding
- u_2, i_2, R_2, L_2 – voltage, current and resistance and inductance of rotor phase winding (re-calculated to stator quantities)
- Ψ_1, Ψ_2 – total magnetic flux of the stator and rotor (recalculated to stator side)
- ω – (rotor) mechanical angular speed
- m_z – load torque
- ω_k – angular speed of a general rotating reference frame $\omega_k = \omega_1$ or 0
- ω_1, ω – magnetic field angular speed, rotor angular speed, where $\omega = \omega_1 - \omega$
- σ – leakage factor $\sigma = (L_1 L_2 - L_h^2)/L_1^2$

For manipulation between various reference frames in the motor model the transformation formulas are used as listed in Tab. 1. All rotor parameters and variables are re-calculated to the stator side.

After inserting real and imaginary components into the complex of variables (e.g. for stator voltage $\overline{u}_1 = u_{1x} + ju_{1y}$ in synchronously rotating reference frame (x, y)), we get the AC motor mathematical model whose equations are listed in Tab. 2 and a block diagram shown in Fig. 1 where $K_1 = 1/(\sigma L_1)$, $K_2 = 1/(\sigma L_2)$, $K = L_h/(\sigma L_1 L_2)$.

Transformation	Matrix notation	Block diagram
$\{a, b, c\} \rightarrow \{\alpha, \beta\}$ from 3-phase system $\{a, b, c\}$ to 2-phase reference frame $\{\alpha, \beta\}$ fixed with the stator (Clark transform)	$\begin{bmatrix} i_\alpha \\ i_\beta \end{bmatrix} = \begin{bmatrix} 1 & 0 & 0 \\ 0 & \dfrac{1}{\sqrt{3}} & -\dfrac{1}{\sqrt{3}} \end{bmatrix} \begin{bmatrix} i_a \\ i_b \\ i_c \end{bmatrix}$	
$\{\alpha, \beta\} \rightarrow \{a, b, c\}$ from 2-phase reference frame fixed with stator $\{\alpha, \beta\}$ into 3-phase system $\{a, b, c\}$ (inverse Clark transform)	$\begin{bmatrix} i_a \\ i_b \\ i_c \end{bmatrix} = \begin{bmatrix} 1 & 0 \\ -\dfrac{1}{2} & \sqrt{\dfrac{3}{2}} \\ -\dfrac{1}{2} & -\sqrt{\dfrac{3}{2}} \end{bmatrix} \begin{bmatrix} i_\alpha \\ i_\beta \end{bmatrix}$	
$\{x, y\} \rightarrow \{\alpha, \beta\}$ from synchronously rotating reference frame $\{x, y\}$ into the stationary frame $\{\alpha, \beta\}$ (Park transform)	$\begin{bmatrix} i_x \\ i_y \end{bmatrix} = \begin{bmatrix} \cos\rho & \sin\rho \\ -\sin\rho & \cos\rho \end{bmatrix} \begin{bmatrix} i_\alpha \\ i_\beta \end{bmatrix}$ $\rho = \omega_1 t$	
$\{\alpha, \beta\} \rightarrow \{x, y\}$ from stator reference frame $\{\alpha, \beta\}$ }into the synchronously rotating frame $\{x, y\}$ (inverse Park transform)	$\begin{bmatrix} i_\alpha \\ i_\beta \end{bmatrix} = \begin{bmatrix} \cos\rho & -\sin\rho \\ \sin\rho & \cos\rho \end{bmatrix} \begin{bmatrix} i_x \\ i_y \end{bmatrix}$ $\rho = \omega_1 t$	

Table 1. Transformation relations between three-phase system and two-phase reference frame and between $\{x, y\}$ and $\{\alpha, \beta\}$ reference frames

	Magnetic fluxes	Relation between fluxes and currents
Stator	$\dfrac{d\psi_{1x}}{dt} = u_{1x} - R_1 i_{1x} + \omega_k \psi_{1y}$	$i_{1x} = K_1 \psi_{1x} - K\psi_{2x}$
Stator	$\dfrac{d\psi_{1y}}{dt} = u_{1y} - R_1 i_{1y} - \omega_k \psi_{1x}$	$i_{1y} = K_1 \psi_{1y} - K\psi_{2y}$
Rotor	$\dfrac{d\psi_{2x}}{dt} = u_{2x} - R_2 i_{2x} - (\omega_k - \omega)\psi_{2y}$	$i_{2x} = K_2 \psi_{2x} - K\psi_{1x}$
Rotor	$\dfrac{d\psi_{2y}}{dt} = u_{2y} + R_2 i_{2y} - (\omega_k - \omega)\psi_{2x}$	$i_{2y} = K_2 \psi_{2y} - K\psi_{1y}$

Table 2. Equations of windings of asynchronous motor model in $\{x,y\}$ reference frame

The corresponding Simulink model is drawn in Fig. 1. The model of squirrel cage motor (rotor voltages = 0) contains 4 inputs and 10 outputs (Tab. 3).

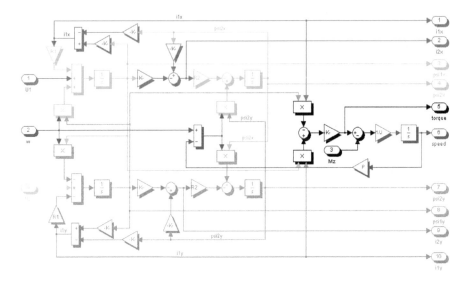

Figure 1. Simulink model of 3 phase squirrel cage asynchronous motor (the variables are denoted in the magnetic field reference frame $\{x, y\}$)

AM model inputs	AM model outputs
• U_1 input voltage (axis x or α)	• current $\overline{i}$ (4 components)
• U_2 input voltage (axis y or β)	• magnetic fluxes $\overline{\Psi}$ (4 components)
• M_z load torque	• motor torque M
• ω_k reference frame angular speed	• rotor angular speed

Table 3. Notation of inputs and outputs of the asynchronous motor model

3.2.1. Modeling of supply source

The asynchronous motor can be set into motion by various supply modes and control platforms:

- by *direct connection* to the supply network or to the frequency converter
- by *frequency starting* (with continuously increasing frequency of the supply voltage from the frequency converter)

Restrict our considerations to supply from indirect converter with the *Voltage-Source Inverter* (VSI). Based on the inverter control mode the output voltage can be:

- unmodulated (with 120 deg. switching in the power semiconductor devices)
- modulated by PWM

Developing inverter simulation schemes we have in mind two facts:

- the *constant stator flux* (i.e. fulfilling condition of constant ratio: U_1/f_1 = const.) should be preserved at all modes of motor control
- in range of very low frequency there should be kept an increased stator voltage (due to the voltage drop across the stator resistor) – so called V-curves (presenting a dependency of the supply voltage from the frequency). The V-curve can be modeled simply by a linear piecewise line.

The model of the motor supply source taking into consideration all described features is shown in Fig. 2 (signals denoted as SL and op are control signals from the GUI buttons). It has 4 inputs: supply frequency and voltage magnitude, ramp frequency and voltage (to simulate frequency starting). The switches "step/ramp" are controlled by pushbuttons from the GUI control panel.

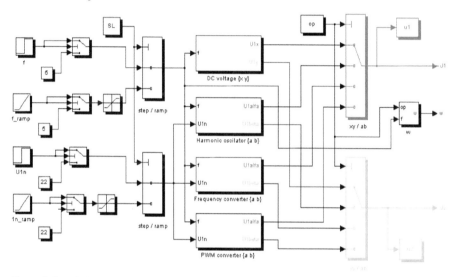

Figure 2. Simulink model of various modes of supply source (DC, harmonic, frequency converter and PWM)

Model of VSI converter (with constant output frequency)

We start to model the inverter output voltage based on a similarity of output converter voltage with the perpendicular harmonic voltages (Fig. 3a). The VSI voltage vector changes its position 6 times per period, after every 60° (Fig. 3b).

Proper switching instants are realized by comparators and switches (Fig. 4). Harmonic oscillator creates a core of the inverter model. Generation of six switching states during period of the output voltage is adjusted by comparing values of the sin/cos signals with pre-set values of $sin\ 60 = \sqrt{3}/2$ for the voltage $u_{1\alpha}$ and value of $cos\ 60 = 1/2$ for the voltage $u_{1\beta}$. The amplitudes of output voltage are adjusted by constants with values 1; 0,5 for $u_{1\alpha}$ and $0,866 = \sqrt{3}/2$ for $u_{1\beta}$.

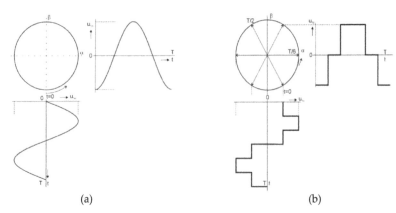

(a)   (b)

Figure 3. Simulink model of inverter

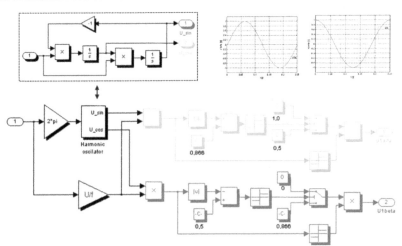

Figure 4. Simulation scheme realizing rectangle voltages $u_{1\alpha}$, $u_{1\beta}$ of the inverter

Model of PWM source

The simplest way to generate a PWM signal uses the intersective method. The three-phase PWM voltage is generated directly in two axes $\{\alpha, \beta\}$ as shown in Fig. 5. The courses of the inverter PWM voltages $u_{1\alpha}$ and $u_{1\beta}$ are shown in Fig. 6. In frequency starting mode of the asynchronous motor, the frequency of supply voltage increases from zero to required final value. To get the stator flux constant, the voltage across the motor has to increase linearly with frequency (U/f = const.), except of very low frequency range (due to voltage drop across the stator resistor). For this purpose, the connection must be completed by a compensating circuit which increases the value of supply voltage keeping the ratio U/f = const (Fig. 7). Up to the frequency of approx. 5 Hz the input voltage is kept constant on 10 % of its nominal value.

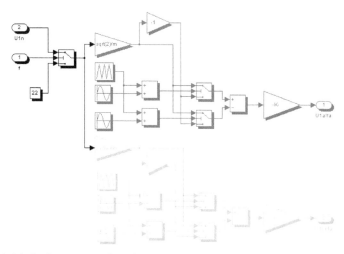

Figure 5. Model of voltages $u_{1\alpha}$ and $u_{1\beta}$ from the inverter with PWM

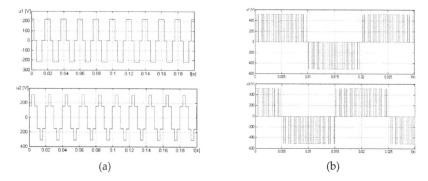

(a)   (b)

Figure 6. Output voltages and $u_{1\beta}$ and $u_{1\alpha}$ from the frequency converter: a) without and b) with PWM

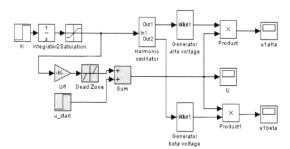

Figure 7. The model of converter realizing the frequency starting under consideration of the law of constant stator flux (U/f = const.)

The model supposes that amplitude of the DC link voltage is changed in the frequency converter. This solution is suitable for drives with low requirements to motor dynamics. The DC link contains a large capacitor what causes the DC link voltage cannot be changed step-by-step. The output inverter voltage can change faster if the PWM control is used. Output voltages of the inverter model with linear increasing frequency and voltage are shown in Fig. 8 (observe a non-zero amplitude of the voltage that at the starting what is consequence of described V-curve block).

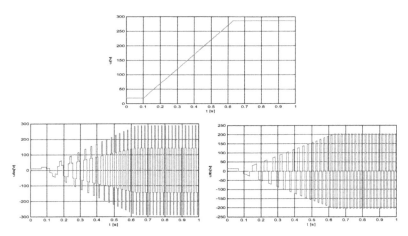

Figure 8. VSI output voltages $u_{1\alpha}$ and $u_{1\beta}$ at increased frequency (the frequency time course is on the top figure)

3.2.2. Model verification

The AC induction motor model was simulated using following motor parameters: R_1=1,8 Ω; R_2=1,85 Ω; p=2; J=0,05 kgm², K_1=59,35; $K2$=59,35; K=56,93.

Time courses of mechanical variables are shown in Fig. 10 (they are the same regardless the used reference frame). Motor dynamical characteristics $\omega = f(M)$ at various modes of supply are compared in Fig. 11.

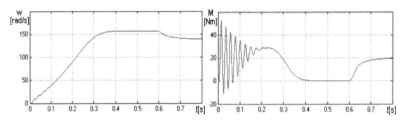

Figure 9. Time responses of asynchronous motor speed and torque at harmonic voltage supply at starting and loading the motor

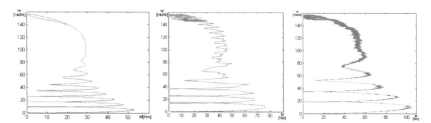

Figure 10. Dynamic characteristic of the asynchronous motor $\omega = f(M)$ supplied: a) by harmonic voltage, b) from frequency converter, c) from frequency converter with PWM

3.2.3. GUI design and realisation

After debugging the motor model (Fig. 11), development of GUI continues with careful design of the program flowchart and design of GUI screen.

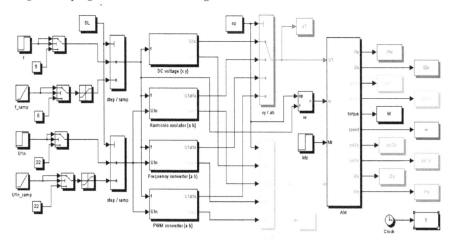

Figure 11. Arrangement of asynchronous motor subsystems in the Simulink GUI model

Description of the GUI functionality

The GUI screen (Fig. 13) consists of several panels. Their functionality is as follows:

- *Input data panel* ("Motor parameters") in the bottom left part. The panel is used to system parameters entry. Their values can be changed by inserting numeric values into editing boxes. There is a possibility to return to original (default) parameters by pushing the button Default (in the pane *Mode*).
- Choice of *Coordinate reference frame system* (the panel on the right top part) enables to display motor output variables:
  - in the synchronously rotating reference frame
  - in the reference frame associated with the stator

- at harmonic supply
- at nonharmonics supply from the VSI
- at nonharmonics supply from the VSI with PWM

- *Output graphs*. Output variables are displayed in four graphs:
  - supply voltage time courses and in two coordinates
  - mechanical variables - motor torque and speed
  - stator currents or magnetic fluxes
  - rotor currents or magnetic fluxes
- The graph to be displayed can be chosen by pushing radio button in the menu *Graphs*. Time courses are chosen by the button *Time*; dependency of one variable on other is chosen by the button *Rectangular*.
- *Mode of starting* the motor can be selected in the panel *Motor supply*:
  - Direct connection to the supply – the button *Step*. The voltage U_1 (effective rms value) and frequency f_1 can be pre-set in the editing boxes.
  - Frequency starting – the button *Linear* enables to pre-set the frequency time rise starting from zero.
- Using the buttons in the panel *Mode* we start *Simulation*, at pressing *Default* (original) parameters are set, and the Simulink scheme is shown by pushing the button *Model* .

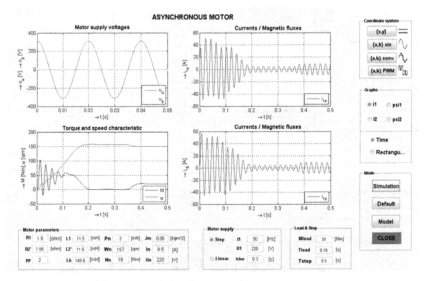

Figure 12. GUI screen of the AC drive with induction machine

Screen outputs

Samples of the screens displaying variables in the stator reference frame $\{\alpha, \beta\}$ are shown in Fig. 13:

a.   time courses at supplying motor by frequency converter – button *Time*)

b.   chracteristics $M = f(\omega)$, $i_{1\alpha} = f(i_{1\beta})$, $\psi_{1\alpha} = f(\psi_{1\beta})$ - button Rectangular)

c.   time courses $i_{1\alpha} = f(t)$, $i_{2\alpha} = f(t)$ at supplying from the PWM frequency converter

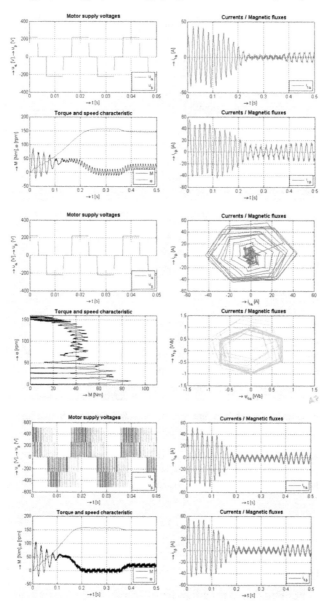

Figure 13. Examples of diplaying various graphs in the GUI for asynchronous motor

3.3. BLDC motor

The Brushless Direct Current (BLDC) motor is rapidly gaining popularity by its utilization in various industries. As the name implies, the BLDC motor do not use brushes for commutation; instead of this they are commutated electronically.

The BLDC motors have many advantages over brushed DC motors and induction motors. A few of these are: (1) Better speed versus torque characteristics; (2) High dynamic response; (3) High efficiency; (4) Long operating life; (5) Noiseless operation; (6) Higher speed ranges. In addition, the ratio of torque delivered to the size of the motor is higher, making it useful in applications where space and weight are critical factors (Indu, 2008).

The torque of the BLDC motor is mainly influenced by the waveform of back-EMF (the voltage induced into the stator winding due to rotor movement). Ideally, the BLDC motors have trapezoidal back-EMF waveforms and are fed with rectangular stator currents, which give theoretically constant torque. However, in practice, a torque ripple exists, mainly due to EMF waveform imperfections, current ripple, and phase current commutation. The current ripple follows up from PWM or hysteresis control. The EMF waveform imperfections result from variations in the shapes of slot, skew and magnet of BLDC motor, and are subject to design purposes. Hence, an error can occur between actual value and the simulation results. Several simulation models have been proposed for analysis of BLDC motor (Jeon, 2000).

3.3.1. Construction and operating principle

The BLDC motor is also referred to as an electronically commuted motor. There are no brushes on the rotor and the commutation is performed electronically at certain rotor positions. In the DC commutator motor, the current polarity is reversed by the commutator and the brushes, but in the brushless DC motor, the polarity reversal is performed by semiconductor switches which are to be switched in synchronization with the rotor position. Besides of the higher reliability, the missing commutator brings another advantage. For the DC brushed motor the commutator presents also a limiting factor in the maximal speed. Therefore, the BLDC motor can be employed in applications requiring high speed (Jeon, 2000).

The BLDC motor is usually considered as a three-phase system and thus it has to be powered by a three-phase power supply. The rotor position must be known at certain angles, in order to align the applied voltage with the back-EMF. The alignment between the back-EMF and commutation events is very important.

A simple motor model of BLDC motor consisting of a three-phase power converter and a brushless DC motor is shown in Fig. 14.

3.3.2. Mathematical model of the BLDC motor

Modeling of a BLDC motor can be developed in the similar manner as a three-phase synchronous machine. Since there is a permanent magnet mounted on the rotor, some dynamic characteristics are different. Similarly, the model of the armature winding for the BLDC motor is expressed as follows:

$$u_a = Ri_a + L\frac{di_a}{dt} + e_a \tag{4}$$

$$u_b = Ri_b + L\frac{di_b}{dt} + e_b \tag{5}$$

$$u_c = Ri_c + L\frac{di_c}{dt} + e_c \tag{6}$$

where L is armature self-inductance, R - armature resistance, u_a, u_b, u_c - terminal phase voltages, and i_a, i_b, i_c - motor input currents, and e_a, e_b, e_c - motor back-EMF.

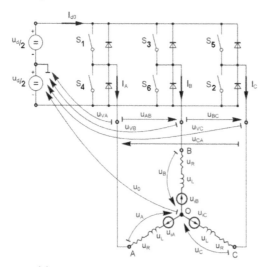

Figure 14. BLDC motor model

In the three-phase BLDC motor, the back-EMF is related to a function of rotor position and the back-EMF of each phase has 120° phase angle difference so the equation for each motor phase is as follows:

$$e_a = K_w f(\theta_e)\omega \tag{7}$$

$$e_b = K_w f(\theta_e - 2\pi/3)\omega \tag{8}$$

$$e_c = K_w f(\theta_e + 2\pi/3)\omega \tag{9}$$

where K_w is back EMF constant of one phase, θ_e - electrical rotor angle, ω - rotor speed. The electrical rotor angle θ_e is equal to the mechanical rotor angle θ_m multiplied by the number of poles p:

$$\theta_e = \frac{p}{2}\theta_m \tag{10}$$

Total torque output T_e can be represented as summation of that of each phase:

$$T_e = \frac{e_A i_A + e_B i_B + e_C i_C}{\omega} \tag{11}$$

The equation of mechanical part is represents as follows:

$$T_e - T_l = J\frac{d\omega}{dt} + b\omega \tag{12}$$

where T_l is load torque, J - rotor inertia, b - friction constant.

3.3.3. Simulink model of the BLDC motor

Fig. 16 shows the block diagram of the BLDC motor SIMULINK model in the rotor reference frame.

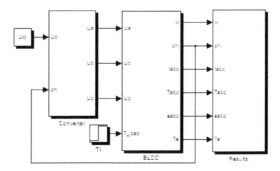

Figure 15. Simulink model of the BLDC motor

Fig. 16 shows detail of the BLDC motor block. Fig. 17a shows Simulink diagram of trapezoidal back-EMF and in Fig. 17b there is Simulink model of sinusoidal back-EMF. The trapezoidal functions and the position signals are stored in lookup tables that change their output according to the value of the electrical angle (Indu, 2008).

Unlike a brushed DC motor, the commutation of a BLDC motor is controlled electronically. To rotate the BLDC motor, the stator windings should be energized in sequences. In order to understand which winding will be energized following the energizing sequence, it is important to know the rotor position. It is sensed using Hall Effect sensors embedded into the stator. Most of the BLDC motors contain three Hall sensors embedded into the stator on the non-driving end of the motor. The number of electrical cycles to be repeated to complete a mechanical rotation is determined by rotor pole pairs. Number of electrical cycles/rotations equals to the rotor pole pairs. The commutation sequences are shown in Tab. 4.

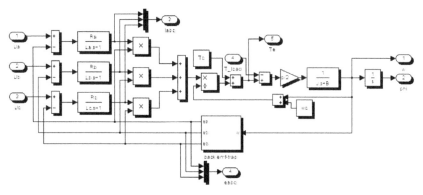

Figure 16. Detailed overview of the BLDC motor block

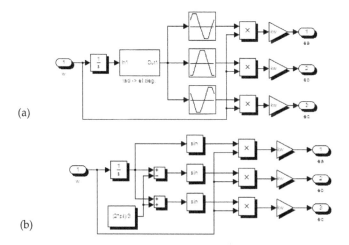

(a)

(b)

Figure 17. Trapezoidal (a) and simusoidal (b) model of the back-EMF

Electrical degree	Hall sensor value (ABC)	Phase	Switches
0º - 60º	101	A-C	S1-S2
60º - 120º	001	B-C	S2-S3
120º - 180º	011	B-A	S3-S4
180º - 240º	010	C-A	S4-S5
240º - 300º	110	C-B	S5-S6
300º - 360º	100	A-B	S6-S1

Table 4. Electrical degree, Hall sensor value and corresponding commuted phase in clockwise rotation of the rotor

3.3.4. Mathematical and simulink model of the three-phase converter

The converter supplies the input voltage for three phases of the BLDC motor. Each phase leg comprises two power semiconductor devices. Fig. 18 shows the scheme of the considered three-phase converter.

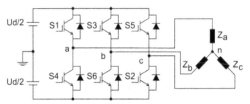

Figure 18. Modelled three-phase converter

Appropriate pairs of the switches (S1 to S6) are driven based on the Hall sensors input. Three phases are commutated in every 60° (el. degrees). The model of the converter is implemented using the equations:

$$U_{an} = S_1 \frac{Ud}{2} - S_4 \frac{Ud}{2} - U_f \tag{13}$$

$$U_{bn} = S_3 \frac{Ud}{2} - S_6 \frac{Ud}{2} - U_f \tag{14}$$

$$U_{cn} = S_5 \frac{Ud}{2} - S_2 \frac{Ud}{2} - U_f \tag{15}$$

where U_{an}, U_{bn}, U_{cn} are line-neural voltages, U_d – the DC link voltage, U_f – the forward diode voltage drop.

Fig. 19a shows the Simulink model of the three-phase converter block. In the simulation we assumed an ideal diode with neglected voltage drop U_f. The *Commutation sequences* block was developed based on the commutation sequence shown in Tab. 4. Converter voltage waveforms that are switched according to the commutation sequences in Tab. 4 are shown in Fig. 19b.

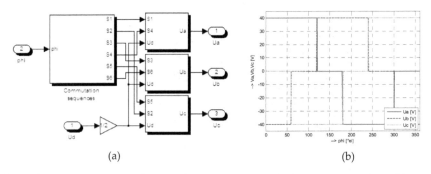

(a)   (b)

Figure 19. Detailed overview of the three-phase converter (a) and voltage source waveforms (b)

3.3.5. GUI of the BLDC motor

The simulated BLDC motor is presented in a graphical user interface GUI (Fig. 20).

By the buttons in the panel *Mode* we start the *Simulation* , put *Default* (original) values and show the Simulink *Model*.

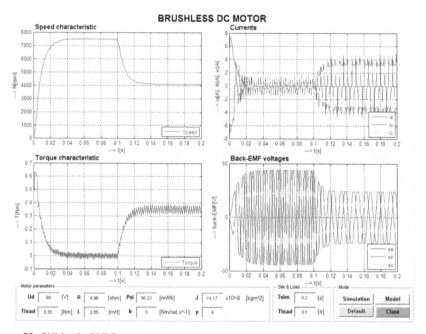

Figure 20. GUI for the BLDC motor

The default parameters of the BLDC motor for simulation are: U_d=80 V, T_l=0,35 Nm, R=4,98 Ω, L=2,05 mH, ψ=56,23.10^{-3} Wb, b=0 Nm/rad.s^{-1}, J=15,17.10^{-6} kgm^2, p=4.

4. Virtual models applied for synthesis of drive systems

MATLAB GUI presents an extremely suitable tool for development of models to support CAD design of drive controllers, whose algorithms are known. Two simple cases are presented below: design of controllers in the frequency and time domains, other cases are mentioned in the subchapter 5.1.

4.1. CAD design of controller parameters for DC motor drive in frequency domain

The DC drive controllers in the *frequency domain* are calculated mostly by using the following criteria:

1. The current controller of the PI type is calculated on basis of the *Optimum Modulus Criterion* (OMC) from the drive system parameters:

$$F_{RI} = K_{RI} + \frac{1}{sT_{iI}} \tag{16}$$

2. After calculation of the current controller parameters and current control loop simplification, the speed controller is calculated based on the *Symmetrical Optimum Criterion* (SOC). It is again of PI type having the transfer function:

$$F_{R\omega} = K_{R\omega} + \frac{1}{sT_{i\omega}} \tag{17}$$

Fig. 22 shows the principal block diagram of the system and in Fig. 23 there is view on the virtual GUI model of speed controlled DC drive.

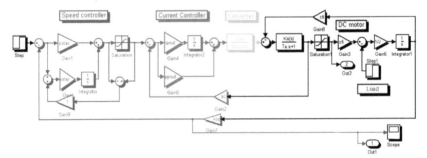

Figure 21. Control circuit of DC motor drive with current and speed controllers

Virtual model features

The user has a possibility to tune controller parameters in each design step according to displayed time response. The GUI screen consists of several panels:

*   *Time response* - the graph with time courses of the motor current and speed. Immediately after change of any system parameter (motor -, drive -, or controller parameters) by a slider or inserting a numeric value into editable box the simulation starts and new time responses are drawn (like in a real drive).
*   *Block diagram* - displays the block diagram of the system
*   *System parameters* are changed by sliders or inserting values into the boxes.

Before starting the model, implicit parameters are set up, but they can be changed later. After pushing the button *Computed value* the parameters of controllers are calculated from the actual values of parameters. Simultaneously a small window appears there with a question whether the calculated values of controller parameters are acceptable or not (if not, user can set up own parameters and can to tune them according to the time responses of the drive). To return to starting values, the user pushes the button *Default* (similar to the system restart).

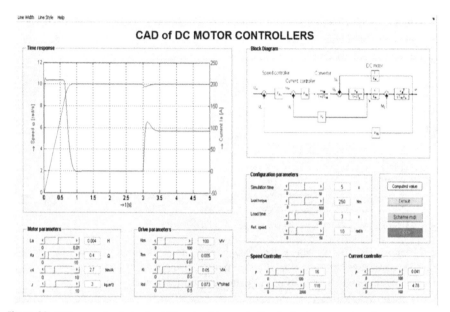

Figure 22. GUI screen for designing DC motor drive controllers in the frequency domain

4.2. CAD design of controller parameters for DC motor drive in time domain

The computing algorithm is different from calculation of the controllers in the frequency domain and the task belongs to more complex one. The computation starts from the state-space model of the DC motor having two inputs in one output, in the form of state equations:

$$\dot{x} = \mathbf{A}.x + \mathbf{b}.u + \mathbf{e}.z = \begin{bmatrix} 0 & \dfrac{K_m}{T_m.K_a} \\[2mm] -\dfrac{K_a}{K_m.T_a} & -\dfrac{1}{T_a} \end{bmatrix} x + \begin{bmatrix} 0 \\[2mm] K_T.K_a \\ T_a \end{bmatrix} u + \begin{bmatrix} -\dfrac{K_m^2}{T_m.K_a} \\[2mm] 0 \end{bmatrix} M_z \tag{18}$$

$$y = c^T x = \begin{bmatrix} 1 & 0 \end{bmatrix} x \tag{19}$$

where **A** is system matrix, x – state vector, **b** – input vector, c^T - output (row) vector **e**-disturbance vector, u – input variable, y - output variable.

The final control structure with the feedback through the state controller vector r^T is clear from the Simulink model Fig. 23. The integrator at the input serves to reject constant or slowly changing disturbances what is a common case.

The state control structure parameters: K_1, r_1 and r_2 are designed by known *pole placement method* where for a prescribed position of poles the required polynomial is compared with the system polynomial and missing parameters of the controller are calculated from a set of linear algebraic equations.

The control structure in Simulink to simulate the system is shown in (Fig. 23).

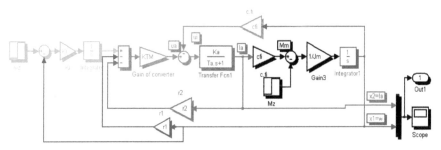

Figure 23. Simulink model of the state-space control of DC drive

Fig. 24 shows the GUI screen of the virtual model that enables to calculate state-space controller parameters and visualize time responses of the current and speed. It is a more complex GUI involving synthesis of the state-space controllers and giving the possibility to tune theoretically calculated parameters.

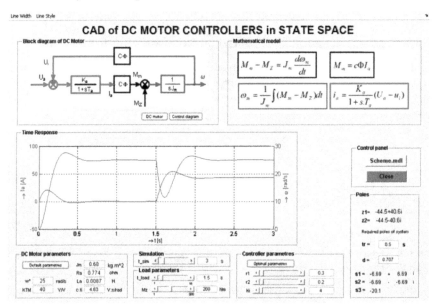

Figure 24. GUI screen for designing DC motor drive controllers in the state space domain

The panel *Controller parameters* serves to setting parameters of the state controller – by tuning or selecting the button *Optimal parameters* to calculate poles position placement.

Here:

- r₁ – feedback from state variable x_1 (motor speed),
- r₂ – feedback from state variable x_2 (motor current),
- Kᵢ – gain of the integrator (to reject steady-state disturbances).

The state controller parameters are calculated automatically on basis of required values of control time and damping (panel *Poles*, the item *Required poles of the system*). In the upper part of the panel the real positions of poles are shown.

5. Experiences with utilization of virtual models

5.1. Utilization of virtual dynamical models

Except of the presented GUI screens of virtual models a series of tens other models from fields of electrical engineering and mechatronic systems was developed to suit institutional needs. They cover topics from Electrical Machines, Power Electronics, Electrical Actuators and Drives, Servodrives, Mechatronic Systems, Control Theory, and others. We have also developed some more complex GUIs, reported e.g. by (Ismeal & Fedák, 2012), calculating artificial intelligence algorithms - to design PID controllers using fuzzy logic and genetic algorithms with various objective functions to evaluate the best PID controller.

The developed GUIs serve as virtual models to clarify phenomena and enhance features of the systems during lectures, and to prepare students for laboratory work. In order students to get more skills and practical experiences prior entering lab their work consists of two phases:

Design and simulation – for a given system motor or drive a student has:

- to derive mathematical model,
- to compose the block diagram,
- to design control law and controllers (in case of drives),
- to verify system behavior by simulation.

Verification and analysis – a student has:

- to verify the design using a virtual reference model,
- to perform system analysis ("to play himself" with the virtual model) in order to investigate system behavior at various values of system parameters and in various working points (small experiments round working point).

5.2. Application of MATLAB compiler in virtual model development

A disadvantage of using GUI MATLAB consists in the fact, that the program can run only on a computer having installed the MATLAB program (and appropriate toolboxes containing instructions that are used in the main GUI program). This disadvantage can be suppressed by development of an executable (.exe) file from the original program. In this case the developer must install the Compiler Runtime program. The MATLAB Compiler creates a standalone executable file from the MATLAB code, which can then run in a runtime engine called *Matlab Compiler Runtime* (MCR). Once compiled, the standalone application, along with MCR, can be shared with other users for free. The only problem is that the original GUI MATLAB program cannot contain any Simulink model (mdl file). As the GUI MATLAB systems usually contain Simulink models, they have to be replaced by MATLAB programs solving mathematical model by various algorithms.

6. Conclusion

The chapter describes principles and methodology of virtual models development in GUI MATLAB for few chosen electrical machines and controlled drives. The models perform analyses of real machines and drives in various working points and they enable easily to show system performance in various working points and to analyze influence of variable system parameters, modes of supply, and control parameters to system behavior. Presented virtual models have been of various complexity – the simpler ones enable virtual analysis of electrical machines and more complex virtual models also deal with algorithms for synthesis of drive controllers.

Strong advantage of developed virtual models consists in the fact user does not need to know the complexity of dynamical system whose simulation scheme is working in the background. He changes only system parameters, selects input signals (shape and amplitude of reference values, forcing and load signals), select mode of calculations and outputs (graphs displaying). The parameters of virtual models can be changed by a slider or by editing numerical values in editable boxes.

Based on the procedure a whole series of virtual models designed in GUI MATLAB has been developed at the authors' institution in recent years which are partly accessible trough the website of the Virtual Laboratory for Control of Mechatronic Systems (KEM TU Kosice, 2010). The virtual dynamical models contribute to e-learning support at teaching and they also serve for preparation of students for laboratory experimentation. Their utilization makes more attractive lectures and considerably enhances explanation of systems properties. By simulation model students generally easier understand physical processes and they are better prepared to the laboratory work.

Shortcoming of developed models consists in the fact they run on computers having installed the MATLAB program. To overcome this, recently our work was concentrated to applications of the MATLAB Compiler to develop execcutable files. It should be noted that this application enables to run MATLAB operation without simulation (i.e. without a Simulink scheme), without 3D virtual reality views and without animation. The advantage on one side makes development of virtual models more difficult using more complex mathematical subroutines. Also some known problems with GUI MATLAB should be noted - cross platform appearance may not be the same and during the GUI development, often must be used tricks and somehow unfriendly techniques.

Author details

Viliam Fedák and Pavel Záskalický
Technical University of Košice, Slovakia

Tibor Balogh
Magneti Marelli, Electronic Systems Division, Industrial Park Kechnec, Slovakia

Acknowledgement

The financial support of the Slovak Research and Development Agency under the contract No. APVV-0138-10 is acknowledged. The work was also supported by Slovak Cultural and Educational Agency of the Ministry of Education of Slovak Republic under the contract KEGA 042TUKE-4/2012 "Teaching Innovation in Control of Mechatronic Systems".

7. References

Galitz, W. O. (2007). The Essential Guide to User Interface Design. An Introduction to GUI Design Principles and Techniques, *Wiley Publishing, Inc.*, ISBN 978-0-470-05342-3, Indianapolis, Indiana

Hill, S. (2011). How to Make an Executable From MATLAB Code, Date of access: Mach 31, 2011, <http://www.ehow.com/how_8686360_make-executable-matlab-code.html>

Indu, B., Ashly, R. & Tom, M. (2008). Dynamic Simulation of Brushless DC Drive Considering Phase Commutation and Backemf Waveform for Electromechanical Actuator. *IEEE TENCON*, Hyderabad 2008. ISBN: 978-1-4244-2408-5

Ismeal G.A. & Fedák V. (2012). Overview of Control Algorithms for DC Motor Drive as a Basis for Development of GUI in MATLAB. *XXVI. microCAD International Scientific Conference*, Miskolc, 2012, 9 p., ISBN 978-963-661-773-8

Jeon, Y.S., Mok, H.S., Choe, G.H., Kim, D.K. & Ryu, J.S. (2000). A New Simulation Model of BLDC Motor with Real Back EMF waveforms. *IEEE CNF on Computers in Power Electronics*, COMPEL 2000, pp. 217 – 220, July 2000

KEM TU Kosice (2010). Virtual Laboratory of Mechatronic Systems Control. , In: Date of access: March 31, 2012, Available from <http://andromeda.fei.tuke.sk/> (in Slovak)

MathWorks (n.d.). Deploytool - R2012a Documentation MATLAB Compiler http://www.mathworks.com/help/toolbox/compiler/deploytool.html

Parspour, N. & Hanitsch, R. (1994). Fuzzy Controlled Brushless DC Motor For Medical Applications. *Industrial Electronic, Control and Instrumentation IECON, IEEE*, Bologna, 1994, ISBN: 0-7803-1328-3

Petropol-Serb, G.D.; Petropol-Serb, I.; Campeanu, A. & Petrisor, A. (2007). Using GUI of Matlab to create a virtual laboratory to study an induction machine. EUROCON, 2007. *The International Conference on Computer as a Tool*, ISBN 978-1-4244-0813-9, Warsaw, September 9-12, 2007

Riaz, M. (n.d.): Simulation of Electric Machine and Drive Systems Using MATLAB and Simulink. University of Minnesota. www.ece.umn.edu/users/riaz/

Saadat, H. (2012). MATLAB Graphical User Interface for EE Students. Date of access: March 31, 2012, Available from <http://people.msoe.edu/~saadat/matlabgui.htm

Permissions

The contributors of this book come from diverse backgrounds, making this book a truly international effort. This book will bring forth new frontiers with its revolutionizing research information and detailed analysis of the nascent developments around the world.

We would like to thank Vasilios N. Katsikis, for lending his expertise to make the book truly unique. He has played a crucial role in the development of this book. Without his invaluable contribution this book wouldn't have been possible. He has made vital efforts to compile up to date information on the varied aspects of this subject to make this book a valuable addition to the collection of many professionals and students.

This book was conceptualized with the vision of imparting up-to-date information and advanced data in this field. To ensure the same, a matchless editorial board was set up. Every individual on the board went through rigorous rounds of assessment to prove their worth. After which they invested a large part of their time researching and compiling the most relevant data for our readers. Conferences and sessions were held from time to time between the editorial board and the contributing authors to present the data in the most comprehensible form. The editorial team has worked tirelessly to provide valuable and valid information to help people across the globe.

Every chapter published in this book has been scrutinized by our experts. Their significance has been extensively debated. The topics covered herein carry significant findings which will fuel the growth of the discipline. They may even be implemented as practical applications or may be referred to as a beginning point for another development. Chapters in this book were first published by InTech; hereby published with permission under the Creative Commons Attribution License or equivalent.

The editorial board has been involved in producing this book since its inception. They have spent rigorous hours researching and exploring the diverse topics which have resulted in the successful publishing of this book. They have passed on their knowledge of decades through this book. To expedite this challenging task, the publisher supported the team at every step. A small team of assistant editors was also appointed to further simplify the editing procedure and attain best results for the readers.

Our editorial team has been hand-picked from every corner of the world. Their multi-ethnicity adds dynamic inputs to the discussions which result in innovative outcomes. These outcomes are then further discussed with the researchers and contributors who give their valuable feedback and opinion regarding the same. The feedback is then collaborated with the researches and they are edited in a comprehensive manner to aid the understanding of the subject.

Apart from the editorial board, the designing team has also invested a significant amount of their time in understanding the subject and creating the most relevant covers. They scrutinized every image to scout for the most suitable representation of the subject and create an appropriate cover for the book.

The publishing team has been involved in this book since its early stages. They were actively engaged in every process, be it collecting the data, connecting with the contributors or procuring relevant information. The team has been an ardent support to the editorial, designing and production team. Their endless efforts to recruit the best for this project, has resulted in the accomplishment of this book. They are a veteran in the field of academics and their pool of knowledge is as vast as their experience in printing. Their expertise and guidance has proved useful at every step. Their uncompromising quality standards have made this book an exceptional effort. Their encouragement from time to time has been an inspiration for everyone.

The publisher and the editorial board hope that this book will prove to be a valuable piece of knowledge for researchers, students, practitioners and scholars across the globe.

List of Contributors

Christophe Batard, Frédéric Poitiers, Christophe Millet and Nicolas Ginot
Lunam University - University of Nantes, UMR CNRS 6164 ,
Institut d'Electronique et de Télécommunications de Rennes (IETR), France

A.B. Campo
Instituto Federal de Educação, Ciência e Tecnologia de São Paulo, Brazil

Tomas Vydra and Daniel Havelka
Czech Technical University in Prague, FEE, Department of Electromagnetic Field, Czech Republic

Jacques Fanjason Ramahaleomiarantsoa and Nicolas Héraud
Université de Corse, U.M.R. CNRS 6134 SPE, BP 52, Corte, France

Eric Jean Roy Sambatra
Institut Supérieur de Technologie, BP 509, Antsiranana, Madagascar

Jean Marie Razafimahenina
Ecole Supérieure Polytechnique, BP O, Antsiranana, Madagascar

Sven Fagerstrom
Pacific Gas and Electric (PG&E), Fresno, CA, USA

Nagy Bengiamin
California State University Fresno, Fresno, CA, USA

Ergin Kosa and Levent Trabzon
Mechanical Engineering, Istanbul Technical University, Istanbul, Turkey

Umit Sonmez
Mechanical Engineering, Sharjah University, Dubai, United Arab Emirates

Huseyin Kizil
Metallurgical and Materials Engineering, Istanbul Technical University, Istanbul, Turkey

Kosol Oranpiroj, Worrajak Moangjai and Wichran Jantee
Rajamangala University of Technology Lanna Chiangmai, Thailand

Khalid Chikh, Mohamed Khafallah and Abdallah Saâd
Hassan II University, National Higher School of Electricity and Mechanics (ENSEM), Department of Electrical Engineering, Energy and Electrical Systems Research Group, Morocco

Adel Aktaibi and M. Azizur Rahman
Memorial University of Newfoundland, Canada

Mostefa Ghassoul
Chemical Engineering, University of Bahrain, Bahrain

M. Ould Ahmedou, M. Ferfra and M. Maaroufi
Mohammadia School of Engineering (Mohamed V University), Rabat, Morocco

M. Chraygane
Ibn Zohr University, Agadir, Morocco

Octavio Ramos-Leaños
École Polytechnique de Montréal, Canada

Jose Luis Naredo
Cinvestav-Guadalajara, Mexico

Jose Alberto Gutierrez-Robles
University of Guadalajara, Mexico

Viliam Fedák and Pavel Záskalický
Technical University of Košice, Slovakia

Tibor Balogh
Magneti Marelli, Electronic Systems Division, Industrial Park Kechnec, Slovakia

Printed in the USA
CPSIA information can be obtained
at www.ICGtesting.com
JSHW011504221024
72173JS00005B/1199

9 781632 401892